BATTLE STATIONS

ALSO BY STEPHEN L. MOORE

Patton's Payback: The Battle of El Guettar and
General Patton's Rise to Glory in North Africa

Rain of Steel: Mitscher's Task Force 58, Ugaki's Thunder Gods,
and the Kamikaze War off Okinawa

Uncommon Valor: The Recon Company That Earned Five Medals of
Honor and Included America's Most Decorated Green Beret

As Good as Dead: The Daring Escape of American POWs
from a Japanese Death Camp

The Battle for Hell's Island: How a Small Band of
Carrier Dive-Bombers Helped Save Guadalcanal

Texas Rising: The Epic True Story of the Lone Star Republic
and the Rise of the Texas Rangers, 1836-1846

Pacific Payback: The Carrier Aviators Who Avenged
Pearl Harbor at the Battle of Midway

Battle Surface!: Lawson P. "Red" Ramage and the
War Patrols of the USS Parche

Presumed Lost: The Incredible Ordeal of America's
Submarine POWs during the Pacific War

Relic Quest: A Guide to Responsible Relic Recovery
Techniques with Metal Detectors

Savage Frontier: Rangers, Riflemen, and Indian Wars
in Texas, Volume IV: 1842-1845

Last Stand of the Texas Cherokees: Chief Bowles and
the 1839 Cherokee War in Texas

War of the Wolf: Texas's Memorial Submarine,
World War II's Famous USS Seawolf

Savage Frontier: Rangers, Riflemen, and Indian Wars
in Texas, Volume III: 1840-1841

Spadefish: On Patrol with a Top-Scoring World War II Submarine

Savage Frontier: Rangers, Riflemen, and Indian Wars
in Texas, Volume II: 1838-1839

Eighteen Minutes: The Battle of San Jacinto and the
Texas Independence Campaign

Savage Frontier: Rangers, Riflemen, and Indian Wars
in Texas, Volume 1: 1835-1837

Taming Texas: Captain William T. Sadler's Lone Star Service

The Buzzard Brigade: Torpedo Squadron Ten at War
(with William J. Shinneman and Robert Gruebel)

BATTLE STATIONS

How the USS *Yorktown* Helped Turn the Tide at Coral Sea and Midway

STEPHEN L. MOORE

CALIBER

CALIBER

An imprint of Penguin Random House LLC
penguinrandomhouse.com

LIBRARY OF CONGRESS CATALOGING-IN-PUBLICATION DATA
has been applied for.

ISBN 9780593186671 (paperback)
ISBN 9780593186688 (ebook)

Printed in the United States of America
1st Printing

May God keep us safe tomorrow.
—Ensign John d'Arc Lorenz,
USS *Yorktown*, June 3, 1942

★ CONTENTS ★

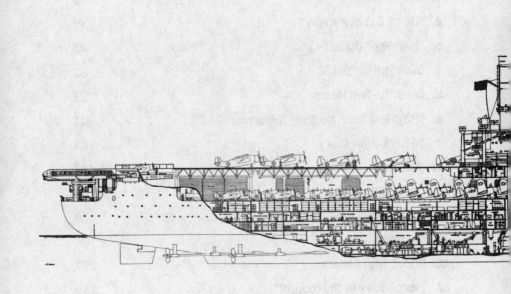

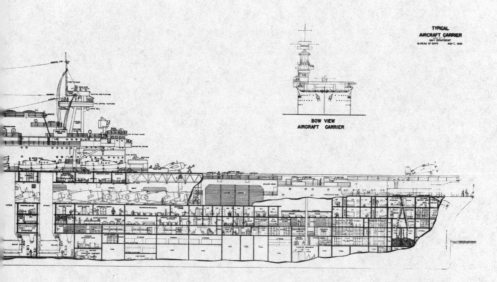

TYPICAL
AIRCRAFT CARRIER

NAVY DEPARTMENT
BUREAU OF SHIPS   NOV 7, 1942

BOW VIEW
AIRCRAFT CARRIER

BATTLE STATIONS

PROLOGUE

George Weise blinked his eyes and wondered if he was dreaming. In his hazy state, he was only vaguely aware of what was real. The smell of charred flesh was horrific but blue emergency lanterns provided insufficient light to see much detail in the compartment.

Weise was lying in a bunk in Sick Bay, three decks below the flight deck. His aircraft carrier *Yorktown* was listing dangerously to port, more than twenty-six degrees. Bomb and torpedo damage had wrecked the ship, and the crew had been forced to abandon ship. Weise was immobile. His left leg was fractured and his left arm had been placed in a temporary cast. His fractured skull made his head pound. Everything was foggy, but Weise thought he was hearing a voice.

Maybe I'm just hallucinating, he reasoned.

Then the voice called again.

"Weise!"

Straining to see in the dim blue light, he finally made out the form of another sailor lying four bunks away. It was seventeen-year-old Seaman Norman Pichette, who had also served as a ship's gunner during the battle against Japanese aircraft.

"How bad are you hurt?" asked Pichette.

Weise quickly related his poor condition. He had been manning a .50-caliber machine gun during the Japanese dive-bomber attack. His gun was located on the dual-searchlight platform on the island superstructure, forty feet above the flight deck. He had poured bullets into the last diving Japanese plane he remembered seeing. But then it had released its bomb, one that penetrated deep inside the *Yorktown* before exploding.

The detonation blew fire and smoke back up through the carrier's smokestack with a violent blast. Weise's head was slammed against the barrel of his gun with enough force to fracture his skull. The same concussion tossed his body high over the railing of his gun platform and sent him plunging forty feet down to the flight deck.

When he came to seconds later, machine-gun slugs were ripping through the wooden flight deck near him as another Japanese plane strafed the carrier. Blood seeped from his head, and the right side of his body was paralyzed. His left leg and arm had been shattered by the impact with the flight deck.

Medical personnel had carried Weise to an emergency aid station just below the flight deck, where his fractured arm was placed in a temporary cast and his left leg was secured. But his head wounds were another story. Shipmates carried him three decks below to Sick Bay, where surgeons would have to work on his skull.

Weise had been unconscious for these two moves but woke up to hear alarms ringing through the ship, announcing an enemy torpedo-plane attack. In another moment of consciousness, he heard the call over the loudspeaker to abandon ship. A short while later, everyone was gone from Sick Bay, save two pharmacist's mates making a last-minute check for survivors. Their assessment of him had stunned Weise to his core.

"Leave him and let's go!" said the senior medic. "He's going to die anyway."

When Weise next regained his senses, he saw only the bodies of several deceased shipmates. He cursed a blue streak—angry, hurt, and frightened.

I don't want to be left on board a sinking ship, he thought.

Although he had no sense of time, it was now more than fourteen hours since his carrier had been abandoned. *Yorktown* was still somehow afloat. His anger momentarily replaced by hope, Weise asked Pichette about his wounds.

Pichette's abdomen had been ripped open by shrapnel from a bomb that exploded just off *Yorktown*'s stern. Someone had administered morphine and placed him in a bunk while doctors and pharmacist's mates raced to save other lives. Pichette was still unconscious when the call came to abandon ship. Like Weise, he had been left for dead.

They were now two dying men, discarded and forgotten, deep in the bowels of a ghost ship.

"What can we do?" Pichette asked.

Weise's will to survive was still strong. He coached Pichette, telling him he was their only hope since his legs were still intact.

"The ship is still afloat, so there must be destroyers nearby keeping watch," Weise reasoned. "Go topside and see if you can get some help. Go to a machine gun and start shooting."

Pichette carefully wrapped his midsection in sheets to hold his intestines in place, and departed into the darkness. His painful odyssey would be further challenged by climbing steel ladders up toward the hangar deck. Weise watched his fellow gunner depart, hoping for the best. It was the only chance they had. Darkness engulfed him once again as he lapsed back into unconsciousness.

★ CHAPTER ONE ★

CARRIER DOWN

Stanley Vejtasa was ready. Far below him, twisting frantically on the brilliant blue ocean, was the most desirable target an American dive-bomber pilot could ask for—a Japanese aircraft carrier. It was 1100 on May 7, 1942, in the Coral Sea, about thirteen hundred miles east of Australia, and now Vejtasa's fourteen-hundred-plus hours of flight-time experience were about to receive the ultimate test.

The junior grade (jg) lieutenant glanced down the length of his plane's wing, beyond the blue oval emblazoned with a large white star, and saw that his wingman was in proper attack position. Slightly ahead of Vejtasa was his skipper, Lieutenant Commander Bill Burch, preparing to dive. It was Burch who had given him his nickname nearly two years ago. Looking over the six-foot-two, blue-eyed, blond-haired pilot who hailed from

5

the farmlands of Circle, Montana, Burch had declared, "You are now Swede." In truth, the moniker was more a result of the skipper struggling to properly pronounce Vejtasa.[1]

Swede Vejtasa was one of seventeen pilots making this strike from Scouting Squadron Five (VS-5), based off the carrier USS *Yorktown* (CV-5). The aircraft he was flying was a Douglas Dauntless SBD dive-bomber, one that he considered highly efficient and very maneuverable against opposing aircraft. Under his plane's belly was a thousand-pound semi-armor-piercing bomb, the most lethal load his Dauntless could carry. It was Swede's job to plant his ordnance through the flight deck of the veering flattop far below.

His quarry was the Japanese carrier *Shōhō*, an eleven-thousand-ton vessel capable of carrying thirty aircraft. The name *Shōhō* translated to "Happy Phoenix." As *Yorktown*'s air group approached, Vejtasa believed she was only lightly damaged. *Shōhō* was just emerging from a merciless pounding by the air group from sister carrier *Lexington* (CV-2), whose dive-bombers and torpedo planes had already slammed at least two bombs and five torpedoes into the flattop. But the carrier was still underway, and Swede could only see small amounts of black smoke rising from what he assumed was a single bomb hit.

Vejtasa watched Burch release his half-ton bomb at twenty-five hundred feet before pulling out. *Shōhō*'s yellowish-colored wood flight deck shuddered as the bomb exploded dead center. Swede plunged another five hundred feet closer before he pulled the manual-release handle to jettison his own ordnance, two thousand feet above the carrier. Heavy g-forces pressed Vejtasa deep into his seat as he fought to pull his bomber out of its steep dive. He recovered just above the wave tops. From his rear cock-pit, Commander Walter "Butch" Schindler—riding as an attack observer in place of Swede's regular rear gunner—shouted, "You got a hit!"[2]

Diving behind VS-5 were eight pilots of *Yorktown*'s other SBD squadron, Bombing Squadron Five (VB-5). Fourth in their order was Lieutenant (jg) Bill Christie, a twenty-five-year-old pilot from Michigan who had been enjoying a leisurely drive to Virginia Beach with his wife when the Japanese attacked Pearl Harbor five months earlier. Since mobilizing for war, Christie had made several combat attacks on Japanese ships and instal-lations in the Marshall Islands, at Lae, New Guinea, and Tulagi Harbor. But his sights were now set on the supreme prize: sink-ing an enemy carrier. Here was a chance to avenge his shipboard roommate, a pilot lost in action back on February 1.[3]

Christie's bomb ripped through *Shōhō*, leaving the warship a blazing wreck as he cleared the fleet. His squadron's rendezvous outside the Japanese fleet was far from coordinated, as many pilots circled about the scene. Lieutenant Commander Joe Tay-lor's Torpedo Squadron Five (VT-5) from *Yorktown* finished off the Japanese carrier with additional torpedo hits on her star-board side. Within ten minutes, *Shōhō* plunged beneath the surface.[4]

A perfect attack, thought Vejtasa.

As *Yorktown*'s dive-bombers left the sinking carrier, they were attacked by several Mitsubishi A6M Navy "Zero" fighter planes. Christie's rear-seat gunner, Seaman First Class Lynn Forshee, got off only one short burst of his .30-caliber Brown-ing machine gun before it jammed. He stood up and fired his

.45-caliber pistol at a passing plane, which came so close, he could see the Japanese pilot's face. Christie joined with another VB-5 pilot for the return trip, but they were jumped by a Zero floatplane en route. Forshee, having cleared his machine gun, returned fire until both he and the enemy pilot were short of ammunition. As the Zero prepared to break off, the pilot fired one last parting shot at Christie's SBD—a round from a signal flare gun. It looked like a huge cannonball coming at him, but did no damage.[5]

Vejtasa tangled briefly with another Zero that made a run on his skipper's dive-bomber. His rear-seat passenger, Schindler, got in his own shots before VS-5's pilots cleared the contested zone and settled in for the long flight back to their own home carrier. Vejtasa, Christie, and the other aviators of *Yorktown's* air group had done their jobs, sinking the first aircraft carrier lost by the Imperial Japanese Navy (IJN) in the Pacific War.

The *Yorktown* pilots droned toward home through a dense bank of rain clouds, silently hoping their own flight deck was still intact.

———

By being on the offensive on May 7, *Yorktown's* air group was carrying out the first order of good task force defense: knock out your opponent before he can launch his own strike.

Closer to home, the second line of defense lay in the carrier fighter squadrons and protective combat air patrols (CAPs). Defending the U.S. carrier task forces fell upon the pilots of *Yorktown's* Fighter Squadron Forty-Two (VF-42) and *Lexington's* Fighter Squadron Two (VF-2). Lieutenant Commander Charles

"Chas" Fenton, skipper of VF-42, had seventeen Grumman F4F-3 Wildcat fighter planes at his disposal. Fenton was aloft at 1041 with a division of his CAP Wildcats when *Lexington*'s radar detected a bogey—an approaching unknown plane. Two of his pilots succeeded in shooting down a four-engine Kawanishi Type 97 reconnaissance flying boat around 1100, just ten miles from *Yorktown*'s task force.

Fortunately for the American carriers, no large-scale enemy counterattack materialized during the ensuing hours. The world's first-ever carrier battle was in full swing, and lessons were being learned with each passing hour. And history was recorded: For the first time, opposing warships neither sighted nor fired directly upon each other. The *Yorktown* and *Lexington* air groups returned triumphantly about two hundred miles home from sinking the carrier *Shōhō*, having sustained only the loss of three dive-bombers.

Admiral Isoroku Yamamoto, commander in chief of Japan's Combined Fleet, had planned to continue his country's dominance of the Pacific by taking control of the Australian territories of New Guinea and Papau to support the capture of Port Moresby—the capital and largest city of Papau—on about May 7. Preceding this effort, Yamamoto planned to occupy Tulagi Island near the key Solomon island of Guadalcanal, where his military could establish a seaplane base and garrison for further operations in the Coral Sea area.

The offensive, dubbed Operation Mo, or the Port Moresby Operation, was a southerly move intended to severe the line of communication between the United States and Australia. Yamamoto had involved three carriers of Japan's Combined Fleet—the twenty-five-thousand-ton fleet carrier *Shōkaku* and the twenty-nine-thousand-ton *Zuikaku*, plus the light carrier *Shōhō*. Learning of the Japanese plans through signals intelligence, the U.S. Navy had sent two carrier task forces and a joint Australian-American cruiser force into the Coral Sea to oppose Operation Mo.

Yorktown's Task Force 17 (TF-17) had rendezvoused with Rear Admiral Aubrey Wray Fitch's Task Force 11, built around the large thirty-six-thousand-ton carrier *Lexington* on May 1. Overall command fell to Rear Admiral Frank Jack Fletcher, who flew his flag on *Yorktown*. His flagship, commissioned in September 1937, was America's fifth-ever aircraft carrier, thus carrying the hull number CV-5. At 770 feet in length, *Yorktown* displaced 25,500 tons, was capable of a top speed of 32.5 knots (37.4 mph), and could carry more than five dozen aircraft into combat.

The U.S. Navy's first aircraft carrier *Langley* (CV-1) had been commissioned in 1922, less than twenty years after Orville and Wilbur Wright's first motor-powered airplane had flown for mere seconds above the sand dunes near Kitty Hawk, North Carolina. Lead ship of the *Yorktown* class, CV-5 was completing her fifth month of wartime operation as she and sister carrier *Lexington* squared off against Yamamoto's force in the Coral Sea.

Japanese landings on Tulagi had commenced on May 3, 1942. The invasion was supported by a task force of destroyers, minesweepers, a large minelayer, troop transports, sub chasers, and two auxiliary minesweepers. The first step in thwarting further

Japanese advancements called for a forceful aerial assault on the newly seized Solomon properties. While Fitch's TF-11 refueled on May 4, Fletcher used his *Yorktown* air group to launch three strikes against Japanese shipping and key ground installations in the Guadalcanal and Tulagi areas. *Yorktown*'s dive-bombers and torpedo planes had torpedoed a Japanese destroyer and forced her to run aground. Three minelayers were sunk and four observation seaplanes were destroyed, in addition to various other invasion-force shipping being damaged.

Now, three days later and two hundred miles away, the *Lexington* and *Yorktown* air groups had struck first against Yamamoto's carriers. While they were in the process of sinking *Shōhō*, Japanese strike groups launched from *Shōkaku* and *Zuikaku* made their own attacks. Capable of operating up to eighty-four aircraft, *Shōkaku*-class carriers displaced 31,600 tons but were the fastest warships yet designed by the Japanese. Their sleek hulls and robust power plants allowed these flattops to maneuver at speeds as high as 34.5 knots. Instead of finding Rear Admiral Fletcher's American carriers, strike planes from these behemoths discovered only the fleet tanker *Neosho* and her escorting destroyer *Sims*. Seventy-eight planes from the MO Striking Force bombed and sank *Sims* and fatally crippled the oiler.

Round one in the world's first carrier battle went to the Americans.

Yorktown's third level of defense lay in the guns of her screening warships and on the carrier itself. During the late afternoon of May 7, the gunners received their first true test.

Japanese reconnaissance planes reported American carriers in the vicinity. At 1615, *Shōkaku* and *Zuikaku* launched a late-afternoon search-and-strike group comprising a dozen Aichi D3A1 Type 99 carrier bombers (nicknamed "Vals" by the Allies) and fifteen Nakajima B4N2 Type 97 torpedo planes (code-named "Kate"). Some of these planes were intercepted by *Lexington* and *Yorktown* fighters thirty minutes before dusk, and aerial shoot downs ("kills") were made. As the late-afternoon dogfights carried on about thirty miles from the ship, the men on Fletcher's *Yorktown* were at battle stations.[6]

Yorktown bristled with armament: seventy-two guns of .50 caliber and higher. Her gun crews were well trained and prepared for the fight, and under the direction of Commander Ernest Judson Davis, a 1925 Naval Academy graduate. His battle station was located on an open platform on *Yorktown*'s elevated bridge structure, where he had a clear view of any incoming raiders. Hailing from Beaufort, North Carolina, Davis was a likable Southerner considered something of a gunnery genius by his peers.

Just days after the December 7 surprise attack on Pearl Harbor, Davis had toiled to upgrade his armament in the Norfolk Navy Yard. *Yorktown*'s most powerful guns were five-inch, .38-caliber heavy cannons, located on all four sides of her flight deck, fore and aft. These eight guns were the longest-range weapons, capable of firing fifty-five-pound projectiles to a maximum range of eighteen thousand yards (more than ten miles) at the rate of fifteen per minute.

Closer to her island superstructure, *Yorktown* had sixteen 1.1-inch (28mm) .75-caliber guns. Lighter and faster than the

5-inch guns, these intermediate-range weapons could fire at a rate of 150 rounds per minute to a maximum range of seven thousand yards. There were four sets of quad 1.1-inch mounts located in gun tubs on the edge of the catwalk, fore and aft of the island on both the port and starboard side. Prior to the Pearl Harbor attack, *Yorktown's* next-most-powerful guns had been .50-caliber Browning machine guns mounted in various positions along the outer perimeter of her deck. At Norfolk, Davis had received the welcome orders to replace the smaller .50-calibers with two dozen 20mm Oerlikon cannons. With a blistering rate of fire of more than three hundred rounds per minute, the 20mms could lob shells out to sixty-eight hundred yards, but were most effective against low-flying aircraft approaching to within a thousand yards.

Norfolk Navy Yard workers and the ship's crew had positioned the new 20mm guns all around the ship. But Davis, wanting all the firepower he could muster, ignored orders from Washington to turn over his two dozen .50-caliber machine guns. Twenty-four guns at six thousand rounds apiece sounded like a lot of firepower to him, so Davis had the .50-calibers sprinkled throughout the carrier—in gun tubs along the catwalks on the edges of the flight deck, high atop the island superstructure, and just below the flight deck, both fore and aft. [7]

Now, as the Japanese strike group tangled with American CAP fighters near dusk on May 7, *Yorktown's* gun teams were primed for their first real shooting match. Among them was seventeen-year-old John Hancock, a six-foot, hundred-thirty-pound second-class seaman. His battle station was far forward on the fo'c'sle deck, manning the portside .50-caliber Browning water-cooled machine gun. Lanky and athletic, he had been the second baseman when his high school baseball team won the state championship in Atlanta in 1940. During his senior year of high school in Alma, Georgia, Hancock had been inspired at the town's post office by a Navy recruiting sign that read, "Join the Navy and learn how to fly." The banner showed a dashing young pilot, his goggles pushed up on his head as he stood on the wing of his plane.[8]

That did the trick for Hancock, who enlisted on October 27, 1941. But less than six weeks later, the Japanese sidelined his flight aspirations by bombing Pearl Harbor. On December 13, he reported on board *Yorktown*, where he was assigned to the deck force with a battle stations gunnery billet. Hancock quickly came to appreciate the skills of his Southern gunnery boss, Ernie Davis. The lieutenant commander often barked through a loudspeaker to direct his crews, and his Carolina twang was often a source of humor to his men. During one gunnery drill en route to the Pacific, the SBDs were making dive-bombing attacks on a sled towed behind the ship. Davis ordered the gun crews to unload their weapons and to track the diving planes with their guns for practice.[9]

As the SBDs approached, Davis got on the PA and hollered in his slow drawl, "Heah they come!"

A watch officer standing nearby hollered back: "Sho' nuff? Well, shut my mouth!" Hancock thoroughly enjoyed the ship-wide laughter that ensued.

Manning another .50-caliber, high atop *Yorktown*'s island superstructure, was Seaman First Class George Weise, who had turned twenty-one just weeks earlier. Growing up in Astoria,

New York, he had made good money during high school working as a caddie. He had carried clubs for the likes of Byron Nelson, Eddie Arcaro, and Joe DiMaggio. Upon graduation, he had planned to marry his high school sweetheart, Jean May Smith. But both sets of parents were against this plan, so with war appearing to be imminent, Weise enlisted in the Navy on August 6, 1940.[10]

Although his heart was still heavy with thoughts of Jean, Weise proceeded to boot camp. Two months later, he reported on board the *Yorktown*, where he spent his first six months toiling belowdecks. Unsatisfied, he next became a yeoman striker in the executive officer's office, but found this assignment also not to his liking. He transferred to the 4th Division and, in time, became coxswain of the 4th Division motor launch.

For his battle station, Weise was first assigned to the crew of a five-inch mount on the port quarter. By the time he was well trained on this weapon, he found himself reassigned to one of the ship's highest .50-caliber machine guns. His weapon was located more than forty feet above the flight deck, in between two thirty-six-inch searchlights on the center of the carrier's smokestack. Although less familiar with his new gun, he was reassured by having a supervising gunner's mate stationed on the stack platform and an able loader, Seaman Second Class Joel W. Sledge. An eighteen-year-old farm boy from Colquitt County, Georgia, Sledge had left the fieldwork behind to join the Navy because, as he later put it, "I was tired of staring at a mule's ass." Weise suffered very few weapon malfunctions and soon considered himself to be a good shot.[11]

Hancock, Weise, and dozens of other gunners now eagerly

peered through their sights, awaiting the chance to fire their guns against the enemy for the first time in their five months of war.

The approaching Japanese strike group was picked up by *Lexington*'s radar at 1747. The contact was forty-eight miles out, but many of the twelve U.S. fighter planes currently flying combat air patrol over the task forces were low on fuel. A four-plane VF-2 division under *Lexington*'s fighter squadron skipper was vectored out to investigate. In the meantime, orders were issued on both U.S. carriers for all available fighter planes to be scrambled.[12]

One of the first VF-42 pilots to jump into a cockpit was Lieutenant (jg) Scott McCuskey. He was eager for action. Hailing from Little Rock, Arkansas, the twenty-seven-year-old fighter pilot was considered something of a hotshot. In February 1942, during *Yorktown*'s air strikes against Japanese forces in the Gilbert and Marshall islands, McCuskey and his wingman, Ensign Johnny Adams, had scored the first aerial kill for their air group.

In full view of TF-17, Adams and McCuskey had made firing passes on a large four-engine Japanese seaplane and set fire to it. Their slugs created an explosion that blew off the Type 97's twin-ruddered tail, sending it plunging into the ocean just miles from the *Yorktown*. McCuskey had bellowed over the radio, "We just shot his ass off!"[13]

When they landed, McCuskey and Adams were mobbed by excited flight deck crewmen—who had prepared a strange costume to be given to the fighter pilots who scored the first shoot down for CV-5. The fezlike hat and heavily decorated jacket were shared by the two comrades in the ensuing celebration.

On May 4, three months after their first shared kill, McCuskey and Adams had participated in *Yorktown*'s air strikes against Japanese bases in the Solomon Islands. Near Tulagi, they attacked Japanese shipping but became separated from their division mates. As the fuel tanks in their Wildcats ran dry, the pair was ultimately forced to make landings on the beach on Guadalcanal's southeast coast. That evening, the destroyer *Hammann* located the downed pilots and sent a whaleboat ashore to recover them. McCuskey and Adams were transferred back to their carrier from *Hammann* the following day. Chas Fenton, skipper of *Yorktown*'s VF-42, was incensed. As a section leader, McCuskey had cost the ship two irreplaceable Wildcat fighters in the midst of a major conflict. Fenton found McCuskey at fault for not properly staying with his division leader and grounded the pilot for two days.[14]

Two days later, on the evening of May 7, McCuskey was technically still grounded. But with a call to scramble all available fighters to intercept the incoming Japanese strike group, he took it upon himself to join the fray. He was in the cockpit of an F4F, warming the engine, when his executive officer, Lieutenant Commander Jimmy Flatley, raced onto the deck.

Flatley was aware of skipper Fenton's grounding of the young pilot. Orders were orders. He quickly motioned for McCuskey to vacate the plane as he climbed onto its wing. McCuskey begged to be given one of the other planes so he could fly out to engage the incoming enemy. Flatley shook his head, knowing that to give in would show weakness in his ability to discipline his pilots.[15]

Flatley departed with eleven VF-42 planes to join the VF-2 fighter pilots already airborne from the *Lexington*, plus another four-plane CAP division already aloft. McCuskey made his way down to *Yorktown*'s hangar deck and found that mechanics had one last flyable F4F. He persuaded his air department superiors to allow him to take it aloft. Hoisted to the flight deck via one of the carrier's massive aircraft elevators, McCuskey's F4F was shortly roaring down the flight deck.[16]

But McCuskey did not score any kills in this action. The approaching *Zuikaku* and *Shōkaku* planes were intercepted by VF-42 and VF-2 Wildcats pilots who claimed eight planes destroyed. Most of the Japanese aviators headed for their home carriers through foul weather. By 1830, the sun had set, and the U.S. carriers began recovering their aircraft in the darkness.

At this point in the Pacific War, American carrier air groups were not trained for night operations. Confusion ensued, and in the process, Task Force 17 experienced one of the stranger events of the war. In the midst of landing her own fighters, *Yorktown* was buzzed by several Japanese Type 99 carrier bombers. Flashing identification code letters, the enemy pilots came in low over *Yorktown*'s flight deck, trying to determine if they were approaching one of their own carriers for landing.

Swede Vejtasa, topside to watch the landings, immediately sensed that something was wrong. The unknown aircraft were approaching from the wrong side to make proper landings. As one flashed past just above deck level, Swede caught enough of a glimpse to realize it was not an American plane. "How the hell he escaped without catching a wire, I don't know," Vejtasa recalled.[17]

Gunnery Officer Ernie Davis was quick to figure out the situation. Grabbing his bullhorn, he bellowed from the bridge, "Those aircraft in the landing pattern are not friendly! Repeat—not friendly!" One of *Yorktown*'s air officers, Lieutenant Commander Robert "Pappy" Armstrong, added his own unique cry over the loudspeakers: "Stand by to repel boarders!"[18]

Some of TF-17's screening warships opened fire on the Japanese planes, and *Yorktown*'s gunners joined in. The action was brief and the confusion complete. John Hancock on his forward .50-caliber and George Weise on his island structure machine gun weren't sure exactly what the hell was going on. But *Yorktown*'s aft .50-caliber gunners and her starboard 20mm mounts took aim on the enemy planes.

The Japanese aircraft soon scattered and made their way back toward their own carriers in the darkness. *Yorktown* and *Lexington* recovered the last of their airborne fighters save one—Ensign John Baker of VF-42. While dodging the friendly fire of task force gunners, he became lost in the night and was unable to find a flight deck to land upon. His plane disappeared from radar and was never heard from again. Another F4F landed on *Yorktown* with a number of fresh .50-caliber bullet holes from friendly fire.

Hancock had not opened fire, but his adrenaline was pumping. The Japanese now clearly knew exactly where the American carriers were located. All signs pointed toward intensified attacks the following day. Although he was excited over the prospects of finally using his guns in action, Hancock was exhausted by the time the PA system announced that all hands could secure from general quarters. "Being young and dumb," he remembered, "I slept like I had been poleaxed."[19]

★ CHAPTER TWO ★

"DON'T GET IN MY WAY"

Since the surprise attack on Pearl Harbor in December, the Imperial Japanese Navy had advanced largely unchecked through the Pacific Theater. As carrier-launched warplanes created havoc on the U.S. Pacific Fleet in Hawaii, other Japanese forces had attacked the Philippines, Guam, Wake Island, and the British territories of Malaya, Singapore, and Hong Kong.

Within months, Japan's vast new empire included a defensive perimeter that ranged from western Alaska to the Solomon Islands. With its battleship fleet crippled in Hawaii, the U.S. Navy turned to its submarine force and its aircraft carriers to prevent the enemy's advance from severing American supply lines to allied Australia. On February 1, 1942, *Yorktown*'s task force had participated in the first tactical air strikes and naval artillery attacks against Japanese garrisons in the Marshall and Gilbert islands.

The early U.S. carrier raids conducted during the first months of the Pacific War had little long-term strategic impact. But the efforts raised morale for the servicemen and for the American public. On April 18, Lieutenant Colonel Jimmy Doolittle even led sixteen B-25B Mitchell medium bombers from the deck of the carrier *Hornet* to bomb the Japanese capital of Tokyo. While further bolstering homeland spirits, the Doolittle Raid also strengthened Admiral Yamamoto's resolve to destroy the American carrier fleet.

On May 8, in the Coral Sea, two of those vessels—*Yorktown* and *Lexington*—were ripe for the picking of Yamamoto's aviators.

———

Through the bluish haze of cigarette smoke in VF-42's ready room, Scott McCuskey saw his name chalked on the board, assigned to escort the dive-bombers and torpedo planes of *Yorktown*'s carrier attack group. His suspension had been lifted, and his solo sortie the previous evening had gone unpunished.

But first, it was paramount to find the enemy before the enemy struck first. At daybreak, as the sun climbed into clear blue skies over Task Force 17 in stark contrast to the stormy weather of the previous day, *Lexington*'s Dauntless dive-bombers were dispatched to search for the Imperial Japanese Navy carrier fleet.

McCuskey would have to wait out the next hours until

positive contact reports were received. Other VF-42 pilots were launched for early-morning CAP duty to protect the task force. The Grumman Wildcat was better suited to tackle the dreaded Japanese fighters than a Dauntless dive-bomber. The F4F fighter could be pushed more than seventy miles per hour faster than an SBD, could climb six hundred feet per minute faster, and had twice the number of forward-firing .50-caliber Browning machine guns.

But with only thirty-one available Grumman F4F fighters to cover both strike groups and CAP duties over both *Lexington* and *Yorktown*, Rear Admirals Jack Fletcher and Aubrey Fitch resorted to an unusual plan for the day: dive-bomber crews would be utilized to supplement the task force defense. Reasoning that their wing guns and rear-seat gunners could be effective against slower, low-flying Japanese torpedo planes, divisions of Dauntless crews were duly assigned to "anti-VT" duty on May 8.

On *Yorktown*, this duty was handed to two divisions of Bill Burch's VS-5 squadron. Swede Vejtasa was incensed to find his name on the list. Instead of flying out to attack Japanese carriers, he and half of his squadron would be playing defense, an assignment that required hours of maintaining station off the bows of the two American carriers to combat any enemy torpedo planes that should appear. Around 0730, Swede and seven other VS-5 crews were launched as *Yorktown's* deckhands hurriedly respotted her flight deck with a strike force. To Vejtasa, it was a bad use of good SBDs, but he had little recourse.

Once airborne, he took up his defensive position, flying lazy circles ahead of the task force while awaiting word from *Lexington*'s scouts.[1]

———

Warren Heller used the morning hours of May 8 to prepare for the worst. Because he was one of thirty pharmacist's mates serving on *Yorktown*, it was his job to help save lives if his ship was damaged due to enemy attack.

Heller's battle station this day was a relatively new one, but he dutifully checked his medical supplies and made ready. Through *Yorktown*'s early months of war, he frequently served in the ship's main medical facility, dubbed "Sick Bay," which was located on the third deck—two decks below the hangar deck, which on *Yorktown* was considered the main deck. On a normal day in this compartment, Heller helped tend to patients suffering from colds and skin infestations like athlete's foot and jock itch, or to those in need of stitches from an untimely meeting with a steel hatch frame. On May 8, there were few patients in Sick Bay, save one sailor recovering from an appendectomy.

The previous evening, Heller had had his closest taste of war when his ship's gunners had fired on the three Japanese planes making their errant approaches. Energized by the action, he had had but a few hours of sleep before the bugle blare of general quarters sounded over the loudspeakers on May 8. He sprang to life, dressing and racing to his battle station. Sleeping quarters for hospital corpsmen were one deck above the ship's main Sick Bay on the carrier's port side, just above the waterline. The heat was stifling. The odor of perspiration permeated the air, adding a flavor of its own to the uncomfortable dankness as Heller climbed a steel ladder to reach the hangar deck. He headed forward to his battle station, wondering if his ship would be as lucky this day in dodging enemy air attacks.[2]

Lexington's air group was launched on a morning search at 0625. *Yorktown*'s own air group was an hour late in sending up its first aircraft of the day—four CAPs and eight SBDs to handle anti-torpedo-plane patrol. In previous months, Heller had enjoyed watching the takeoffs and landings of the air group. He was technically assigned as the medic for Bombing Squadron Five and had long held a general quarters station on the island structure.

But not this day. His boss, Ohio native Jim Wilson, had other plans for him. A seasoned Navy veteran with fourteen years' service, Wilson was a no-nonsense chief petty officer who had previously served on two other carriers. The Japanese attack on Pearl Harbor was a day he would never forget. December 7, 1941, was the day his son, Richard, was born, to his wife, Florence, in Norfolk. On the same day, he lost a brother, Chief Warrant Officer Neil Wilson, on board the battleship *Arizona*, when it exploded from a Japanese bomb hit.[3]

While in port at Tongatabu prior to the Coral Sea action, Wilson had decided that he needed an experienced pharmacist's mate to be in the first aid station in the forward part of the ship. Should the main Sick Bay be knocked out by an enemy attack, he reasoned that a secondary medical facility should be ready. The new aid station was located in officer's country, immediately below the flight deck near the wardroom.

Although Heller was to be in charge, the reassignment did not appeal to him. For months, he had been assigned to Battle

Dressing Station No. 1, located in the afterpart of the island structure. As a medic for VB-5, he pointed out to his chief, he should remain on the flight deck. But Wilson decided that, for the good of the entire medical department, a medic like Heller was needed to take over the new Battle Dressing Station No. 2 forward.[4]

Heller's background certainly qualified him to run the new station. Raised in Bridgeport, Connecticut, he had struggled to make the most of his first twenty-two years. His father's business had crumbled during the Great Depression and his parents' marriage had dissolved. His younger sister, Jean, remained with his mother, but Warren was forced to live with other family members as a teenager. His early dreams of becoming an architect were shelved as he watched architects struggle to make a living in the midst of the nation's financial crisis.[5]

Heller shifted his focus to medicine, deciding it was a more stable occupation. He attended the Rockland State Hospital of Nursing and obtained his RN (registered nurse) license from the New York State Board of Nursing. Heller had gone to work in a psychiatric sanatorium in White Plains, New York, hoping to one day continue his education to become a physician. In pursuance of that endeavor, he began attending Columbia College.[6]

In 1940, he was dating Helen Amelia Fleming, an attractive nurse who was equally strong-willed in her medical occupation. That year the war in Europe began to have repercussions in America. Young men his age were beginning to be drafted into the military. Heller decided to join the Navy Reserve, where he could serve as a pharmacist's mate, should he be called up. Helen didn't think too much of that idea, but Warren and

Helen were married on December 26, 1940, after his completion of his third semester at Columbia. He was called to active
duty in the U.S. Navy in February 1941, forcing him to put
medical school on hold and leave his young wife at home. In
November 1941, at age twenty-two, Heller became a father.[7]

Fresh from a North Atlantic convoy-escort mission, *Yorktown*
made port in Portsmouth, New Hampshire. Heller received a
seventy-two-hour leave and hitchhiked four hundred miles
across New England to see his new son, Warren. He returned a
day late to find *Yorktown* had already sailed to Virginia. Heller
faced a captain's mast for overstaying his liberty; for his punishment, he was confined to the ship for a month. Since he
didn't have anything to do off ship, the penalty wasn't much of
one.[8]

On board *Yorktown*, he had made two close friends within
the medical department. When Chief Wilson assigned him to
run the new medical station just prior to the Coral Sea battle,
Heller asked his boss to assign one of his two best friends—
Pharmacist's Mate (PhM) Second Class Ralph Stewart—with
him. Prior to the war, Stewart had been a chiropractor in Los
Angeles, and he had implored Heller to partner with him in
chiropractics after the war. Their small medical compartment,
roughly ten feet by twelve feet, was liberally stocked with first
aid items: tourniquets, sterile battle dressings, antiseptics, Vase-
line gauze, bandage scissors, tannic acid solution, needles, su-
ture material, morphine sulfate syrettes, and more. Secured to
the bulkheads were wire mesh and canvas basket stretchers
that other corpsmen could use to haul casualties to their station
or down below to the main Sick Bay.[9]

Heller's other close friend on *Yorktown* was PhM3c Edmund Koslowski, described by Heller as "a pimply-faced, gangly chap who had worked on the family tobacco farm back in Kentucky." Koslowski's battle station was now the one Heller had long manned, Battle Dressing Station No. 1 at the base of the island structure. During flight operations, Koslowski stood on the first landing of the after-island-structure ladder with a first aid bag. In case of an accident, he could be down the ladder and onto the flight deck in an instant.[10]

The trio of pharmacist's mates was tight, often enjoying liberty together. During *Yorktown*'s most recent stop in Honolulu, Heller had been teased by his buddies when he naively came to learn of a particular vocation still being legally practiced in the Hawaiian Islands. Strolling through Honolulu, they came to a building with a long line of sailors queuing up in front. The overhead sign read SENATOR ARMS.

Oblivious, Heller said, "That must be a very good movie for those guys to be waiting so patiently to see."[11]

Koslowski laughed. "Hell, that's no movie house. That's a whorehouse!"

"Come on, fellows, you're kidding me," said Heller.

Stewart and Koslowski hustled their buddy to the front of the line so he could find out for himself. The first sailor queried gave a very matter-of-fact reply: "I'm waiting to get a piece of ass."

"How much does that cost?" asked Heller.

"Two bucks," said the sailor. "But I understand it's going up to three next week."

That event was far removed from Warren Heller's mind on

the morning of May 8. Koslowski was on his ladder perch near Battle Dressing Station No. 1, while Heller and Stewart stood ready at their new forward station. For the time being, the trio could do little more than ride out the morning hours. Once *Yorktown* launched her morning CAP and anti-VT dive-bombers, she resumed her base course, and the waiting game on the Coral Sea continued.

Bill Roy had a plan. Through the first five months of the Pacific War, his carrier had escaped direct enemy attack. But this day, odds were stronger that the Japanese Navy might send carrier-strike groups against the American fleet. Should such a battle ensue, Roy had a vision of filming a documentary of the action.

As one of *Yorktown's* photographer's mates, William Glenn Roy yearned for flexibility. His "office" was the carrier's photography lab, located on the third deck, far removed from direct view of enemy aerial attacks. His lab included developing chemicals, a variety of handheld still cameras, movie cameras, and even special aerial-photography cameras. He intended to put these tools to use to record the action, and he had taken steps to do so.

The twenty-one-year-old Roy hailed from rural Alabama, but had completed high school in Lake City, Florida, in 1939. Roy opted to join the military when Germany invaded Poland. During his first duty, on board the battleship *Arkansas*, his interest in photography was noticed by the ship's executive officer. In high school, Roy had worked for a commercial photographer, experience that helped net him the role of becoming the *Arkansas* ship's photographer. In July 1941, he applied for and was assigned to the Navy's photography school in Pensacola, Florida. Upon completion of the comprehensive four-month course, he was rated as a photographer's mate third class, and reported on board *Yorktown* on December 6, 1941, in Norfolk, Virginia.[12]

With *Yorktown*, he had sailed from the East Coast after the start of the war as the carrier transited the Panama Canal, visited San Diego, and then proceeded to Pearl Harbor. Roy had witnessed all of *Yorktown*'s early 1942 Pacific actions—raids on the Marshall and Gilbert islands on February 1 and against Lae and Salamaua, New Guinea, in March. During his carrier's subsequent month of battle cruising, his duty station during flight quarters was on the port side of the flight deck near the No. 2 arresting wire, to film landings and takeoffs.

Bill Roy's photography skills had come into play on the night of May 3, the eve of his carrier's strikes against Tulagi. Commander Murr Arnold, the ship's air officer, was in a quandary. His aviators were ill prepared, without proper maps of the South Pacific. Arnold managed to procure a geography book that included a detailed map of Tulagi and the Solomons chain. He visited *Yorktown*'s photo lab and asked Roy to produce a hundred eight-by-eight-inch copies of the map on photo paper for the use of his pilots in the morning. Roy worked into the night in his lab and delivered the prints to Arnold before dawn.[13]

The raids made by the *Yorktown* air group were deemed a success. Roy felt some satisfaction in having played a small part in the opening of a naval action that would come to be known as the Battle of the Coral Sea. Three days later, he felt further jubilation when his ship's aviators helped sink the *Shōhō*. As his air group prepared for further carrier strikes on May 8, Roy had a premonition that this day might bring closer battle action.

He took his idea to the ship's executive officer, Commander Dixie Kiefer, that morning. Forty-six-year-old Kiefer, a 1919 Naval Academy graduate, was one of the Navy's pioneering aviators. Heavyset and kindhearted, he had only been *Yorktown*'s XO for three months, but had quickly become a favorite among his crew. Although the Navy was officially dry, Kiefer had convened the first "Yorktown Cocktail Meeting" a month earlier in the Coral Sea to allow his aviators a shot of whiskey to calm their nerves before battle.[14]

After hearing out Roy's wishes, the commander granted his request. Roy had already commenced work on shooting stock footage throughout the ship. Now he planned to film and photograph the heart of the carrier's command center by being amid the action on the bridge, which contained the pilothouse, the radar center, and the conning tower.

Roy wore plain dungaree pants and a shirt, and stuffed his pockets with extra film. Although steel helmets were required of sailors standing watch anywhere topside, he decided not to wear one in order to better handle his photographic equipment. On the bridge, he informed the skipper, Captain Elliott Buckmaster, of the special project he had been granted permission to undertake.[15]

"Don't get in my way," Buckmaster told him. "But you can stay on the bridge and do your job."

Buckmaster was ever present on the bridge. While at sea, he

never slept in his own private quarters far below. He preferred to rest in a little emergency cabin on the bridge where his meals were carried up to him on a tray. At night, he never used lights because of the time it took his eyes to adjust. If he received any orders, he remained in the dark and had someone read them to him.[16]

Buckmaster was firm but fair in his treatment of the crew. At age fifty-two, he had been in the Navy two-thirds of his life. Appointed to the Naval Academy from Virginia, he graduated in 1912 and was assigned to the battleship *New Jersey*. By 1934, he held his own command, putting the destroyer *Farragut* into commission. Following his early surface ship duties, Buckmaster entered naval aviation flight training at Naval Air Station (NAS) Pensacola.

In 1938, he was assigned to *Lexington* as her executive officer, then promoted to captain in 1939. Buckmaster was commanding officer of NAS Ford Island in Pearl Harbor until January 1941, when he was appointed *Yorktown*'s third commander. Although qualified as an aviator, he had not served in a squadron. But being a naval aviator qualified him as a true "brown shoe" leader on an aircraft carrier. Surface officers wore black shoes with their military uniforms, unlike the brown shoes worn by commissioned naval aviators. To his pilots, brown-shoe Buckmaster was one of them.

But *Yorktown*'s new skipper was burdened with an executive officer, Commander Joseph J. "Jocko" Clark, who made it known that he had eleven years' more flight experience than his new skipper. Clark challenged many of Buckmaster's decisions. Tall and dignified, Buckmaster appeared to have an icy disposition to those who did not know him well. But he endeared himself to his air group in bypassing his bullish exec to seek advice from his squadron commanders and his air officer. He was unafraid to let them try new ideas, much to the disdain of Jocko Clark. When Clark was promoted and transferred to a new assignment in February 1942, Captain Buckmaster certainly felt no regrets.[17]

The *Yorktown* was a virtual floating city, with a complement of twenty-two-hundred-plus officers and men. Buckmaster had led them unscathed through air attacks against Japanese bases in the Pacific in early 1942. When tensions ran high, he allowed his men to release a little steam. On April 10, after more than three months of battle cruising without liberty, his carrier was running short of all vital supplies. Chief Pay Clerk Phil Dahlquist had reported that *Yorktown*'s freezers were down to their last five steaks. He suggested they be raffled off, and the "*Yorktown* Jamboree" was held that day.[18]

The carrier's amidships aircraft elevator was lowered to within a foot of the hangar deck. From this stage, a series of acts entertained the crew who gathered on the hangar deck while others peered down from the flight deck. Chief Electrician's Mate Walter Fox, a *Yorktown* plank owner (the name for an an original commissioning member) dubbed the "Swami of Granby Street," performed hypnosis acts on volunteers and served as the master of ceremonies. First Class Musician Ed Oakley led the ship's twenty-piece orchestra through catchy tunes. Each band member was a graduate of the U.S. Navy School of Music in Washington, DC, and was assigned regular battle stations when Oakley was not leading them in practice.

Fireman Second Class Sidney Flum—dressed as a bearded lady—and Seaman Second Class Pete Montalvo danced the "jumping jive."

The names of the raffle winners were drawn from a box and the five lucky men were seated at a fancy table on the ship's elevator. The final steak dinners were served to them by a fourteen-year-old sailor named John Underwood, who had lied about his age to enter the Navy. Underwood was dressed as a waitress, complete with a blond wig, knee-length white hose, and soup bowls for breasts.

Captain Buckmaster did not attend the festivities, but he fully realized the value of maintaining the spirits of fighting men. Now, less than a month removed from this sidebar to the war, *Yorktown*'s crew was in the midst of the world's first carrier battle in the Coral Sea. Buckmaster carried on with his normal routine as Bill Roy captured film during the morning of May 8.

Aside from the skipper, Roy had the rare chance to capture images of TF-17's commander, Rear Admiral Fletcher. Unlike Buckmaster, Fletcher was a black-shoe officer. Since graduating from the Naval Academy in 1902, fifty-six-year-old "Black Jack" Fletcher had served on traditional warships—battleships and destroyers. As a lieutenant in 1914, he had earned the Medal of Honor for rescuing hundreds of refugees during the occupation of Veracruz, Mexico. Promoted to rear admiral in 1939, Fletcher had commanded a cruiser division until the Japanese attack on Pearl Harbor.

He had first hoisted his two-star flag on board *Yorktown* on New Year's Day 1942. His staff included a dozen officers and a larger number of yeomen, enlisted personnel, and mess attendants to take care of his entourage. Of medium height, he was a black-haired, slender man with brown eyes and a weathered, ruddy complexion. Fletcher possessed a manageable ego, had a keen sense of humor, and held little regard for paperwork. He was not one to get immersed in details and lose sight of the big picture. Nor did he unduly interfere with his subordinates.[19]

Fletcher had arisen on this morning after just four hours of sleep. His task force was steaming a hundred eighty miles from the southern fringe of the Louisade Archipelago, a string of volcanic islands off New Guinea. The previous day, his carriers had sunk the light carrier *Shōhō*, and had turned back the Port Moresby invasion force, at least temporarily. Now his two flattops and their hundred seventeen operational aircraft faced the very real possibility of trading blows with the main Japanese carrier-striking force. He and his counterpart, Rear Admiral Fitch, were tasked with sending out scouting patrols and protecting their own vessels until definitive contact was made.[20]

Roy moved silently about *Yorktown*'s bridge, careful not to interfere with Buckmaster or the TF-17 commander. In the process, he captured movie film of a thoughtful Rear Admiral Fletcher and his support staff on the exposed bridge, more than forty feet above the flight deck, peering through binoculars while wearing their steel hard hats.

The stage was set for renewed action in the Coral Sea, and Bill Roy would have a bird's-eye view of all the drama.

———

The Japanese were first to spot their opponent. At 0802, *Yorktown*'s radar picked up a bogey eighteen miles to the northwest.

This Japanese reconnaissance plane reported the American carriers but disappeared from radar during the next quarter hour.

At 0820, the first contact reports of the Japanese carrier fleet were received from *Lexington* scout pilots. The distance: just a hundred twenty miles away. Admiral Fletcher sent word via voice radio at 0837: "Believe we have been sighted by enemy carrier plane." Aubrey Fitch from his flagship, *Lexington*, quickly responded with "Launch striking group."[21]

The launching order dropped like a lighting bolt on both U.S. vessels. Scouts from opposing navies had each spotted the other's carriers. The Battle of the Coral Sea now hinged upon which air groups could strike first and which could inflict the most crippling damage. Aviators scrambled into action from *Yorktown*'s ready rooms.

In VF-42's ready room, Scott McCuskey made quick notes on the enemy's reported position. He copied onto his plotting board the vital Point Option—the place in the ocean where his carrier was expected to be found upon his return from the strike. *Yorktown* would be launching two dozen dive-bombers, each loaded with thousand-pound bombs: seven from Lieutenant Commander Bill Burch's VS-5 and seventeen from Lieutenant Wally Short's VB-5. Accompanying them were nine torpedo-loaded TBDs from Lieutenant Commander Joe Taylor's VT-5. Escorting the strike force would be three sections—six planes total—from VF-42. Freshly ungrounded, McCuskey and his Tulagi wingman, Johnny Adams, were both slated to make the strike. But this day, each pilot would be flying as wingman to another senior pilot.

The *Yorktown* group began launching at 0900. McCuskey's

section leader was Lieutenant (jg) Bill Leonard. Coupled with a second section of Lieutenant (jg) Bill Woollen and his wingman Adams, these four Wildcats were tasked with escorting the slower Devastators. They departed the task force at 0915, flying at two thousand feet at a cruising speed of a hundred thirty knots with the Grummans making gentle "S" turns to prevent them from overtaking the torpedo planes.[22]

From his battle station on *Yorktown*'s fo'c'sle deck, gunner John Hancock watched the strike planes depart. As they formed up and headed out toward the last-reported position of the Japanese carriers, he hoped they would strike the enemy before any strike groups were sent toward Task Force 17. Hancock had been at his gun since 0545. After four hours of waiting, he wondered if he would see any action that day.

A quarter hour later, clarifying reports became available. Another *Lexington* SBD scout plane, piloted by VS-2 skipper Lieutenant Commander Bob Dixon, began spying on the Japanese fleet. It consisted of the carriers *Shōkaku* and *Zuikaku*, plus six destroyers and four cruisers. Dixon would continue to monitor the enemy fleet for the next seventy-five minutes as the strike groups from his own *Lexington* and *Yorktown* approached.

After a flight of one hour and fifteen minutes, Burch's leading SBDs caught sight of the Japanese strike force. The dive-bombers remained in sight of the enemy and circled through a mass of clouds while waiting for the slower TBDs and their four F4Fs to catch up. Everyone was eager. Lieutenant John Powers, leading the second section of VB-5's first division, had boldly stated prior to the flight: "I am going to get a hit if I have to lay it on their own flight deck."[23]

Seventeen thousand feet below, the white wakes of warships slithered across the shimmering blue ocean surface. For the moment, all was peaceful. There was no indication the enemy had sighted them. Burch and Short passed word for the SBDs to circle in the clouds and wait for Taylor's torpedo planes to catch up. Closer to the enemy fleet, the American strikers encountered a warm frontal zone of cloud banks and rain squalls. Lieutenant (jg) Bill Christie of VB-5 felt the seventeen minutes wasted, while waiting for the slower Devastators to arrive on the scene passed like hours. Sputtering gray pockets of rainstorms did not help his mood.[24]

Yorktown's dive-bomber crews were much relieved when the VT-5 torpedo planes finally appeared. McCuskey was ready, but so far no Japanese Zeros had appeared to challenge his strike force. He worried that the opportunity for surprise was slipping away. Lieutenant Turner Caldwell, second-in-command of VS-5, noted *Shōkaku* turning into the wind to begin launching planes and *Zuikaku* steaming toward a nearby rain squall.

All hopes of surprise evaporated when the Japanese ships suddenly began firing on the circling American warplanes.

It was 1057 when VT-5 skipper Taylor finally radioed his Naval Academy classmate VS-5 skipper Burch: "Okay, Bill, I'm starting in."

It was time to attack.

———

John Hancock felt the breeze change direction against his face. Thirty minutes after *Yorktown*'s strike group had departed for the Japanese fleet, the carrier was turning back into the wind, making fifteen knots of speed for additional flight operations. By 0945, *Yorktown* had landed her first morning CAP fighters and had launched her second combat air patrol. Swede Vejtasa and seven of his VS-5 Dauntless teams remained on patrol, holding station just ahead of *Lexington* and *Yorktown* to watch for approaching Japanese torpedo planes.

Hancock chatted with his loader, Stuart Motley, to pass the time. They were young men, full of nervous energy. Their air group had taken care of an enemy aircraft carrier the previous day. Now they wondered which country's aviators would find the other country's fleet first. They did not have long to wonder.

Warrant officer Vane Bennett was the first to receive indications that *Yorktown* had been sighted. His ship's CXAM radar could determine the bearings and ranges of aircraft within a radius of eighty miles from the ship. The ultrahigh-frequency radar waves operated in a line-of-sight method; they did not bend or dip over the horizon and offered no indication of a contact's altitude. On board both *Yorktown* and *Lexington,* a fighter director officer (FDO) tracked the unidentified aircraft or bogeys and was responsible for directing airborne fighter planes out to intercept. Today, Lieutenant Frank "Red" Gill on board *Lexington* would act as the key FDO for all fighters aloft from both carriers. *Yorktown*'s acting fighter director officer this day was Commander Oscar "Pete" Pederson, the air group commander.[25]

Yorktown had been one of the first half dozen ships of the U.S. Navy to receive the CXAM radar in October 1940. Manufactured by the Radio Corporation of America (RCA), the seventeen-by-eighteen-foot antenna—which looked like a large

bedspring—was mounted high atop the carrier's island structure. It was connected to a radar plot located in a corner of the
compartment in the island known as Air Plot. The CXAM set
was managed by thirty-four-year-old Radio Electrician Bennett,
one of the Navy's most seasoned radar experts.

In 1922, in his rural home in Bladen, Nebraska, fourteen-
year-old Bennett had built a radio receiver with copper wire
wrapped around an oatmeal box. The instructions came from
Popular Mechanics magazine. After joining the Navy three
years later, Bennett had been one of six chief petty officers selected for special radar training at RCA's New Jersey plant.
Each of the six was assigned to the first six ships to receive the
CXAM radar. Having been advanced to warrant officer rank,
Bennett had operated *Yorktown*'s radar since its arrival. No one
knew it better.[26]

At 0932, the rotating antenna locked onto a new target. Bennett reported that a bogey had been detected thirty-nine miles
out from the ship. Lieutenant Vince McCormack's fighter division was vectored out to investigate by Gill, but found nothing.
The unknown contact got as close as twenty-five miles to the
U.S. task forces before disappearing. Further cause for alarm
was received on board Aubrey Fitch's flagship, *Lexington*, at
1000. One of her returning SBD scout planes radioed that a
dozen unidentified aircraft had been spotted forty-five miles
out from TF-17. Three minutes later, lookouts on *Yorktown*'s
bridge reported visual sighting of a single aircraft fifteen miles
away and closing. At 1007, Rear Admiral Fletcher ordered Fitch
to launch additional aircraft to help fend off what he believed
to be an incoming enemy air strike. *Yorktown* buttoned up and

prepared for action. On the hangar deck, the gasoline lines were drained at 1008 as flight operations were halted.[27]

McCormack and his VF-42 wingman, Ensign Walt Haas, had been directed northward toward the single bogey radar had seen. They tallyhoed the bandit, found to be a lumbering Kawanishi Type 97 flying boat operating from Tulagi. The two-pilot Wildcat section made three firing passes on the big plane, and their bullets created smoke. Japanese aviators fired back at the Grumman fighters from turrets and gun hatches on the Kawanishi, but it was a short fight. During his third firing pass, Haas saw the plane explode directly in front of him.[28]

From *Yorktown*, a black plume of smoke rising from the ocean surface could be seen on the horizon at 1015. It marked the spot of the kill made by McCormack and Haas. During the next half hour, additional F4F fighters and SBD dive-bombers were launched from both *Lexington* and *Yorktown* to bolster the task force's outer defenses. The bogey had not been an enemy air strike, but certainly the Japanese knew where the American fleet was located.

Bennett's radar team was part of *Yorktown*'s communications department. His vigilant department leader was Commander Clarence "Jug" Ray, a 1925 Academy graduate best known for his ever-present tobacco pipe. When Ray had joined the carrier, he told Captain Buckmaster that if he could not have the privilege of smoking his pipe on the bridge, the skipper might as well get rid of him. Buckmaster acquiesced, making him the only pipe smoker on the bridge.[29]

When Pearl Harbor was attacked, Ray had been enjoying lunch with his wife and young son in Virginia Beach. He raced back to the ship, where his duties during the next five months covered everything from secret dispatches to the operation of *Yorktown*'s top secret air-search radar set.[30]

On the morning of May 8, Jug Ray was exhausted. He had been up most of the night, sending out operational orders and sorting through countless dispatches. During the early morning, Ray had just turned in for a quick nap when he was awakened by the predawn general quarters as flight operations commenced. Determining that the ship was not in immediate danger of air attack, he turned in again to get some more rest in Air Plot. He told the radioman on watch to wake him in thirty minutes, figuring he needed fifteen minutes "to get the spiderwebs out of my eyes before we were hit."[31]

While Commander Ray dozed, his ship's CAP had downed the snooping Kawanishi. At 1039, his radio gang monitored a report that *Yorktown*'s strike group had sighted a Japanese carrier. Throughout the ship, there was excitement—and the hope—that *Yorktown*'s planes might knock out the enemy before they could launch. But any lingering doubts as to whether the Japanese had already sent out their own attack group were quickly dispelled. At 1055, Vane Bennett's radar set locked in on a large group of enemy planes. They were sixty-eight miles out and closing the distance. Based on the strong contact registering on both the *Lexington* and *Yorktown* CXAM radar sets, there was little doubt that this was the anticipated enemy air strike.

Lexington turned into the wind to launch additional CAP fighters and Dauntless dive-bombers to tackle anti-VT duty. Lieutenant Commander Jimmy Flatley scrambled another division of VF-42 at 1103 to join the intercept after *Lexington* FDO Red Gill broadcast the call, "Hey, Rube!" An old carnival barker phrase, this message indicated to all airborne defensive planes to return to their assigned defensive positions near their carriers.[32]

The Japanese strike force was only minutes away from a visual sighting of the American carriers. Lieutenant Gill began issuing various intercept orders to the first line of defense—his available F4Fs and SBDs. Their success, or lack thereof, would deterine how many warplanes made it past the defensive curtain to face the second level of defense—antiaircraft gunners on the carriers, destroyers, and cruisers.

Gunner John Hancock could feel his pulse increasing as radio reports broadcast the countdown. Enemy airplanes might be in sight at any minute.

As Japanese strikers approached TF-17, the *Lexington* and *Yorktown* air groups were already making their own strike. Joe Taylor's lumbering VT-5 torpedo planes reached the scene shortly before 1100, and *Yorktown*'s dive-bomber squadrons prepared to push over.

Rear-seat gunner Lynn Forshee could see the Japanese carrier *Zuikaku* heading toward a nearby rain squall as his SBD circled. Looking over at one of his fellow radiomen, Forshee tapped out signals on his helmet to verify that both were on the proper radio setting. Bill Burch's Scouting Five began their dives first, intent on releasing their thousand-pound bombs on the other enemy flattop, *Shōkaku*. The first six Dauntless pilots landed only near misses against the swerving warship, which raised huge pillars of seawater that splattered onto its flight deck.

The VS-5 and VB-5 pilots suffered a familiar problem in their dives on the enemy carrier: Rapidly changing air temperatures during their seventy-degree plunges caused both their windshields and telescopic sights to fog over. Forshee's pilot, Lieutenant (jg) Bill Christie, felt that lining up a target ship by peering over the side of his cockpit was not a good way to proceed, but he had gotten used to this odd necessity.[33]

Burch's seven VS-5 dive-bombers scored only near misses, but Christie's VB-5 fared better. He believed he scored a direct hit. *Yorktown's* Dauntless crews landed at least two direct hits on *Shōkaku*, and brilliant orange-red fires erupted on her flight deck. Among those scoring was Lieutenant Jo Jo Powers, who had vowed he would get a hit even if he did not return. His plane was hit by antiaircraft fire during his descent, wounding both him and his gunner. But Powers dived his flaming SBD to five hundred feet before toggling his bomb. As the thousand pounder shredded *Shōkaku's* flight deck just aft of her island structure, his plane slammed into the Coral Sea a short distance away. For his actions in pressing home his attack to make a hit, Powers would posthumously receive the Medal of Honor.

Yorktown's Dauntlesses were assailed by Japanese Zeros even before they could complete their dives. Firing both 7.7mm machine guns and 20mm cannons, the Mitsubishi fighters doggedly pursued VS-5 and VB-5 planes as their pilots fought to clear the antiaircraft gunfire from the Japanese warships. Ensign Davis Chaffee's 5-B-16 was shot down near the task force, killing both the pilot and Lynn Forshee's good friend Seaman First Class John Kasselman. *Shōkaku* was burning furiously in the distance as Forshee and other *Yorktown* rear-seat gunners blazed away at the swirling Zeros during their retreats. Forshee's pilot, Christie, applied full throttle as he pushed his SBD toward the welcoming cover of a nearby storm front.

Sixteen Zeros from *Shōkaku* and *Zuikaku* swarmed over the *Yorktown* strike planes. McCuskey's first view of trouble was in the form of two *Shōkaku* Zeros that swung in to attack the VF-42 escorts. As a Mitsubishi moved in to fire on his F4F, McCuskey gunned his Grumman into a sharp climbing turn. As he nosed back down to gain speed, he lined up his sights on a second fighter and pressed his trigger. McCuskey's four .50-caliber wing guns blinked rapid bursts of red flame as his bullets raked the Zero from stem to stern. The Zero rolled onto its back and slammed full tilt into the ocean.[34]

A third Zero latched onto McCuskey, forcing him to turn sharply into his opponent to dodge the bullets. In a series of twisting dives and sharp climbs, he struggled to evade the efforts of two Japanese fighters that chased his F4F through the cloud cover. At one point, he plunged to within a hundred feet of the wave tops before he was able to pull out. When he was finally able to shake his opponents, McCuskey was separated from his comrades, so he set a course for home. He and his VF-42 pilots had shot down two Zeros that had attempted to attack Joe Taylor's torpedo planes.[35]

Lexington's strike group moved in next, adding another thousand-pound-bomb hit to *Shōkaku*. The Japanese carrier was left heavily damaged and unable to conduct further flight operations. The surviving *Lexington* and *Yorktown* air groups fought their way through slashing Zero attacks and turned for home. McCuskey throttled back to conserve fuel and droned all alone in the direction of Task Force 17, unaware how his own *Yorktown* had fared against Japanese strikers.

CHAPTER THREE

"MAN YOUR GUNS!"

By 1107, radar showed the approaching enemy planes to be twenty-two miles out from *Yorktown*. The FDOs on both carriers coached their airborne fighter divisions out to intercept. Lieutenant Swede Vejtasa and the eight VS-5 SBDs on anti-torpedo-plane defense could expect enemy contact within minutes.

Should any Japanese torpedo planes and dive-bombers make it through the CAPs and the steel curtain of antiaircraft fire, the carrier was vulnerable. Any bomb or torpedo damage must be tackled swiftly to save lives, to shore up damage, and to maintain the seaworthiness of the ship. This role fell squarely upon the shoulders of Lieutenant Commander Clarence Edward Aldrich. As the ship's first lieutenant and senior damage control officer, he was in charge of teams of specialists positioned throughout the ship. They stood ready on the hangar deck, at the base of the flight deck, in the engineering compartments, and in multiple places on the third deck.

Forty-two-year-old Aldrich, reared in New England, had more than twenty years of experience in a wide variety of warships. As the Japanese strike group approached, he was in his element. His command post was Central Station, a compartment located five decks below the flight deck. In the event his ship was damaged, he was trained to act as the quarterback, calling the plays and directing each of his key teams. Aldrich was connected to repair parties throughout the ship via telephone talkers wearing headsets. Sound-powered telephone circuits were used to relay orders throughout *Yorktown*. On each headset, a microphone transducer converted sound pressure from a user's voice into an electric current. This was then converted back to sound by a transducer at the receiver nodes. This ingenious system was the means of quickly communicating crucial data to Aldrich's Central Station.

Lieutenant Ralph Patterson, Aldrich's assistant, was directly in charge of more than a half dozen repair parties, each strategically positioned at key points throughout the carrier. Patterson was distanced from First Lieutenant Aldrich so both men could not be killed by the same bomb or torpedo hit. Patterson's job was to feed all key data to his boss and personally accompany some of the repair parties into any severely damaged areas to supervise their work.

Fireman Third Class Gene Domienik was among the four-dozen-plus men assigned to Repair Party Five. He had enlisted in the Navy from Detroit with the permission of his parents while still seventeen, hoping to secure a stable job during the Great Depression. He had joined *Yorktown* three weeks prior to the Pearl Harbor attack and was assigned to the engine rooms. But the previous evening, Domienik had been pulled from his normal duty station and ordered to stand his battle station as a member of Repair Five.

Gene had taken part in damage control drills on a regular basis: how to handle a fire hose, how to put out an oil fire, how to properly use emergency respirators, and how to help carry wounded men on stretchers. Stationed below in a compartment adjoining the crew's main mess hall, Domienik found it was too crowded to lie flat on his belly—the preferred position to avoid being cut down by shrapnel from an explosion. So he idly chatted with a friend from the ship's boiler room. For the moment, there was nothing further he could do. He had already said extra prayers before hitting the sack the previous evening.[1]

Repair Five was under charge of Lieutenant Milton Ernest Ricketts, a twenty-eight-year-old Baltimore native who had graduated from the Naval Academy in 1935. Nicknamed "Rick" by his classmates, he was described in the *Lucky Bag* yearbook as being "easy going, even tempered, generous to an extreme." After graduation, Ricketts had served for two years on the carrier *Ranger* (CV-4) before marrying his sweetheart, Betty Jane Huffaker, in 1937. Ricketts then became an original commissioning member (known as a "plank owner") of the new carrier *Yorktown*.[2]

Ricketts was intimately familiar with *Yorktown* from stem to stern. As commander of one of Aldrich's repair parties, he was wise to tap two veteran petty officers—Chief Machinist's

Mates Duke Davis and John Homes—to help direct the men of Repair Five. His damage control party included a pair of brothers, Machinist's Mate Second Class Bill Kowalczewski and Fireman Second Class Victor Kowalczewski, who had been stationed side by side for nearly two years. But two days before the Coral Sea battle, Ricketts decided they should be split up in the event of a catastrophe. Bill was directed to move to a passage just abaft the galley and to remain there with another team until after the attack.[3]

Chiefs Davis and Homes spotted a newcomer among their already crowded compartment. Gene Domienik was still chatting with his fellow engineer when one of the M Division chiefs caught his attention and asked, "What are you doing here?"[4]

Domienik explained that he had been ordered to join Repair Five for the battle. The chief ordered him to move into the adjacent mess hall. No sooner had he left Repair Five than all hatches and compartments were sealed for Condition Zed—the maximum state of readiness of subdivision and watertight integrity of the ship's survivability systems.

In his new compartment, Gene saw cooks, various enlisted men, and another damage control team. Repair Party Four was under command of Carpenter Boyd McMurry McKenzie. As a thin and wiry teenager growing up in Maryville, Tennessee, McKenzie had been nicknamed "Skeeter" by classmates—a moniker unknown to most of the green youngsters serving under him. The warrant officer was seasoned, having risen in rank from chief carpenter's mate during nearly three years of service on *Yorktown*. His experience and a full head of prematurely gray hair made McKenzie a father figure to his repair team.

The mess hall grew stagnant with the hatches and ventilation system secured. Beads of sweat formed on McKenzie's brow as he surveyed the four dozen men of his Repair Four. They could feel the ship picking up speed, preparing to fight off the incoming Japanese attack. McKenzie's chief petty officers sorted out the vast assemblage of men in the mess hall. The engineering group was told to occupy the starboard side while the deckhand group was moved to the port side of the compartment. Domienik took a prone position on the port side near a main hatch that led toward the forward part of the carrier. In the event of a fire, the engineering men were ordered to fight fires in Sick Bay and after compartments, while the deckhands would move forward to combat any fires and damage.[5]

Domienik listened to the chatter coming from a nearby telephone talker. Manning the sound-powered headset was ship's musician Stanford Linzey, nicknamed "Deacon" for leading a regular Bible study group on *Yorktown*. As battle talker for Repair Four, Linzey's job was to relay vital messages from McKenzie to another battle talker, musician Bill Smith, in Central Station. Smith in turn passed the messages to Commander Aldrich. Linzey and Smith were careful to remember specific frame numbers and hatch numbers in their communications, directions that could prove vital to mobilizing repair teams in the event of a catastrophe. For the moment, repair party members were either seated or lying flat on the deck. They had been cautioned by McKenzie that standing in the compartment could be fatal in the event of an explosion.[6]

Domienik listened to the reports from Linzey and from the overhead loudspeaker system as the enemy planes drew closer.

He said silent prayers and wished he could dig a hole in the deck of the ship.

———

By 1111, Vane Bennett's radar had the enemy attack group only fifteen miles out. On the bridge, Captain Buckmaster changed course a minute later and increased *Yorktown*'s speed to twenty knots. The sea was smooth, with visibility out to thirty miles. Two minutes later, he ordered flank speed—twenty-five knots.

Working alongside the skipper was a new battle stations officer of the deck, Lieutenant (jg) John Greenbacker. Hailing from a dairy farm near Meridan, Connecticut, Greenbacker had been so determined by the seventh grade to attend the U.S. Naval Academy in Annapolis that his junior high friends began calling him "Annapolis" in jest. But he did not come from a privileged family, and entering the Navy's private training school required Greenbacker to secure a congressional appointment while he was still in high school.[7]

After a year of college at Connecticut State, and having never been to sea or even south of New York in his life, Greenbacker entered Annapolis in 1936. Soon after graduating in 1940, he was assigned to *Yorktown*, where he fell under the direction of communications boss Jug Ray. As ship's secretary, he was custodian of all classified and registered publications.[8]

On May 8, he had a new battle stations assignment. During the previous day's action in the Coral Sea, Greenbacker had been duly assigned as Rear Admiral Fletcher's flag secretary. Desiring more action, he had requested and been granted permission to qualify as officer of the deck. Instead of standing a normal four-hour watch in the communications department, he would remain on the bridge for as many hours as the ship was at general quarters. He was now into his sixth hour of duty.[9]

Greenbacker was excited as the radio crackled with news of incoming Japanese planes. Because he was battle stations officer of the deck, it was his job to help the captain maneuver the ship once the enemy attackers were overhead. Greenbacker took station on the starboard side of the bridge with a junior officer less than six months out of the Naval Academy, Ensign Norm Tate. Helping coach the skipper from the port side of the bridge were Lieutenant (jg) Cecil Gill and Chief Quartermaster Earnest Parton. Instead of staying under the protective steel plating of the pilothouse, Buckmaster spent more of his time out on the exposed wing of the bridge, high above the flight deck. Tate and Greenbacker kept a running commentary of the position of escorting destroyers and cruisers to ensure that *Yorktown* avoided any potential collision while under attack. The incoming aircraft would be the responsibility of lookouts and the skipper to monitor.[10]

Yorktown's bridge and conning tower were crowded. Chief Petty Officer Joe Burger presided over the mass of enlisted men it took to steer the ship through danger—the helmsman, the skipper's Marine orderly, the telephone talkers, and the yeomen to log the ship's movement. The ship's navigator, Commander Irving "Jim" Wiltsie, stood ready in the conning tower with the steering, main engine, and whistle controls. Adding to this throng was photographer Bill Roy, who had been granted free run of the bridge area to document the attack.

Stationed a good hundred twenty feet away from the pilot-house was the ship's popular executive officer, Commander Dixie Kiefer. From his station in Battle II—on the after end of the bridge platform—Kiefer was far enough removed that a single bomb hit was unlikely to wipe out both of *Yorktown*'s senior officers. Should Buckmaster be killed or severely wounded while on the bridge, it would be Kiefer's job to step in and take acting command of the carrier.[11]

Greenbacker silently prayed that the task force combat air patrols were doing their jobs.

———

Lexington's fighters made the first intercepts against the sixty-nine Japanese strike planes at 1116. Seven F4F pilots from her VF-2 would claim eleven certain or probable kills. Jimmy Flatley and six of his *Yorktown* VF-42 pilots would turn in claims for an additional nine enemy planes destroyed. Dauntless crews from both carriers fanned out on anti-VT-plane duty shot down five Kate torpedo planes and one Val dive-bomber, but they paid heavily for these successes.[12]

Lieutenant Swede Vejtasa and seven VS-5 comrades were about eight miles north of their own task force. *Zuikaku* torpedo planes suddenly flashed through their formation at more than a hundred eighty knots. A bright glint in the sun was the only warning he had before three Zeros ripped into the leading four-plane SBD division. Vejtasa yelled into his mike, "Attack from the rear!"[13]

But it was too late for some. Four *Yorktown* dive-bombers were sent plunging toward the ocean in flames. All eight pilots and gunners, including Swede's shipboard roommate, perished. Vejtasa threw his Dauntless into a series of radical counterma-neuvers as 7.7mm machine-gun bullets ripped into his plane and 20mm cannon shells burst all about him.[14]

During the next fifteen minutes, he called on every bit of experience and every trick he knew. He twisted, turned, and fired his wing guns while his gunner fought valiantly from the rear cockpit. At one point, Vejtasa put his SBD into a violent skid, sliding out from under an approaching Zero so close their wingtips nearly scraped. His Dauntless was hit several times, and a small piece of shrapnel bloodied his leg. But Swede would be credited with downing one of his Japanese opponents.

By the time the Zeros were gone, Vejtasa was exhausted. He had expended most of his ammunition, and he believed he had personally destroyed one of the Zeros. But half of his VS-5 squadron mates had perished in the battle. Vejtasa found him-self all alone in the sky. He swung his plane back around to-ward *Yorktown* to see how his ship had fared against the surviving Japanese strikers.

The fighters and SBD crews had done their best. It was now time for the ship's gunners to take over. Gunnery Officer Ernie Davis took an exposed position on top of the pilothouse to direct the fire. Using the flight deck loudspeaker system, he coached gunners toward incoming targets with a voice as clear and calm as though he was conducting yet another gunnery drill.

Ernie's assistant gunnery officer, Lieutenant Elgin Blaine Hurlbert, assisted with the gunnery control from Sky Control, a tiny unprotected platform just above *Yorktown*'s bridge. The husky thirty-seven-year-old Californian was called "Oxy" by his fellow officers after his alma matter, Occidental College. Hurlbert was a solid leader. The efficiency of Davis and Hurlbert as a team was respected by their prepared gun crews.

Among them was Ensign John d'Arc Lorenz, a twenty-three-year-old from Portland, Oregon, who had joined *Yorktown* in January 1941. Months later, Lorenz had secured permission from Davis to transfer to submarine duty, but the carrier's previous executive officer denied him, apparently believing him to be better suited for gunnery. Lorenz had since excelled in his role as battery officer for a quadruple-mount 1.1-inch/.75 caliber antiaircraft cannon group.[15]

His Mount 3, located just aft of *Yorktown*'s island structure, was adjacent to Ensign Charles Broderick's Mount 4. Each gun crew consisted of twenty men, and he was nearly as familiar with Broderick's crew of Mount 4 as he was with his own team. Boatswain's Mate Second Class Henry Johnson was gun captain of Lorenz's Mount 3. Stocky and tough natured, Johnson often talked to the ensign about the "true love" back in Kentucky he hoped to marry. He kept his gun crew in line. "He was very well built, and could have handled any half dozen of the rest at a single time," Lorenz recalled.[16]

Quad 1.1-inch gun mounts such as Mount 3 were nicknamed "Chicago Pianos" due to their similar size and appearance and in reference to the tommy guns once used by Chicago gangsters. These antiaircraft weapons were prone to jams, often requiring a gunner's mate to lie on his back underneath the mount, equipped with wrenches and hammers to clear them.

This task fell to Gunner's Mate Third Class Edward Zimmerle, who had been part of the Lorenz team for eight months. Zimmerle loved to talk about his guns. But it had taken Lorenz quite some time to get him to share some details about his home life.

Mount 3's pointer was easygoing Seaman Rupert Gibson. Seated on the left side of the quad, Gibson used a spokeless hand wheel to elevate the barrels and fire the guns via a foot pedal. Seated directly across on the right side in the trainer's seat was Gunner's Mate Third Class Walter Maurice, who used his wheel to rotate the mount into the desired firing direction. Supporting the whole team were a dozen other men serving as loaders and ammunition handlers.

The Lorenz crew was one of many teams about to receive their baptism of fire under direct enemy assault. Farthest forward on the fo'c'sle deck, Gunner's Mate Third Class Doug Word was in charge of a pair of .50-calibers. Standing ready on the port side was gunner John Hancock, with loader Stuart Motley, a young second-class seaman from Virginia. Across from them to starboard was another .50-caliber, manned by a pair of second-class seamen, gunner Leroy Hicks and his loader, Bill Howard.[17]

"As inexperienced kids, we had not been exposed to blood and mayhem except in the movies," Hancock recalled. As the air battles swept toward his carrier, he felt a rush of excitement comparable to trotting out onto the baseball field back in his high school days. Hancock asked Motley to break out an extra canister of .50-caliber ammunition to speed things up if necessary.[18]

The ship's loudspeaker system kept a running report of the location and altitude of the incoming strike. Hancock listened to Gunnery Officer Davis calling out directions to his gunners, preparing them for their first big action. The lieutenant commander's next order, hollered into the mike with his best North Carolina twang, elicited a smile from Hancock:

"Yankees, take covah! Southerners, man yo guns!"

———

From the starboard wing of *Yorktown*'s bridge, John Greenbacker could see some of the incoming torpedo planes tumbling in orange flame toward the blue sea.

At 1118, *Yorktown*'s guns opened fire. At this point, the enemy torpedo planes had separated into attack groups, too far distant for effective firing of anything but the 5-inch guns. The gun crews opened at a range varying from eight to ten thousand yards. The 1.1-inch Chicago Pianos kicked into action as the Japanese planes closed to four thousand yards. Finally, at two thousand yards, the smaller 20mm and .50-caliber gun teams commenced firing.[19]

Buckmaster estimated that four Kates from the first approaching group were shot down prior to making their drops. Still, three Kates approached to within dropping distance, five hundred yards from the port quarter. The officers of the deck called out the bearings to their skipper. As soon as their first three torpedoes were seen to hit the water at 1119, Buckmaster ordered, "Full right rudder!"

Battle helmsman Howard Kiser cranked the large silver

wheel to starboard as Buckmaster shouted to his engineering gang, "Emergency flank speed!"

As *Yorktown* heeled hard to the right to dodge the incoming torpedoes, Bill Roy was filming the action. Amidst the sudden staccato firepower of all the ship's guns, his six-inch lens caught one Kate roaring down the carrier's port side after making its drop. It was close enough to fill three-quarters of Roy's lens view. He could clearly see a large white "H" on its fuselage—an insignia he was later told was a squadron commander's logo. Roy saw the pilot angrily shaking his fist a second before the plane was hit.[20]

Seaman George Weise was likely responsible for this torpedo bomber's demise. High above the flight deck, he had a commanding view of the battle from his searchlight platform on the side of the smokestack. The Kate was just skimming the wave tops, too low for the trajectory of *Yorktown*'s 5-inch guns. But it was a perfect target for his .50-caliber. The machine-gun bullets slammed straight into the cockpit just after the pilot had completed his torpedo drop.[21]

Trailing smoke, the Japanese plane made a radical wingover to the right, then slammed into the ocean just off *Yorktown*'s port quarter. In the excitement of the moment, Kiefer even joined the action, assisting Joel Sledge with loading Weise's machine gun. Afterward, Kiefer credited Weise with this shoot down and promised to recommend the youngster for a commendation.[22]

Having previously served on a battleship, Roy was stunned at how nimbly his captain conned their massive flattop. White wakes of the torpedoes sped toward his ship. The flight deck oscillated as *Yorktown* bent into the hard turns, but Buckmaster put his ship in between their paths. Roy considered it real seamanship that his skipper had maneuvered to allow the first three torpedoes to run harmlessly past the port side close aboard.

By this time, the remaining Japanese torpedo planes had rounded *Yorktown*'s stern more than eight thousand yards out. Under heavy fire, these Kates were forced to drop farther out. As they were seen to release, the skipper called, "Full left rudder!"[23]

With this maneuver, he presented the smallest possible target—his carrier's stern. Two torpedoes passed down the starboard side. Another attacker was forced to drop early, at about two thousand yards out. His torpedo streaked by, just ahead of the bow.

Ernie Davis's gunners had performed well. Lieutenant John Huntley's forward 5-inch crews were credited with downing at least three torpedo planes, while Lieutenant John Wadleigh's after 5-inch gunners claimed four kills. The entire action had lasted less than five minutes, and Buckmaster's alert maneuvering had spared his ship from damage. But sister carrier *Lexington* was less fortunate, as she was swarmed by *Shōkaku* and *Zuikaku* torpedo planes. At 1120—during the same moment *Yorktown* was twisting frantically—two Japanese torpedoes struck *Lexington* with tremendous explosions. Slowed to twenty-five knots and assuming a seven-degree list to port, the Lady Lex nonetheless charged forward, still very much in the fight.

Once the enemy torpedo squadrons had completed their runs, thirty-three Val dive-bombers prepared to push over into dives on both American carriers. At 1121, the flight commander,

Lieutenant Commander Kakuichi Takahashi, split his group, sending nineteen *Shōkaku* Vals against *Lexington*. These pilots held their dives to fifteen hundred feet before releasing. A pair of 242-kilogram high-explosive bombs slammed into Lady Lex, while near misses exploded close enough to rip her hull and spray shrapnel into exposed sailors.

The remaining fourteen-plane *Zuikaku* bomber group pushed on toward *Yorktown*, which had thus far dodged the Japanese torpedo planes successfully. But her luck was about to change.

CHAPTER FOUR

DEVASTATION BELOW

John Hancock had no time to rest. It was 1124, a mere five minutes after the Japanese Kates had first started their torpedo runs. From his position on the fo'c'sle deck forward, he now spotted the high specks of enemy bombers starting into their dives.

This time, Hancock began firing even before Lieutenant Commander Davis passed any such orders. He led his shots, aiming just ahead of each diving plane. Once a bomber began its pull out, Hancock shifted his line of fire to walk tracers in toward the rear-seat gunner's cockpit.[1]

In the heat of battle, he discarded every rule of thumb Doug Word had taught him. "I didn't know any better," Hancock later admitted. "I held the firing lever down and overheated the barrel on that .50-caliber Browning until the hoses burst." Word instinctively snatched the jacket off the gun, removed the red-hot barrel, and tossed it over the side. In a matter of seconds, he had installed a fresh barrel, covered it, and turned the water-cooling system back on. "Fire in short bursts so you don't over-heat the gun!" he yelled at Hancock.

Captain Buckmaster remained on the open bridge for the best view. The first enemy dive-bombers were coming in from port to starboard, plunging directly out of the sun. He saw that their paths would carry them directly across *Yorktown*'s flight deck. Just as each plane released, he shouted orders for Howard Kiser to spin the rudder hard over to maneuver the ship toward the point of each dive. By this effort, he hoped to swing his carrier away from the path of each falling bomb.

The skipper succeeded in dodging direct hits from the first bombers. But their explosives began landing close enough on the port and starboard quarter to cause damage. Buckmaster noted that some of the near misses off his starboard quarter were so violent that they raised the ship's screws clear of the water.[2]

Bill Roy dashed about the bridge, continuing to film this second wave of attackers. Standing exposed on the starboard wing, he suddenly saw the flight deck below beginning to splinter. Bullets from a strafing Japanese Zero were chewing up the wooden surface. Roy instinctively pulled back into the wheelhouse, as Buckmaster crouched below the steel side shielding. One chief petty officer on the bridge was slightly wounded in the left shoulder by the strafing, but Roy was untouched. Battle stations OOD John Greenbacker, also on the bridge's starboard wing, watched in awe the dirty pillars of water reaching for the clouds. At least six near misses shook *Yorktown* so mightily that Greenbacker at first assumed some of them to be direct hits.[3]

Two near misses off *Yorktown*'s starboard bow pierced the ship's sides with shrapnel in numerous places above the waterline. One bomb grazed the edge of the catwalk, just abaft 5-inch gun mount No. 3, before it exploded only fifty feet from the hull. Aviation Ordnanceman Judson Brodie, a VF-42 mechanic, had been seated beneath the wing of a fighter plane just before the Japanese aerial attacks commenced. He and a fellow mechanic, Paul Meyers, had been discussing what they wished to do when the war was over.

As the Japanese dive-bombers approached, Brodie jumped up and raced down the flight deck to seek cover in the island structure. Meyers and three other VF-42 enlisted men opted to stretch out in the steel netting just below the starboard catwalk to avoid bomb splinters that might sweep across the flight deck. But the bomb that clipped the catwalk exploded almost directly below them. When Brodie returned minutes later to check on his friends, he found that three of the four had been hit by bomb shrapnel. His buddy Meyers was grayish colored and lay mortally wounded from a large chunk of metal that had ripped through his groin area.[4]

At 1127, three minutes into the bombing attack, *Yorktown* took a direct hit.

Fifteen hundred feet above the waves, an Aichi Type 99 Val released a 250-kilogram (551 pound) semi-armor-piercing bomb. Its delayed-action fuse allowed it to penetrate deep into *Yorktown*'s vitals before it exploded. It struck the flight deck—made of three inches of pine timbers above a tenth-inch steel plate—six feet to the starboard of exact center at frame 108. As it passed through the flight deck and the quarter-inch-thick steel gallery deck below, it left a hole fourteen inches in diameter through each. Passing through the gallery deck, the bomb went through Ready Room No. 3, used by Bombing Five.[5]

The ready room was nearly empty, as the aircrews were all aloft on a strike. The duty telephone talker was Aviation Machinist's Mate Third Class Budd Beistell. In less than a second, he saw the bomb plunge through his compartment, glance off a steel safe, and continue downward. Stunned, Beistell announced over his headset to the bridge, "Sir, I think a bomb just passed through here!"[6]

The bomb proceeded through the first, second, and third decks. It finally exploded fifty feet deep in the ship, midway between the third and fourth decks at frame 107 in compartment C-402-A, the aviation storeroom. The point of explosion was directly above the forward engine room located on the fourth deck where Chief Engineer Jack Delaney was stationed.

Repair Party Seven, stationed on the hangar deck far above the point of explosion, was the first unit to suffer. The four dozen sailors and repair specialists of this damage control team were under command of forty-two-year-old Chief Aviation Machinist's Mate Art Powers. One of his men, Seaman Emil Puksar, saw the bomb crash through the overhead and punch a hole through the deck only four feet from where he stood. As it passed through, the bomb tore away half of the skull of Seaman Pat Palumbo. He became the first nonaviator member of *Yorktown*'s crew to be killed by enemy action.[7]

As Palumbo crumpled, curious members of Repair Seven

ran to look through the new hole in the hangar deck. The up-rushing explosion killed Seaman Walter Krupinski, injured an-other man, and cost Seaman Ed Pettipas an eye. Aviation Mechanic Bill Josen, who was nowhere near the hole, was killed by shrapnel that ripped through the opening. The explosion tossed Chief Powers across the hangar deck. A piece of red-hot shrapnel hit him in the buttocks. The only thing keeping the shard from digging deeper into his flesh was the fact that it first pierced his wallet, which was stuffed full of cash.

Seconds before the bomb hit, the men of Lieutenant Milton Ricketts's Repair Party Five had been sweating out the attack. Five levels below the flight deck, they were stationed in C-301-L, a crew's messing compartment. Machinist's Mate First Class Tom Fuller had been sitting on the starboard-side hatch with his friend Claude Dawson. During the attack, Fuller moved over to where battle stations talker Toney Pancake was manning the sound-powered headset. They sat facing aft, with their backs resting against the amidships gedunk, the ship's service counter.[8]

In an instant, the compartment was obliterated in a blind-ing flash and a deadly wave of heat. Chiefs Homes and Duke Gault were killed instantly, along with three dozen other mem-bers of Repair Five. Ricketts was horribly burned when he was slammed into a fireplug that badly injured his skull. Twenty-six-year-old Worth Hare, seated near Fuller and Pancake, had been on board *Yorktown* since 1938. Hare somehow survived the explosion but fell unconscious, suffering from severe burns to the exposed skin on his arms and the back of his neck.[9]

Near Hare, only a handful of Repair Five men were still alive. Fireman First Class Bob Good was badly wounded, suffering from severe burns and shrapnel wounds. Another badly injured survivor was Fireman Second Class Sid Flum, who had delighted the crew with the jitterbug dance he and buddy Pete Montalvo had performed weeks earlier during the *Yorktown* Jamboree. The young sailor in previous months had developed a close friendship with three fellow New Yorkers of Repair Five: Bob Hunt, Charlie Steiniger, and Carmine "Paddy" Racioppi. The quartet had gone through boot camp together, come on board *Yorktown* together, and partied together during liberties ashore. Prior to the battle, Flum had visited ship's chaplain Frank Hamilton to pray in memory of the father he had lost three years prior. When he had entered the galley to join Repair Five at battle stations, he told his friends he wished to be alone to sort through his feelings.[10]

His friends complied with his wish, remaining some distance from him in Compartment C-301-L. The force of the bomb blast killed Steiniger and Hunt instantly. Racioppi and Flum fell wounded. A wave of heat and dust engulfed Flum, setting his clothes on fire. Seaman Second Class Jack Sutter, badly injured himself, hurried over to help smother the flames before Flum collapsed, unconscious and frightfully burned.[11]

Some of the men survived due to being partially protected by a small metal partition. Those wearing regulation blue chambray shirts with short sleeves received second- and third-degree burns on their arms and faces, while the rest of their bodies were spared. One survivor had been wearing a long-sleeved jumper. At the moment of the explosion, he had been sitting with his arms folded on his knees and his head resting on his arms. Although his hair was singed, his skin was not burned, except for severe burns around his ankles due to his trousers being rolled up.[12]

The dead and dying were everywhere. Screams and moans filled the compartment as Milton Ricketts regained his footing. He was badly burned and his head had been crushed against the fireplug. Somehow, the lieutenant summoned the strength to move. He opened the valve to the fireplug beside him and partially played out the fire hose. He began directing a heavy stream of water into the fires that had erupted. His swift action prevented the fires from quickly spreading, but his body was failing. The fire hose dropped from Ricketts's hands as he died from his wounds.

The blast had knocked Machinist Tom Fuller unconscious. When he began to regain his senses, the compartment was dark and filled with smoke. The starboard side where Ricketts's crew had been was now a scene of unspeakable human carnage. The battle talker near him, Pancake, was dead also. Fuller's face and arms throbbed from severe burns, and he was bleeding from various shrapnel wounds. He vaguely distinguished a sudden bright white light as someone opened the watertight door forward on the port side before he passed out again.

―――――――

Carpenter Boyd McKenzie's Repair Party Four was stationed in the compartment adjacent to Repair Five. Ship's musician Stan "Deacon" Linzey, wearing a pair of battle talker headphones, had been deep in thought and prayer as the attack commenced. As the ship's guns boomed above, fellow musician

Gordon Roop suddenly confided, "Deacon, I've been doing some praying."[13]

"Don't feel alone, mate," replied Linzey. "Many of us are praying."

Then the bomb hit. The ship lurched sideways, and the deck surged upward, tossing Linzey into the air. He was still collecting his senses when the bulkhead door leading to the adjacent compartment, C-301-L, burst open. Heavy smoke poured into Linzey's mess hall compartment, along with a wounded, bloody sailor. He stumbled through the hatch, his clothes tattered, his face and hands burned, one leg hanging uselessly.

"We've been hit," he said. "I'm blind. They've been blasted to hell."[14]

Worth Hare, seriously burned, was among those who regained consciousness and found enough strength to help others. He helped Tom Fuller and other stunned survivors stumble through the black smoke toward the safety of Repair Four's adjacent compartment. Boyd McKenzie was the first man of Repair Four to charge into the thick smoke entering the galley area.[15]

The men who followed him were met by a grisly scene. Dozens of members of Repair Five were already dead, while survivors writhed in pain from severe burns. McKenzie found his mentor, Lieutenant Ricketts, lifeless beside the fire hose he had been using to assault the fire. McKenzie ordered other men to take over the firefighting while he scrambled to help anyone still alive.

The warrant officer found fireman Sid Flum sprawled out on the deck, moaning from severe burns. McKenzie scooped him up and sprinted aft for Sick Bay, hoping to save at least one life. He handed Flum over to the medical personnel and turned to head back toward the scene of devastation. One of the doctors tried to detain him, telling McKenzie he was too badly wounded to do anything more for the time being.

Confused, McKenzie suddenly realized that his clothing was splattered crimson with Flum's blood.

"This isn't my blood!" he yelled, and sprinted back toward the mess hall.

Yorktown's trained medical professionals were quickly over-whelmed with dozens of serious casualties. The senior medical officer, Captain William Davis, had a staff of about thirty pharmacist's mates, two dental officers, and five other medical doctors, including the air group's senior flight surgeon, Lieutenant Commander Charles Yanquell. Davis's main Sick Bay was located on the third deck, several compartments aft of the bomb explosion. His ward included two dozen bunks, two surgical beds, a quiet room with two other surgical beds, a dressing room, a dental office, a general treatment room, and an isolation ward of a dozen bunks.[16]

In order to protect supplies and render quick first aid service, medical supplies and equipment had been distributed between five emergency dressing stations prior to the battle. After the bomb hit, Davis sent Lieutenant (jg) Edward Kearney, one of his junior medical officers, forward to assess the casualties. Kearney was among the more skillful surgeons on *Yorktown*. Prewar, he had been educated at Manhattan College and the Columbia University of Physicians and Surgeons. His previous residencies included Thomas Jefferson Medical

Center in Philadelphia, Queens General Hospital in New York, and Boston's City Hospital.

One of his volunteer stretcher-bearers, a musician first class named Frank Baldino, was a young saxophonist from Rhode Island. He had received a year of professional music schooling in Washington before joining *Yorktown*, but his medical experience was nil.

Seconds after the bomb explosion, Kearney called to Baldino, "All right, let's go!"[17]

Baldino was trembling, unable to move. Kearney poured him a shot of medicinal whiskey. "Drink this," he ordered. Baldino downed the harsh liquid, then followed Doc Kearney out of Sick Bay. The pair moved forward through the passageways, transiting the areas of the scullery and bakery compartment until they reached a dogged hatch that led into C-301-L.

They forced the door open, but Kearney was unable to enter due to the smoke and flames. But once he and Baldino worked their way in, they found men burned so badly, they were unable to move. Baldino helped hold each wounded man as Kearney worked IV needles into them. The young musician had to look away.[18]

Among the mortally wounded members of Repair Five encountered by the emergency medical team was Fireman Second Class Victor Fazzi from Cranston, Rhode Island. He and Baldino were close friends. Their mothers knew of their tight bond, and in their letters always asked their sons how the other young man was doing. Baldino could see that his friend was dying. Fazzio lay on the deck, his glistening eyes peering desperately up at him.[19]

"Hey, Doc, can we do something for my buddy here?" Baldino asked.

Kearney gave the wounded man one final look and shook his head at Baldino. But one dozen other members of Ricketts's Repair Five would survive their ordeal, including Flum, Hare, Good, Racioppi, and Fuller. Boyd McKenzie and members of his midship repair party worked diligently in the smoke-filled compartment to save lives.

Among the first to enter C-301-L with McKenzie was Bill Kowalczewski. He borrowed a gas mask and plunged through the smoke. The flashlight he had borrowed was barely able to penetrate the thick black smoke. Frantically searching through the bodies, Bill was horrified to find his worst fears realized. He located the body of his brother, Victor Kowalczewski, on the deck. Victor had likely been killed instantly by the concussion. There was not a mark on his body.

Painter Third Class Bill Carpenter helped guide two Repair Five survivors to safety before returning to fight the fires. Although severely burned, Carpenter continued to battle the flames until McKenzie ordered him to Sick Bay. Sloshing through water and fighting strangling smoke, McKenzie's Repair Four men carefully pulled bodies from the mangled debris and placed them in neat stacks for corpsmen to tend to. Their work was just beginning.

The Japanese air strikes against *Yorktown* had lasted only thirteen minutes. But to her gunners and damage control parties, the battle seemed to have lasted for an eternity.

At the height of the dive-bomber attack, Vane Bennett's CXAM radar set suddenly ceased to function. He immediately diagnosed the problem to be something with the antenna array high above Air Plot. Bennett raced from his station with his assistant, Radioman First Class Alvin Attaway, in tow. They climbed up to the bedspring-size antenna and set to work with their tools. Bennett would later receive a letter of commendation that cited him for being "exposed to machine gun fire and fragments from our own anti-aircraft fire" while repairing the antenna.[20]

By 1131, the surviving Japanese planes were moving toward a distant rendezvous location. The jubilant flight commander, Lieutenant Commander Takahashi, radioed at 1125 that his aviators had sunk the carrier *Saratoga* (mistaking the carrier *Lexington* that they had actually attacked for her sister ship). They claimed nine torpedo hits and ten bomb hits on *Saratoga*, plus two torpedo hits and at least eight bomb hits on *Yorktown*. Their scorecard was overly optimistic; *Lexington* had taken two torpedoes and two bomb hits, and *Yorktown* was badly damaged by one direct bomb hit and numerous near misses.[21]

The departing Japanese planes were pursued by CAP fighters as the task force gunners slowly ceased firing. During the attack, *Yorktown*'s gunners had expended a record numbers of shells. Her 5-inch gun crews had fired 404 rounds. The four quad 1.1-inch mounts fired 2,906 rounds and two dozen 20mm guns had fired seventy-nine hundred rounds. From John Hancock's .50-caliber machine gun and seventeen others, some 15,800 rounds had been expended.[22]

During the action, John Lorenz's 1.1-inch Mount 3 suffered six misfires. Each required the gun to be recocked before firing. In one case, the gun had to be completely reloaded. Another time, the breach mechanism locked in the rear position. First loader Edward Thornberg used his leg to force the magazine cutout to the down position before it was replaced with a fresh cutout.

As the air strike was cleared, Captain Buckmaster sent orders to his exec, Dixie Kiefer, to hurry below and assess the damage. In his journeys, Kiefer would learn of dozens of acts of heroism that had taken place.

Lieutenant Commander Jack Delaney had narrowly cheated death. The bomb that wiped out Repair Five exploded in the compartment directly above his head. The thirty-seven-year-old Boston native had graduated from the Naval Academy in 1925. In the seventeen years since that time, Delaney had accumulated a wealth of knowledge in his various warship assignments. Since joining *Yorktown* in June 1939, he had been promoted to chief engineering officer. Now he had his hands full, assessing the damage caused by the bomb hit. The explosion wrecked the ship's service center, the soda fountain equipment, the laundry issue room, the ship's service office, and Delaney's engineering office—all located in C-301-1L.

Machinist's Mate Second Class Dwight Dehaven had been one compartment away from the bomb explosion. His battle station was on the third deck amidships at the Boiler Emergency Station, under charge of Lieutenant Charles Reed Cundiff. The twenty-year-old was unscathed as heavy shrapnel ripped through his after boiler station. Cundiff's men escaped injury because they had been trained to lie flat on the deck. But the explosion blew out the fire in the boiler room.[23]

Dehaven went to work, intent on resetting the overspeed governors—the blowers that took the suction from the intake unit. Carrying an emergency battle lantern, he climbed onto a platform to reset them. As he did, *Yorktown* was rocked by an underwater explosion from a nearby bomb hit. His battle lantern fell from the ledge on which he had it propped and smashed. He was left on a perilous perch, fourteen feet above the lower deck and surrounded by complete darkness. Forced to jump from his perch, Dehaven caromed off a workbench, felt his way through the blackness, and finally exited his boiler room in search of proper lighting.

In the forward engine room, the force of the explosion tore loose the overhead insulation. A pair of two-hundred-watt lamps and reflectors was ripped from the sockets. Dust and dirt dropped on the control platform on the starboard side. The explosion produced similar results in the nearby steering motor room. Electrician's Mate First Class Donald Wilson, a twenty-six-year-old *Yorktown* plank owner who hailed from Dexter, Iowa, was amazed by the effects of the blast. During more than five years of gunnery practice he had previously experienced in the motor room, no dirt had ever been jarred loose until May 8. "The sound was like a freight train underneath you, in a tin barn in a hailstorm, and a dust storm coming in an open window," Wilson recalled. "Our lights were only visible as a glow due to the dust."[24]

In Boiler Rooms 8 and 9, dense smoke and choking fumes forced the sailors to evacuate the lightless compartments. The men exiting Fireroom No. 9 reported a fire, but this was later found to be a flareback in the burners due to the concussion. Chief Engineer Delaney also ordered the crew of Boiler No. 7 to evacuate their space, as superheat could not be utilized in the present wrecked condition of the room. Reports of two condensers being contaminated with salt water further added to the challenges of the engineers.

Water Tender Ray Davis, a member of the boiler repair party, entered Boiler Rooms 8 and 9 despite smoke and gas to investigate the extent of the damage. Largely through his efforts, the boilers were back online about one hour after the bomb hit. Electrician's Mate First Class Lyon Russell, burned by the bomb explosion, refused medical treatment while continuing to carry on temporary repairs with Boyd McKenzie's engineering repair party to electrical circuits in the damaged areas.[25]

Lieutenant Commander Delaney fed a steady stream of updates from his engineering department's Main Control to Captain Buckmaster on the bridge. Two boiler rooms and a fireroom had been temporarily evacuated due to smoke and gas, and two condensers were down at the moment. As the dive-bomber attack was nearing completion, the skipper asked what speed could still be maintained.[26]

"Twenty-four knots," Delaney replied.

"Should the ship slow?" Buckmaster asked.

"Hell no!" said Delaney. "We'll make it!"

Yorktown did indeed maintain twenty-four knots until the last of the Japanese attackers had cleared the area.

———

Damage control officer Clarence Aldrich was flooded with reports at Central Station. Orchestrating the chaos was made more manageable by his two junior assistants, Lieutenants (jg) Don Scheu and Mervin "Mo" Slater. Scheu remained at Central Station, helping to interpret the many reports that came in. Once the dive-bombers had cleared the scene, Aldrich sent Slater to the scene of greatest devastation to help with making repairs and saving lives.

Carpenter McKenzie's Repair Four was still in high gear when Slater arrived. Survivors had been hauled off toward the emergency aid stations, and firefighting teams wearing emergency respirators were making headway against the stubborn blazes. After some of the wreckage had been cleared, McKenzie sent Fireman First Class George Neilson into the worst area. Neilson climbed down through the jagged bomb hole into C-402-A, where he found smoldering stores. A fire hose was passed down to Neilson, who arrested the progress of the fire sufficiently enough to allow boiler repair crews to pass through the area to investigate the boiler damage. Another of McKenzie's valiant repairmen was Shipfitter Clyde Upchurch, who waded into partially flooded compartments, ignoring dangling live electrical cables. Sometimes working in up to four feet of water, Upchurch would spend eighteen hours straight doing damage control, making repairs, and keeping submersible pumps in operation.

Boatswain Edmund Crosby's Repair Party Two was soon dispatched to the scene of the bomb devastation. One of his men,

Shipfitter First Class Norris Hook, was a key repair supervisor due to his intimate knowledge of the ship's inner workings. Hook's efforts helped ensure that countless items of machinery, ventilation, plumbing, and drainage functioned normally during the crisis. His skills as one of *Yorktown*'s most talented welders, and those of comrade Paul Vander, proved vital this day in effecting emergency repairs.

Fireman Gene Domienik was given a bucket and told to follow a boatswain's mate as Repair Four went into action. They bypassed the Repair Five area and scaled a steel ladder into officer's country. Their job was to inspect all compartments for oil and gasoline fumes, damaged hatches, and flooding. They were also to shut down any electric vent motors to prevent fumes from igniting.[27]

When Domienik and the petty officer returned to the next lower deck, their sweep eventually led them back through the devastation of Repair Five. In the adjacent passageway, he saw the bodies of fallen shipmates. One of them was a sailor who had taken Domienik's place in the boiler rooms, and during battle stations had been assigned to Repair Five. Gene had been sitting with the man until he was tapped at the last minute to go join Repair Four. The man's legs were severed below the knees. His eyes were wide open, but no blood flowed from his body. To Domienik, it looked like someone had taken a knife and made a clean cut right through his flesh and bones.[28]

Commander Bill Davis's medical teams worked tirelessly to treat the wounded. Chief Pharmacist's Mate Jim Wilson and seven other male nurses helped take charge, often administering lifesaving first aid without orders from doctors who were fully absorbed in operating on patients.

Other sailors not medically trained pitched in. Machinist's Mate Second Class Leo Adams, admitted to Sick Bay with burns on his legs, disregarded his own care and helped others more critically injured. Ship's baker Arthur Triplett, on duty near the Repair Five compartment, had been hit in the ribs by shrapnel. He made it to Sick Bay and took a seat outside. A corpsman gave him morphine and a shot of Ten High whiskey. The corpsman set the bottle down and moved on to assist other more grievously wounded men. Triplett took the liberty of downing the remainder of the whiskey and soon dozed off.[29]

Wounded men were hauled into Sick Bay on unique zipper stretchers. Conceived by Davis and manufactured on board, the stretchers were lightweight with a binding method that secured patients in order to pass them up and down steel ladders. Near the flight deck, at Dressing Station No. 1, *Yorktown*'s band leader, Ed Oakley, served as the leader of the stretcher-bearers, many being his fellow musicians. Nearest to the explosion, the main Sick Bay quickly received seventeen patients suffering from burns and shock.[30]

Six men carried in had bullet wounds from strafing Japanese planes. Several had broken limbs, and one was missing an eye. Most of those arriving had already been injected with a half grain of morphine, indicated by a tag placed around the wounded man's wrist. Corpsmen were designated to take on specific duties, such as preparing burned skin surfaces for treatment, spraying burns with solutions of tannic acid, and giving water to patients. Elsewhere in the ship, another five dozen men were treated at four different battle dressing stations for injuries ranging from leg fracture to severe burns.[31]

Warren Heller and his close buddy Ralph Stewart had ridden out the attack at their new battle station, the forward-most emergency battle dressing station. Heller would not learn until much later in the day that the third member of his trio, pharmacist's mate Ed Koslowski, had not survived. At the moment the Japanese bomb struck *Yorktown*, he had been standing on the after portion of the island structure on a landing just outside Dressing Station No. 1—the very battle station location Heller had previously occupied for many months. Koslowski was killed instantly by the percussive blast.

Soon after the bomb hit, Heller had received orders over the ship's intercom to report to the main Sick Bay to assist. Leaving Stewart to man the forward station, he hurried aft toward the main medical facility. As he reached the after mess compartment adjacent to Sick Bay, Heller was intercepted by Chief Wilson. The smell of burned flesh in the compartment was suffocating. All about the mess hall, burned men lay moaning on stretchers. Two musicians acting as stretcher-bearers were vomiting their guts out in a corner.[32]

Wilson told Heller to take charge of the burn team, then left. The "team" comprised two puking musicians and a few corpsmen. But Heller went to work. His first step was to administer morphine to all the victims for pain relief. He found that many complained of severe pain in their heel bones as a result of fractures sustained by the sudden buckling up of the deck at the time of the explosion. Those with the most severe burns, third degree, were in less immediate pain due to the fact that the nerve endings in their skin had been destroyed. The medics administered fluids to these victims, both orally and intravenously.[33]

Some of the things Heller noted would lead to changes before *Yorktown*'s next battle. Exposed areas of bodies were singed. Men with full beards had had them singed but suffered no facial burns. Going forward, men would be required to wear long shirtsleeves, full-length dungarees, and shoes to avoid flash burns. Facial hair was encouraged.

In the mess hall and in Sick Bay, Heller's team removed clothing from the burn victims. Sprayers filled with tannic acid solution were used to apply several coatings to burn areas. After this had dried, the corpsmen sprayed silver nitrate solution for a final coating, which created a black eschar, or dark scab. "We worked hard and fast," he recalled. "Knowing that if we could keep air away from the burns, the pleaful requests for morphine would abate. The morphine, itself, became a problem in that many of the recipients would become nauseated, and vomited."[34]

Heller and his makeshift crew spent hours treating the wounded. As the afternoon passed, the chaotic situation slowly stabilized.

On the fo'c'sle deck, John Hancock breathed a sigh of relief as the last Japanese attack plane cleared the area. Gunfire both from his carrier and its screening vessels was dying off. To him, it felt like the sudden calm that swept over a prairie after a violent storm had passed. He was sweating liberally, and the barrel of his .50-caliber machine gun was red-hot. Throughout the battle, he and loader Stuart Motley had whooped and cheered, thinking they had downed many enemy planes. Now he wasn't so sure—the sky had been black with flak bursts, falling planes, and tracers. More important to him was the fact that they had escaped without injury, despite shrapnel that had severed nearby lifelines.[35]

The quad 1.1-inch guns in Mount 3 under Ensign John Lorenz and Mount 4 under Ensign Charles Broderick—located aft of the island structure—had performed well. On Mount 3, pointer Rupert Gibson and trainer Walter Maurice reviewed their efforts, sure that they had accounted for at least half the downed Japanese planes.[36]

Smoke still poured from the hole in *Yorktown's* flight deck. Precious fuel oil leaked from numerous ruptures in her steel sides where near misses had done heavy damage far below the waterline. Deeper inside the ship, repair teams worked without pause to put out fires and shore up the damage. Chief Engineer Jack Delaney's experts labored to restore steam to the Number 7 and 8 boiler rooms. Far above the flight deck, radar officer Vane Bennett and Alvin Attaway continued to work on getting their CXAM set back into commission. Rivets holding the antenna yoke to its pedestal had been sheared away during the action. At 1222—less than one hour after his radar had gone down—Bennett announced that *Yorktown's* radar set was back online.

The bodies of men from Repair Party Five and other departments were carefully transported to other locations for identification. Band leader Ed Oakley oversaw the stretcher-bearers who moved the deceased first to the after mess hall and later to the partial afterdeck for an eventual burial-at-sea service. Bill Kowalczewski and shipfitter Ed Fogarty carried the body of Bill's brother, Victor, topside from where he had fallen with his Repair Five comrades.[37]

Due to the potential of further enemy attacks during the day and for reasons of morale, Captain Buckmaster decided to bury the dead at sea that night. The task of collecting body parts was more than most young men could stomach. Corpsmen offered shots of whiskey to bribe some volunteers to help with the grisly task. Some sailors resorted to morbid humor to get through the stress. Plane captain Truxton King "T. K." Ford was ordered to grab some rags to help clean up oil on the hangar deck. But as he began removing rags from a pail, he was shocked to find that someone had deposited a severed human head in the bottom of the bucket.[38]

Turning to a redheaded fellow VF-42 plane captain, Lynn Rucker, Ford said, "Red, we need more rags." Rucker was equally shocked by his discovery.

Normal operations steadily returned. At 1215, just forty-five minutes after the attack, *Yorktown* turned into the wind to begin recovering her aircraft, which had recently returned from their own carrier strike. First in were two CAP fighters and the four surviving SBDs from the anti-torpedo-plane patrol. Swede Vejtasa was among those landing. He headed below to his ready room, feeling fortunate to have survived his ordeal against the Zeros, but also beaten. He thought it demonstrated the complete stupidity of using SBDs for anti-torpedo-plane patrol.[39]

Following Swede's return, *Yorktown* launched three more

Wildcats to bolster her CAP before settling in to land the rest of her strike group. Bill Burch's VS-5, recently returned from its strike against the Japanese carrier *Shōkaku*, touched down first. One badly damaged Dauntless was forced to ditch near the task force, but its crew was quickly scooped up by the destroyer *Aylwin*. Next to land were the fourteen SBDs of Bombing Five.

Flight operations were briefly suspended around 1250 when another badly shot-up SBD, piloted by Lieutenant (jg) Floyd Moan, crashed during his landing. Unable to slow his dive-bomber due to dive flaps that had been blasted away, Moan missed both the arresting wires and the crash barrier. Both the pilot and his gunner, Seaman Second Class Bob Hodgens, were bleeding from bullet wounds sustained in their fight with Japanese Zeros. Hodgens, sitting facing to the rear, could hear the crash alarm sounding and braced for the impact.[40]

Moan's plane slammed full tilt into *Yorktown*'s island structure. Upon impact, Hodgens's machine gun slammed into the back of his head. His plane's engine ripped free from the fire wall and went bouncing down the flight deck. Willing hands extracted the wounded pilot and gunner from the Dauntless before it was shoved over the side to help clear the deck. Moan and Hodgens were treated at a nearby aid station before being moved belowdecks to the main Sick Bay. There, junior medical officer Ed Kearney operated on Hodgens to remove Japanese bullets and stitch up his head. Both men would survive.

The remainder of *Yorktown*'s strike group made landings until 1300. By that time, her engineers reported to the bridge that two of her abandoned boiler rooms were now back online. By

1313, her No. 9 boiler was also back online. Things were looking up.

A short distance away, fate had not been so kind to the carrier *Lexington*. Fumes from small leaks in her port stowage gasoline tank, caused by Japanese bomb hits, seeped into her motor generator room. At 1247, *Lexington* was in the midst of launching aircraft when sparks ignited a massive explosion that tore through the carrier. Despite the fresh fires, Rear Admiral Fitch allowed flight operations to continue on his flagship. Nine dive-bombers were launched, followed by a number of CAP fighters being allowed to nestle back onto the deck.[41]

Among the F4F pilots hoping to land was Lieutenant Scott McCuskey, who had returned home alone from the Japanese carrier strike. He was low on fuel and had no choice but to head straight for the first flattop he spotted, *Lexington*. No sooner had he landed at 1255 than he was summoned to the bridge to update Fitch. McCuskey informed him that *Yorktown*'s strike group had badly damaged a Japanese carrier. During the interim, his plane was refueled, giving him hope that he could soon be relaunched back to his own carrier.[42]

Due to both U.S. carriers being heavily damaged, Rear Admirals Fitch and Fletcher concurred that their task groups should retire from the battle. *Lexington*'s own strike group soon appeared on the horizon. During the next half hour, many of her SBDs, TBDs, and F4Fs began landing, even as fires raged belowdecks and caused another serious explosion. While her damage control crews labored to contain the fires, another drama was playing out over the airwaves.

Three SBDs from *Lexington*'s air group had become scattered in the overcast skies after departing from the Japanese carrier force. Among them was *Lexington* Air Group Commander Bill Ault, who reported that both he and his gunner were wounded. Around 1400, he opened up on his radio to inquire whether *Lexington* had him on radar. Due to fires and explosions, *Lexington* was forced to shift all communications to *Yorktown.*

In her radio room, the task of tracking the three lost *Lexington* dive-bomber crews fell on the shoulders of twenty-five-year-old junior communications officer Ensign Shelley Lashman and his radiomen. Although his normal duty was in radio central, decoding and encoding messages between the carriers, Lashman spent a half hour pleading with the lost pilots to climb higher and avoid Japanese aircraft. Lashman never heard from them again. The painful final exchanges would remain with him for life.[43]

One of Ault's junior pilots finally reported that he was making for the nearest land. Ensign Harry Wood was fortunate enough to reach Rossel Island, where he and his rear-seat gunner were later rescued. But the *Lexington* Air Group commander and three other aviators were never seen again. In his final transmissions, Ault requested to be given credit for landing a direct bomb hit on a Japanese carrier. At 1454, he repeated that claim in the last radio transmission received on *Yorktown:* "So long, people. We got a 1,000-pound hit on the flattop."[44]

McCuskey's hopes of relaunching from *Lexington* back to his own *Yorktown* were never realized. Once the last of Lady Lex's strike planes had been recovered, deckhands set to work positioning aircraft aft for takeoffs. McCuskey's Wildcat was spotted first among eight F4Fs readied for takeoff. Before the order to launch could be passed, *Lexington* was rocked with yet another tremendous explosion at 1442. The blast lifted the forward elevator more than a foot above the flight deck. Smoke and steam gushed from the carrier, and its hangar deck erupted into flames. McCuskey was shocked to see several sailors run over to his plane and pull his emergency life raft from it to use for abandoning ship.[45]

Over the next hour, *Lexington* deteriorated. Another explosion at 1525 created new fires, damaged her boiler uptakes, and forced the abandonment of key engineering compartments. Within fifteen minutes, fires on the carrier were out of control, and her skipper was forced to shut down all power by 1600. Destroyers moved in close to assist, and Captain Ted Sherman ordered the transfer of wounded personnel and nonessential aviators to begin. By 1707, Sherman passed the word to abandon ship as fires and explosions raged through his vessel.

McCuskey joined more than two thousand *Lexington* sailors in descending knotted lines to reach the ocean below. They were soon hauled on board task force destroyers. Massive explosions hurled debris and aircraft into the air as the abandon-ship process continued. In the end, ninety-two percent of her crew survived, but the U.S. Navy's second aircraft carrier was finished.

Watching CV-2 burn and explode on the horizon was a troubling scene for many *Yorktown* sailors. Her supply officer, Commander Ralph Arnold, had helped fit out *Lexington* and had served on board for three years. During the Coral Sea clash, Arnold had persuaded gunnery officer Ernie Davis to give him an active battle station. Assigned to a pair of 20mm guns on the fo'c'sle deck, Arnold had helped his gun teams with loading during the Japanese attacks. He now felt helpless as he saw his former carrier blazing into the late-evening hours and sad watching her go down.[46]

Photographer Bill Roy, having captured valuable footage of the Japanese attacks earlier, now trained his lens on *Lexington*. Using a six-inch telephoto lens on his 35mm movie camera, he filmed its demise. Roy also snapped still pictures with a twenty-inch lens on his K-1.[47]

At 1830, Captain Sherman finally left his carrier, certain all of his crew still living had been evacuated. He was picked up by a whaleboat from the destroyer *Hammann*, from the decks of which he would witness another destroyer deliver the coup de grâce to his carrier. In order to prevent *Lexington* from potentially falling into enemy hands, the destroyer *Phelps* fired five torpedoes into the blazing wreckage. Just after 1952, *Lexington* rolled over to port and sank with one final explosion that was felt as far as twenty miles away.[48]

By midafternoon on May 8, Warren Heller was feeling some relief from his lifesaving efforts. Most of his patients in Sick Bay were stabilized, and he began thinking how good it would be to finally catch a nap. At that moment, Chief Jim Wilson appeared.[49]

"I'm glad you've got things under control," said Wilson. "But I need you for another detail. I'm sure your men can handle things now."

Wilson handed Heller a stack of pink legal-size forms. In large letters atop each document was: "CERTIFICATE OF DEATH." Wilson detailed Heller to obtain a thumbprint from each of the bodies that had been piled up on the fantail of the hangar deck. Heller made his way aft to the fantail, just above the screws and just under the flight deck. There were dozens of corpses, all laid out in canvas sacks. He stepped up to each one, carefully straddling the body and bending down to examine the attached name card and to match that name with the dog tag still attached to many of the victims. Next, Heller took each cold right thumb and rolled it carefully across the outlined space on the death certificate.

With eighteen certificates for each man, Heller worked quickly and quietly among the bodies. Although he had heard that his close friend Ed Koslowski was among the victims, he was still shocked when he reached his body. *This kid from Kentucky died in my place*, he thought. He felt as if he were attending his own funeral. Heller thought of the months he had stood general quarters in the very spot where Ed had perished, only to be shifted to a new medical station just before the Coral Sea battle. He would later reckon it to be the "fickle finger of fate" that had spared him this day.[50]

Heller had no time for a requiem. He continued the grim task of collecting identifying fingerprints from the rest of the dead. Behind him, sailmakers weighted each canvas sack with bricks and 5-inch shells before stitching them closed. Per Captain Buckmaster's action report, forty men had been killed outright, although others would eventually expire from their injuries. Of the forty bodies on the fantail, only twenty-one were immediately identified by means of their remaining ID tags. The work of identifying, fingerprinting, and preparing the dead for burial at sea was completed at 0200 on May 9.[51]

Soon after, Chaplain Frank Hamilton conducted a somber funeral service. Only a small group of necessary men was on hand to help slide each body down a chute over the side after Hamilton said his prayers for each victim. The skipper felt a large gathering might have had a negative impact on his crew's morale. By 0240, Hamilton's burial-at-sea service was complete.[52]

Heller was thoroughly exhausted. But a long list of severely injured patients still needed his attention back in Sick Bay. Sometime later, when he finally allowed himself to crawl into a bunk, he had been on his feet for seventy-two hours straight. He fell asleep immediately.

CHAPTER FIVE

SEVENTY-TWO HOURS

Yorktown's task group retired from the Coral Sea on May 9. One false report from a scout plane created a scramble of her air group, but the "Japanese carrier fleet" was gone. The ship's navigator, Jim Wiltsie, correctly concluded from his maps that the SBD scouts had merely found a set of reefs with surf washing over them to look like ships' wakes.[1]

Rear Admiral Jack Fletcher's Task Force 17 headed for Tongatabu to assess damages to his flagship. As Yorktown entered the beautiful harbor's lagoon on May 15, Lieutenant John Wadleigh felt a sense of relief. Since the carrier's previous visit to the Tonga Islands just weeks before the Coral Sea battle, an Allied convoy had arrived from the East Coast. Among those now stationed on Tongatabu was a group of Army nurses at the new medical facility. The females were only too glad to accept an invitation to join *Yorktown*'s wardroom for dinner that evening. "Along with dinner went fresh water showers for these modern 'Nightingales,' for the field hospital just landed did not have high priority on the construction of running water facilities," recalled Wadleigh. The reaction of having a half dozen females on board the ship caused emotions to run high among the monastic crew.[2]

The Army nurses stayed through dinner and also for a special performance prior to the evening movies. Ed Oakley and the ship's band put on a concert for the crew. Seated front and center for this concert were several burned and bandaged survivors of Repair Party Five, including Worth Hare and Tom Fuller.[3]

Once the music was complete, the men prepared for the start of the movie. Chief Boatswain's Mate Pop Austin, *Yorktown*'s master-at-arms, suddenly barked, "Attention!" As per an age-old tradition, Captain Buckmaster was the last to be seated. He was met with rousing cheers. "There probably was not one man present who would not have gone into battle with Buckmaster in a rowboat," radioman Lynn Forshee remembered.[4]

Jack Delaney's fuel gang tackled the task or refueling the ship. Word had been passed that *Yorktown* was to proceed to Pearl Harbor as quickly as fueling and inspection of damages could be completed. The aging tanker *Kanawha* (AO-1) was unable to snug up against the carrier due to *Yorktown*'s overhang and the lack of barges to be positioned between the two ships. *Kanawha* was forced to anchor close to the carrier's stern and pass a fuel line over from her bow to the flattop's stern. The long and tedious process, a first for *Yorktown*'s engineers, was the first and last time her crew struggled with this type of refueling.[5]

Rear Admiral Fletcher was concerned with maintaining round-the-clock watches to prevent an enemy surprise attack while his TF-17 was in port. Ensign John Lorenz, normally gun director for one of *Yorktown's* after 1.1-inch antiaircraft mounts, was tasked with harbor patrol on May 18. His enlisted crew was armed with Browning submachine guns and Springfield rifles. Their forty-foot motor launch cruised about the harbor entrance, ever vigilant for signs of the enemy. Lorenz's coxswain ran their boat aground on a reef that night, leaving the crew stranded for two hours. In defense of the hell he caught for grounding the launch, Lorenz replied, "If you'd given me some damned charts, it might not have happened!"[6]

Many crewmen were given the chance to go ashore for brief liberty periods at Tongatabu. John Hancock found little to do other than rent horses with his buddies. "There was nothing on the island but coconut palm trees and brown-skinned gals that wouldn't have anything to do with you," he remembered. Fighter pilot Scott McCuskey made his way back to the ship at Tongatabu. Forced to abandon ship from *Lexington* on May 8, he had been highlined between two cruisers before he was able to finally return to VF-42. There, he found his executive officer, Jimmy Flatley, was returning Stateside to form a new fighter squadron, VF-10, in San Diego. Two of his new fighter pilots, including Swede Vejtasa, had flown SBD dive-bombers at Coral Sea. Vejtasa, Flatley, and the *Lexington* survivors boarded troop transports at Tonga for a long voyage back to California.[7]

But *Yorktown* would not be following them. Fleet Admiral

Chester Nimitz—commander in chief of the U.S. Pacific Fleet—had sent orders to Fletcher to return his task force to Pearl Harbor as quickly as possible. On the afternoon of May 19, *Yorktown* departed Nuku'alofa Harbor in Tongatabu, still trailing thin ribbons of oil from ruptured tanks on her port side. During the weeklong voyage to Hawaii, Captain Buckmaster worked on his Coral Sea battle after-action report. He reported on the events of the battle and the damage sustained by *Yorktown*, and he added seven pages of deficiencies that needed to be addressed. These ranged from the need for aircraft improvements and the number of fighter planes needed to defend the ship, to a second search radar in case his unit went down like it did, recommendations on improving fighter direction, aerial communication needs, modifications to the boiler division for improved damage control, and the need for additional 20mm antiaircraft guns.

Buckmaster stated the conduct of his entire ship's company and air group had been "worthy of the highest traditions of the Naval Service." He cited their "tireless energy, unquenchable enthusiasm, grim determination, and high courage," which had guided their ship through its first major ordeal. Buckmaster concluded with: "I can have no higher honor than to have commanded them in battle."[8]

The sweet smell of the Hawaiian Islands beckoned to those topside as *Yorktown* began launching her air group for Ford Island midmorning on May 27. She stood into Pearl Harbor in the early afternoon, with her crew eager for liberty. They had been at sea since mid-February, marking 101 days since her last departure—broken only by two brief stops in the Tonga Islands.

Hundreds of sailors dressed in whites stood topside in muster formation in the bright sunshine as their flattop rounded Ford Island. Buckmaster moored his ship in Berth 16 at the Pearl Harbor Navy Yard for the night. Expectations were that his carrier would need at least ninety days to properly mend her battle damage. But by 0720 the following morning, May 28, tugs were moving *Yorktown* into Dry Dock No. 1 for emergency repair work. After the caisson was positioned and the dock was pumped dry, CV-5 was left resting on keel blocks.[9]

Once the water receded, a team of experts sloshed around in the muck below *Yorktown*, inspecting her damaged hull plates. Captain Claude Gillett, the yard manager, was joined by Admiral Nimitz in hip boots. He was well-informed on intelligence his specialists had gathered about an imminent Japanese offensive. Every last aircraft carrier at his disposal would be required to turn back the enemy. Turning to the group of repair specialists, Nimitz gave a shocking order: "We must have this ship back in three days."[10]

The reason for the quick turn was known to only a few officers. Yard workers were still swarming on board *Yorktown* when the intelligence documents from Nimitz's staff were delivered. The document—officially CINCPAC Operation Plan no. 29-42—was delivered to the ship's secretary, Lieutenant John Greenbacker. In his position as one of *Yorktown*'s communications specialists, Greenbacker had knowledge that few others possessed. He had learned that after its next action, his ship was scheduled for a long period in the Puget Sound Navy Yard in Bremerton, Washington. There, she would receive a proper refit, proper repairs, new guns, and new radar equipment.[11]

But the documents handed to Greenbacker in Dry Dock No. 1 were beyond his imagination. "The intelligence was most impressive," he recalled. "The entire Japanese plan was described in detail." Rear Admiral Fletcher had already been briefed by Nimitz on the particulars gathered by U.S. Naval Intelligence. Greenbacker soon absorbed the basics: A major Japanese force intended to occupy Midway Atoll, located about thirteen hundred miles northwest of Pearl Harbor. Should this occur, the Hawaiian Islands would become an easier target for Japan to occupy in the Pacific.

Two vast armadas were already underway from Japan, one each toward strategic assault areas of Midway and the Aleutian Islands. Admiral Isoroku Yamamoto's Midway armada was divided into various forces of support, assault, and supply. Vice Admiral Chuichi Nagumo's first carrier-strike force included four of the aircraft carriers that had carried out the December 7 assault on Pearl Harbor—his flagship *Akagi*, plus *Kaga*, *Hiryu*, and *Soryu*. Altogether, some hundred sixty-eight enemy vessels were underway, with attacks against Midway slated for June 4.

To counter this thrust, Nimitz would do well to scrape together thirty-one surface vessels and nineteen submarines. His figures included the battle-damaged *Yorktown*, if Pearl Harbor's repair crews could patch her fast enough to make the voyage to Midway. Greenbacker now understood the seriousness of the situation.

He also learned that when *Yorktown* returned to Bremerton after the upcoming operation, skipper Elliott Buckmaster would be detached to new duties. In preparation for this, the skipper's cabin area was piled high with his personal gear, crated and ready to be moved. It was little inconvenience to Buckmaster, who never used his formal cabin while at sea on war duty. Green-backer knew that it was more than the normal amount a senior officer would carry aboard his ship. When Buckmaster had assumed command of *Yorktown*, he had moved his family into residence in Honolulu, while he moved directly on board from his previous command at Ford Island.[12]

Buckmaster's gear included personal documents and mementos from a career in the Navy. Knowing the seriousness of the upcoming battle, his exec, Dixie Kiefer, pleaded with the captain to move his belongings ashore for safekeeping.

"No," Buckmaster replied. "I hate to violate the old rule that you should never get separated from your gear."

He explained to Kiefer that *Yorktown* might not return to Pearl Harbor after the coming action. Should the ship be sent directly on to Bremerton, he might never be able to reclaim all of his personal belongings. And so they remained on board for the upcoming Midway operation.

Seventy-two hours. That was the demand Chester Nimitz had placed on the Pearl Harbor Navy Yard to bring *Yorktown* back into fighting condition.

Such expectations required an army. Some fourteen hundred workers went to work with drills, hammers, and acetylene torches. They burned away damaged plates and installed new watertight patches to the hull. Riggers and welders cut out crumpled sections of steel and installed new sections to patch up *Yorktown*'s charred innards. Orange sparks and blue welders' torches burned through the night of May 28. The Navy Yard even called on the Hawaiian Electric Company to stage rolling blackouts in Honolulu and other settlements to help meet the excessive power demands of the repair crews.[13]

Nimitz had suspended liberty on May 26 until further notice, but he allowed it for the returning carrier task force sailors who would soon be sailing into harm's way once again. *Yorktown* sailors not directly involved with the ship repairs were allowed to leave dry dock during the day to visit their favorite bars and cathouses in Honolulu. Others in the ship's construction and repair department had no such luxury. Carpenter Boyd McKenzie worked closely with the Navy Yard teams to help patch up his ship. "Some of the repairs being made were not of a permanent type," he observed. But McKenzie understood: He had picked up enough scuttlebutt to learn that the U.S. fleet was being rushed out to meet a Japanese fleet.[14]

Those *Yorktown* sailors allowed to take liberty in Honolulu made the most of their short time. Seaman George Weise, who manned the .50-caliber on the ship's smokestack during battle stations, was amused by the actions of his trusty loader. Joel Sledge returned to the carrier, boasting, "I have been screwed and I have been tattooed. Now I am ready for anything." On one arm, Sledge now sported a tribute to his mother. Freshly inked on the other was "U.S.S. Yorktown."[15]

Gunner John Hancock spent the day roaming about Honolulu and Diamond Head, killing time with his buddies. They had been thoroughly warned about speaking of what action they had seen or even using the name of their ship. "They kept a real eye on us," Hancock recalled. "They said there were multiple Japanese spies still on the island and they didn't want us to tell anybody anything."[16]

Fighter pilot Scott McCuskey enjoyed no downtime in Honolulu. He was among the sixteen VF-42 pilots shuffled from Ford Island to Naval Air Station Kaneohe on Oahu for rapid flight training. McCuskey found that his squadron would be flying a new Grumman variation of the Wildcat fighter, the F4F-4. It sported two additional guns than his former F4F-3 model had, but the new aircraft was found during checkout flights from Kaneohe to be heavier and less maneuverable. His new fighter had six guns, now limited to about two hundred rounds per gun—twenty seconds plus of firepower, instead of forty-odd seconds of firepower.[17]

Even more disturbing to McCuskey was the fact that his VF-42 skipper and executive officer had been relieved. In their place, Lieutenant Commander John Smith "Jimmy" Thach and his XO, Lieutenant Commander Don Lovelace, would be coming on board Yorktown with VF-3, a squadron previously attached to the carrier Ranger. The revamped Fighting Three included a few seasoned pilots, but also a number of flight rookies straight out of the Navy's Advanced Carrier Training Group (ACTG). "They changed our name, which really upset us," McCuskey recalled. He and fifteen former VF-42 pilots, along with their entire shipboard complement of gunners and mechanics, would sail forth for the Midway operation as VF-3.

The balance of Yorktown's air group was revamped as well. Joe Taylor's VT-5 was replaced by Lieutenant Commander Lance

"Lem" Massey's VT-3. His torpedo squadron had been marooned in Hawaii since their carrier *Saratoga* had been torpedoed months earlier. Among his pilots was Chief Aviation Pilot Wilhelm George "Bill" Esders, who hailed from St. Joseph, Missouri. The twenty-nine-year-old had enlisted in the Navy in 1934 and had been accepted into flight training three years later. He was now an old-timer with Torpedo Three, having joined the squadron in 1938 to learn to fly its TBD-1 Devastator torpedo bombers.[18]

His VT-3 had spent the past months ashore on Oahu at NAS Kaneohe Bay, awaiting the chance for a fresh carrier deployment. During that time, Esders's former skipper had been transferred, replaced in early April by Massey. Esders had little time to get to know him well, but he learned that Massey had previously served as executive officer of VT-5 and had participated in *Yorktown*'s raids in the Marshalls. While CV-5 was being repaired, Esders and his fellow pilots were informed that a major conflict with the Imperial Japanese Navy was brewing. "The skipper told us we were going to see action," he remembered.[19]

Bill Burch's long-tenured VS-5 was also cast ashore, its place on *Yorktown* filled by Lieutenant Commander Max Leslie's VB-3, another former *Saratoga* outfit. Each squadron would be maintained by enlisted personnel still on the carrier from the previous units. The only other squadron retained in the hurried shuffling was Lieutenant Wally Short's Bombing Five. With VB-3 now on board, undue confusion was likely for airmen and deck personnel when orders to "spot bombers for launch" were issued. In the days ahead, Captain Buckmaster would settle the issue by temporarily designating Bombing Five as Scouting Five (VS-5), a move that did not sit well with Short's pilots.[20]

Lieutenant Bill Christie felt it was a disgrace to have their squadron designation changed. "The fact that VB-5 was, to a high degree, the only combat-tested squadron, we really felt put down by having our designation changed and being placed in a position as the 'new boys' rather than the other way around," he recalled. "After all, this was our ship and who the hell were these other guys!"[21]

As her air group was sorted out ashore, Yorktown's repair work in Dry Dock No. 1 continued around the clock. Commander Clarence Aldrich, the ship's first lieutenant, worked tirelessly to see that as much battle damage as possible could be shored up in less than three days. Working closely with Aldrich as his new assistant damage control officer was Lieutenant Oxy Hurlbert. The longtime assistant gunnery officer was pulled from Ernie Davis's team to help offset the death of Lieutenant Ricketts at Coral Sea. "As one involved with the repairs, I had to be told why the work was to be rushed so and why we had to accept a patching rather than a real repair job," Hurlbert recalled. Among the scuttlebutt he picked up was that Yorktown would be serving in a backup role, with her air group supplementing the striking power of Task Force 16's carriers Hornet and Enterprise. Under that premise, Hurlbert theorized his crew could accept the minor hazard of a less-than-perfect repair.[22]

But the volume of stores and ammunition being loaded onto Yorktown left others to wonder how much of a "backup" role she would be playing. Warrant Gunner Maurice Witting, responsible for the ordnance used by both the ship's gunnery department and the air group, could not be fooled. Due to the amounts and types of bombs and torpedoes Witting was directed to load, it became evident that his ship was going out as soon as possible on a "big one."[23]

Hundreds of sailors were put to work off-loading provisions. A large dry dock crane swung railroad cars onto the flight deck to be unloaded. Commander Ralph Arnold, *Yorktown*'s supply officer, supervised this process. "We had to make it an 'all hands evolution' to get them struck below," he recalled. Goods were hustled below to the hangar deck, where they were then further distributed to galley and storeroom spaces through the carrier. For his part, Arnold managed to sneak in only four hours of sleep the first night and none the next.[24]

Chief Commissary Steward Calvin Callaway, a *Yorktown* plank owner, worked his cooks, bakers, and mess cooks tirelessly on packing the ship full. One of his cooks, Mississippian Tom Saxon, smuggled a white rabbit on board in the process, leaving some to wonder whether it was truly a pet or the makings of a future stew.[25]

Ensign Bryan Crisman, the ship's disbursing officer and assistant paymaster, was ordered by Arnold to have enough cash on hand to pay the entire twenty-two-hundred-man crew in full as soon as the carrier returned to Bremerton. Crisman had roughly $200,000 on hand in his disbursing office one deck below the hangar, but he picked up an additional $3,000 in coins and $500,000 in currency. His coins amounted to $500 in pennies because he had run short of pennies on the previous cruise.

"Don't let this happen again, Ensign," Arnold had said. When he picked up the cash for the upcoming cruise, a contingent of a half dozen ship's Marines was assigned to guard and carry the currency and coins. The $500 in pennies required one Marine just to carry it.[26]

Yorktown was still in her dry dock on the morning of May 28, as Rear Admiral Raymond Spruance's Task Force 16 put to sea. Headed by the carriers *Enterprise* and *Hornet*, the TF-16 warships were Midway bound a full two days ahead of when *Yorktown*'s TF-17 was expected to move out.

While battle damage was hastily repaired, Commander Dixie Kiefer urged his officers to strive to replace even the luxury items on his carrier. During the return to Pearl Harbor, the XO had met with a small team that included the ship's service officer, Lieutenant John Wadleigh. "Get the soda fountain and store operational pronto," Kiefer had ordered. Major areas of Wadleigh's department, including the ship's store and soda fountain, had been destroyed by the Coral Sea bomb. While the yard workers patched the hull, Wadleigh's team packed the ship's store with snacks and installed storage cabinets and more than $10,000 worth of new ice-cream-making equipment.[27]

Personnel changes were minimal due to the emergency status. One of *Yorktown*'s senior medical officers, Lieutenant Commander Charles Yanquell, departed for a new assignment. Coming on as the replacement surgeon was Lieutenant (jg) Joseph Pollard from the 14th Naval District dispensary in Honolulu. He had graduated from the U.S. Naval School of Aviation Medicine in Pensacola only a week after the Pearl Harbor attack. Reporting on board at 2000 on May 27, before the ship went into dry dock, Pollard had time to learn his way about the medical staff.[28]

He found that he would be assisting Lieutenant Nicholas Dobos as the assistant flight surgeon. Captain Bill Davis was senior medical officer, and his right-hand man was Lieutenant Commander Augustus French, a thirty-nine-year-old former civilian surgeon who hailed form Lawrence County, Kentucky. Pollard would share a stateroom with the junior medical officer Ed Kearney. He learned there were two other doctors: Lieutenant Dewey Jackson and Commander James Lough, the latter a dental officer.

Another new officer to join *Yorktown* in Hawaii had to pull strings just to get permission. Ensign John William "Jack" Crawford Jr. had been schooled at MIT in the use of radar and was itching for a fleet assignment. Raised in New Hampshire, he had been slated to graduate from the Naval Academy in 1942. But with the rush to war, Jack's class was advanced to graduation on December 19, 1941. His original orders to report to the battleship *Oklahoma* were dashed when the ship was destroyed in the Japanese attack on Pearl Harbor.[29]

Eager to fight, twenty-year-old Crawford instead found himself marooned as a "gopher boy" for a flag lieutenant. Months ticked by as he worked with the 14th Naval District, hoping to join *Yorktown* to put his CXAM radar training to practical use. That chance finally came when CV-5 entered the dry dock to repair her Coral Sea damage. At the base officer's club that afternoon, he found that five of his Academy classmates were already serving on *Yorktown*. Over a drink, Crawford explained his desires to get on board during the next few days.[30]

Ensign Mo Slater, who was not even allowed to disclose the name of his vessel, advised expediency. "I'd be aboard by nightfall," he said.

Crawford immediately set out on a quest, but his transfer was denied. A duty officer finally told him that it would take the approval of the district commandant's chief of staff. Snatching up the transfer papers, the young ensign tracked down the captain at a Honolulu movie theater. When he was pulled from the movie to meet the anxious young officer, the captain was furious.

"You mean you got me out of the movies so you can go to sea?" he growled as he walked away.

Crawford followed him, continuing to plead his case. Disgusted but moved, the captain finally signed the papers. He thrust them back at the redheaded ensign and snapped, "Mr. Crawford, you keep doing business this way, and you're headed for trouble!"

Neither man had any idea at that moment just how prophetic the statement would prove to be. Crawford hurried to report on board his new carrier. Deciding that "a good sailor and his baggage are never parted," Crawford brought aboard several suits of dress blues and whites, his Academy sword, and a prized pair of leather-cased 7x50 Bausch & Lomb night-vision binoculars. The latter had been awarded to him at the academy by the American Legion for making top honors in government studies.

He found Dixie Kiefer stressed with a thousand details in readying his ship for combat again. Crawford was assigned to the ship's service department, unsure of any other details about his duties. "Look, get on the watch list," Kiefer told him. "And get as familiar as you can with the ship."[31]

Crawford made his way around *Yorktown*, trying to soak up as much as he could in the overnight hours. He finally went to sleep, exhausted, in his new stateroom. When he awoke the next morning, his carrier was getting underway.

By 0900 on May 29, the dry dock was reflooded. By the time *Yorktown* was eased out of her two-day berth, all of her major engineering vitals that could be fixed in a short time had been fixed. Three of the destroyed superheater boilers simply could not be repaired in two days. For the upcoming battle, the carrier's normal top speed of thirty-two knots would be out of the question.

Elliott Buckmaster conned his flattop into the channel and past Ford Island, where many yard workers were still hard at work. As *Yorktown* maneuvered through Pearl Harbor, the last of these men dropped over the side to a waiting launch. The seventy-two-hour orders from Nimitz had been carried out as best as they could be. Soon after entering the open seas out from the Hawaiian Islands, Ernie Davis put his gunnery department through some routine 5-inch gunnery practice. His teams had shot down Japanese planes at Coral Sea, but he was hoping for better. "His remarks were that we had lived through an attack by Jap air groups in the Coral Sea," recalled Lieutenant John Wadleigh, "but we needed more hits per gun per minute and we might need them very soon."[32]

As *Yorktown* left Hawaii in her wake, Buckmaster took the

opportunity to address his entire crew over the ship's PA system. He said they would be defending Midway Island against Japanese attack. Afterward, they would be heading to Bremerton for repairs and a long-overdue overhaul. Cheers broke out throughout the ship.

In the room they shared, John Wadleigh and Lieutenant Bill Crenshaw swapped stories about West Coast duty and wondered what Bremerton would be like as a wartime boomtown.[33]

CHAPTER SIX

"MAY GOD KEEP US SAFE TOMORROW"

J ohn Hancock now had a front-row seat for air operations.
At Coral Sea, he had manned a .50-caliber machine gun
on the fo'c'sle deck, just below the forward end of *York-town*'s flight deck. Gunner's Mate Doug Word had commended
the young seaman for his ambition, energy, and relentless fir-
ing. "I grew up in the South, shooting quail," Hancock recalled.
"My daddy taught me how to lead 'em. Word told them I had
done pretty good at Coral Sea, so they moved me to where I
would have a larger field of fire."[1]

Hancock's new battle station was another .50-caliber Browning. This one was mounted on the after end of the island structure, affording him a roughly three-hundred-degree firing area.
As *Yorktown* cleared Oahu on May 29, he looked aft toward the

white wake frothing behind the ship. Hancock could see the new air group circling as they prepared to land by squadron.

On the edge of the flight deck, between the number two and number three arresting wires, photographer Bill Roy was filming the landings with his 35mm black-and-white movie camera. As the F4F Wildcat fighters settled into the groove to catch a wire, he filmed one rookie ensign who botched his landing. Roy saw the fighter plane drop too sharply, gathering speed, then bouncing off the deck, missing both the arresting wires and the crash barriers. The ensign's F4F slammed into the back of the plane just ahead, that of VF-3 executive officer Don Lovelace.[2]

Lieutenant Joe Pollard, the new assistant flight surgeon, ran toward the wreckage to assist. He found that the incoming plane's propeller had slashed through Lovelace's cockpit. One blade had fractured the pilot's skull and the next had ruptured his carotid artery. There was nothing he or anyone could do for Lovelace.[3]

Roy grabbed his still camera and snapped images of the aircraft wreckage. But as corpsmen moved in to try to save the dying officer, he put his camera down. Lovelace's body was carried down to the ship's morgue as deckhands worked to clear the two destroyed Wildcats. *A hell of a way to start out a battle*, Roy thought.

Jimmy Thach, the new fighter squadron skipper, gathered his pilots to coach them through the grim loss. There was an important mission ahead, and his pilots must protect the carrier at all costs against Japanese attacks. Lieutenant (jg) Scott McCuskey was shaken up over the loss of his XO. In Thach's reshuffling of the squadron, Lieutenant (jg) Dick Crommelin stepped up to the executive officer position and McCuskey was fleeted up to VF-3 gunnery officer.[4]

As such, McCuskey and the enlisted men of his former VF-42 were now tasked with trying to get the new VF-3 Wildcat guns ready in time. He worked with Chief Aviation Ordnanceman Cecil McCarty to properly mount and sight in each gun. Using a stand, each F4F's tail was raised to put the aircraft into a horizontal attitude so that the guns could be aimed at a boresight-pattern target supported by a structure several hundred feet down the flight deck. McCuskey watched the tracers through the gunsight to make sure each gun, firing out to seaward, was properly aligned to converge on its target. The arduous task of hauling each Wildcat to a safe firing position and sighting in the new guns would consume McCuskey's entire voyage toward Midway.[5]

Yorktown's wardroom was somber due to the loss of Lieutenant Commander Lovelace, but Captain Buckmaster needed his officers sharp. His TF-17 was pressing forward toward Midway, aiming to rendezvous with *Enterprise* and *Hornet's* TF-16 before the expected Japanese offensive commenced. About an hour after the air group was taken on board, the skipper called his officers to the wardroom for their first briefing on the Midway operation.

Communications officer Jug Ray went through the fine details of the captured Japanese plans, which went as far as even naming each of the Japanese carriers that would soon be faced. Ensign Jack Crawford couldn't believe the extent of the information. He wondered how so much detail was available and how Admiral Nimitz was so convinced by it that he would risk the most important ships available in his Pacific Fleet. He was surprised to find that many of his new classmates didn't appear to share his concerns.[6]

But Ensign John Lorenz was shocked to hear that the U.S. Navy knew every detail of their enemy's plans. But he felt some assurance by the time Commander Ray finished his briefing. He thought, *We're about to give the Japs the surprise of their lives.*[7]

Task Force 17 steamed northwest for three days toward its scheduled rendezvous with Task Force 16. On June 1, *Yorktown*'s group met the tankers *Cimarron* and *Platte* to take on fuel while underway. Throughout the voyage, men implemented new battle procedures from the lessons learned at Coral Sea. Surgeon Joe Pollard noted that antiflash clothing, steel helmets, and gas masks were issued to all hands. In his Battle Dressing Station No. 1, just below the island superstructure, he and his corpsmen rechecked their medical equipment. Pollard even had a shipfitter repair the large overhead water tank and fill it with drinking water for emergency use.[8]

At 1600 on June 2, *Yorktown*'s task force finally rendezvoused with the *Enterprise* and *Hornet* force at a position dubbed Point Luck, about 325 miles northeast of Midway. Rear Admiral Fletcher assumed tactical command of the three-carrier force, which also included eight cruisers, fifteen destroyers, and 221 operational aircraft.[9]

En route to Midway, pharmacist's mate Warren Heller was on duty in Sick Bay one morning when a water tender came in complaining of stomach pains. In short order, Heller determined he was suffering from an acute case of appendicitis. Junior medical officer Ed Kearney examined the young engineer and agreed with the diagnosis. *Yorktown*'s medical staff decided that emergency surgery was the only way to save him.[10]

As the operating room—little more than a cubbyhole—was prepped, Heller felt little anxiety. During three years of medical training before the war, he had assisted on a number of appendectomies. Kearney and Heller scrubbed their hands and donned surgical gloves and gowns, while the young sailor was carefully laid on the sterile table and the ship's dentist, Commander James Lough, administered the ether anesthesia.[11]

Once Lough confirmed the patient to be under, Kearney used his scalpel to create a five-inch opening in the infected area. Heller applied gauze pads for compression at the bleeding points. Just as Kearney began his incision into the peritoneum, the ship's bugle blared general quarters. Sailors raced about the ship toward their battle stations, and the mighty carrier swung into the wind to begin flight operations. The turn of the ship caused antiseptic solutions to slosh around and spill onto the steel deck.

The jostling of the vessel added difficulties to the surgery. Every motion had to be perfectly timed and controlled to avoid any injury to the exposed gut. But Kearney expertly removed the inflamed appendix and clamped off the appendiceal artery. A short while later, Kearney carefully stitched up his patient and Heller helped apply the dressing.

The surgical team received well-deserved congratulations from their superiors, and the water tender was secured for recovery. Heller felt great relief in helping to save the man's life. But his thoughts turned toward the impending battle.

How many will be sacrificed in the days to come?

Other departments were busy with last-minute battle preparation on June 3. Based on all available intelligence, the Japanese were expected to attack Midway the following day and air strikes against the enemy fleet were expected. Jug Ray provided another briefing for *Yorktown's* officers in the wardroom. He knew that Midway-based search planes had located vessels of the enemy's Midway occupation force, but their carriers had yet to be sighted. Over a cup of coffee with engineering officer Jack Delaney, Ray shared his firm belief that the Japanese flattops would certainly be spotted on June 4.[12]

Elsewhere through the ship, department leaders were in full preparation mode. Plane captain T. K. Ford and his comrades retained from the old VF-42 worked through the night on *Yorktown's* new VF-3 fighter planes, making sure all would be serviceable by morning. Boiler division officer Reed Cundiff made sure that flashlights were secured in the overheads for all of his B Division compartments. Should the carrier lose lighting as she had at Coral Sea, Cundiff wanted his engineers fully prepared.[13]

Jack Crawford, having been on board for only five days, had no specific department duties when he was not on watch. He spent the evening of June 3 discussing the expected battle with four pilots from Lem Massey's Torpedo Squadron Three. He found the aviators to be subdued, knowing that they would likely be facing Japanese Zero pilots while flying antiquated Devastator torpedo planes. Newer Grumman TBF planes had just missed being delivered to *Yorktown*, but these men were determined to make the most with their old TBDs. Crawford was impressed with their bravery and commitment.[14]

Others used their time to reflect on the upcoming battle. Lorenz passed the evening with his closest friend, Ensign Joe Zawacki, who hailed from Bradford, Pennsylvania. One year removed from the Naval Academy, Zawacki similarly commanded an eighteen-man *Yorktown* gun crew. The pair talked for hours while smoking cigars and speculating on what they would endure the following day.[15]

Around 2000, Lorenz parted ways with Zawacki and headed for his stateroom. He was still wondering how his gun crew would perform, should enemy strike planes again assail *Yorktown*. He thought of his fiancée, Delight McHale, a beautiful and elegant young woman from St. Paul. They had met at a college dance at the University of Portland, where Lorenz danced with her and immediately fell in love. Now he studied her picture on his desk and paused to scribble a brief note on a sheet of paper.[16]

He flipped out the light and crawled into his bunk. He began praying. He was certain he was not alone in seeking divine intervention in the battle—the feeling of impending danger was everywhere.

On his sheet of paper, he had scrawled only six words:
May God keep us safe tomorrow.

Hours before sunrise, *Yorktown* was alive with activity. Her task force was about two hundred miles north of Midway, while Vice Admiral Nagumo's carriers lurked in the darkness roughly two hundred forty miles northwest of the atoll. The lessons learned at Coral Sea were still fresh in Rear Admiral Fletcher's mind: It was key to find the enemy carriers before they found his own.

Throughout the ship, duty messengers roused weary pilots and gunners from their staterooms and bunks. Anxiety ran high among the airmen who had yet to experience their first strike against a Japanese carrier force. Aviation Radioman Third Class Lloyd Childers, raised in Oklahoma City and still relatively new as a TBD rear gunner, had a sense this would be a big day. His Torpedo Squadron Three was slated to carry in live torpedoes. June 4 was noteworthy to Childers for another reason. It was his twenty-first birthday. He dressed quietly, deep in thought. Lloyd placed his wristwatch and wallet on a shelf in the bunk-side locker he shared with his brother, Aviation Machinist's Mate Third Class Wayne Childers. "Wayne," he said, "if I don't come back from this flight, these are yours."[17]

The aviators assembled in their respective ready rooms for their briefings. Childers, already nervous about how he would fare in a lumbering TBD, was not encouraged by the words shared by Lieutenant Commander Lem Massey in VT-3's ready room. The skipper told them that if only three planes made it through the flak and fighters to launch their torpedoes, then their job had been done. As they walked out, everyone else was joking and laughing. Childers was not.[18]

Pilots and gunners were dismissed in shifts between 0300 and 0400 to eat breakfast before air operations commenced for the day. Breakfast was steak and eggs, a true luxury after the scant ration of *Yorktown*'s previous battle cruise. To Childers, it felt like a last meal for condemned men.

Spotted on the flight deck were six Wildcats for dawn CAP duty, plus ten SBDs of Wally Short's newly designated VS-5. Scott McCuskey was among the half dozen F4F pilots who began launching at 0431 into the predawn darkness. *Yorktown*'s scout planes searched a northern semicircle as far out as a hundred miles, but turned up nothing during their two hours aloft. The morning search teams were circling back above *Yorktown* by 0630, waiting to be landed after a fresh rotation of CAP Wildcats could be launched.

After McCuskey landed, he made his way to the ready room. His next assignment, chalked onto the blackboard, did not sit well with the veteran pilot. First, he would be flying with a rookie wingman again—Ensign Mark Bright—instead of his longtime wingman, John Adams. Second, he found out that he and Bright had been penciled in for the strike plane fighter escort. He had done that at Coral Sea, and he had nearly been shot to hell. He thought that duty ought to be spread around the squadron.[19]

McCuskey learned that things were heating up near Midway. During his first morning flight, Midway-based PBY Catalina search planes had started sending in sighting reports of the

Japanese forces. The first had been at 0534, a vague message that stated only, "Enemy carriers." Another PBY pilot eleven minutes later sent the warning: "Many planes heading Midway." Fletcher was now aware that Japanese carriers were somewhere in the vicinity and that a large air strike was apparently inbound for Midway Island.

Jack Crawford was on the bridge, standing duty as assistant OOD, when the "many planes" message came through. The bearing of the inbound Japanese planes matched the intelligence briefing of the previous evening. This message and other data received on the bridge before 0800 convinced Crawford of the accuracy of the intelligence. He was no longer a skeptic.[20]

At 0552, another PBY sent a contact report of two enemy carriers and battleships at a location a hundred seventy-five miles from the U.S. carrier forces. Fletcher signaled Rear Admiral Spruance to have his TF-16 dash ahead and launch strike groups as soon as better position reports on the Japanese carriers were obtained. *Yorktown* dropped behind long enough to recover her morning search planes, then surged forward at twenty-five knots to catch up with *Enterprise* and *Hornet*.[21]

Spruance's TF-16 raced ahead until 0700. At that point, *Hornet* and *Enterprise* turned into the wind to begin launching their strike groups toward the last-known position of the two enemy flattops. Delays and running-rendezvous procedures would consume the better part of an hour. But by 0800, a force of a hundred sixteen strike planes was on its way: sixty-seven dive-bombers, twenty-nine torpedo planes, and twenty escorting fighters.[22]

For the time being, Scott McCuskey could do nothing more

than wait. *Yorktown's* flight deck was fully spotted with strike planes, but Fletcher, hoping for better scouting report intelligence, delayed sending them off. Still irritated at being assigned to strike group escort duty, McCuskey used his idle time to coach Bright.

They'd enjoyed no prior practice time together to sharpen their skills as a team. He told Bright that Zeros had flown circles around him at Coral Sea as if he were sitting still. "I thought it was going to be my last day on this good Earth. Those Zeros made a believer out of me," McCuskey told him.[23]

He discussed tactics that skipper Jimmy Thach had instilled in fighter pilots. They would use the so-called Thach Weave to cover each other's tail with defensive scissor moves. "I'll shoot them off you and you shoot them off me," he told Bright, "because there's no way to outmaneuver them one to one."

Their moment of truth would come soon enough.

★ CHAPTER SEVEN ★

THE PRICE FOR GLORY

O n *Yorktown*'s bridge, Captain Buckmaster caught enough garbled radio messages to learn of the Japanese air strikes on Midway. The tiny white-sand atoll—located at the southwest end of the Hawaiian island chain thirteen hundred miles from Oahu—contained a seaplane base and airstrips capable of fielding medium bombers. Midway's aerial defenses were launched with a fury as PBY reports and radar warned of the incoming enemy planes. Bombers and torpedo planes took to the skies from the sandy airstrip in search of the enemy fleet. Eighteen Marine F2A-3 Buffalo and six F4F-3 Wildcat fighters engaged the incoming Japanese strike group but fifteen of them were shot down by the Zeros.[1]

Midway was bombed and strafed thoroughly by the Japanese. By 0700, the strike group was retiring back toward the

IJN carrier group with intentions of mounting a second air strike against the island. During the next ninety minutes, various small groups of American strike planes launched from Midway made valiant attacks against Admiral Nagumo's carrier. The Army Air Force, Navy, and Marine pilots failed to score a single hit and their squadrons paid the price in terms of heavy losses. Any potential damage to the Japanese flattops now rested solely in the hands of U.S. carrier-based strike groups.

The morning strike against Midway had been outlined in the U.S. intelligence operational plans. Buckmaster's young officer of the deck, Lieutenant John Greenbacker, had remarked on how thorough the code breakers' intelligence was proving to be. Everything was proceeding as if on a playlist.[2]

Buckmaster was alarmed that he had mentioned the classified report. "Don't even talk about it!" he told Greenbacker.

By 0820, Rear Admiral Fletcher was becoming concerned that his carrier might be caught off guard by an enemy strike group. Not wishing to keep fully fueled and armed aircraft in such a vulnerable position, he held a conference with Buckmaster and *Yorktown*'s two senior air officers—Murr Arnold and Oscar Pederson. Their decision was to send two-thirds of *Yorktown*'s air strength out to attack, while holding seventeen SBDs of Wally Short's VS-5 in reserve with six fighters.[3]

The change of plans worked in Scott McCuskey's favor. He learned that skipper Jimmy Thach would escort the strike group with only a half dozen F4Fs. He would be held in reserve for CAP duty, one that he preferred. Shortly after 0830, he felt

Yorktown swinging southeast into the wind to begin launching her strike planes.

First off would be twelve TBDs of Lem Massey's VT-3. With a maximum distance expected to the enemy carriers, the slower torpedo planes were to simply head toward the target. They would be followed by the second-slowest aircraft, seventeen SBDs of Lieutenant Commander Max Leslie's VB-3, heavily loaded with thousand-pound bombs. Last off the deck would be six of Thach's faster F4F-4 Wildcats, allowing the entire strike group to make a running rendezvous en route.

Chief Aviation Pilot Bill Esders, decked out in full flight gear, leather flight helmet, and goggles, swung into his cockpit. He would be flying in the number-two position as wingman for Lieutenant Commander Massey. One plane back from Esders was that of Chief Harry Corl. Radioman Lloyd Childers climbed into Corl's rear compartment and keyed his mike to address his pilot. "Today is my twenty-first birthday," Childers said. "Presumably, today I am a man, so let's celebrate."[4]

Laden with aerial torpedoes, Massey's squadron lifted off without incident and proceeded on course at the slow speed of a hundred knots. Leslie's seventeen dive-bombers followed, circling the task force for twelve minutes so as not to overtake the Devastators too quickly. Finally, at 0905, Thach's half dozen nimble Wildcats climbed into the sky and set their airspeed at a hundred forty knots.

Ensign John Lorenz, gun director at one of *Yorktown*'s after 1.1-inch gun mounts, watched the entire launch process. His crew had been at their battle stations for hours, so this spectacle helped ease some of the monotony. He watched the sky fill with circling dive-bombers until the strike force set out toward the enemy. Within minutes, the anxious tension returned to his gun crew. *War is nine-tenths waiting,* thought Lorenz. *Now let's hope they all return.*[5]

Leslie's faster dive-bombers climbed for altitude and soon caught up with VT-3. When his SBDs approached fifteen thousand feet, Leslie hand-signaled his pilots to arm their bombs. As the first pilots flipped the electric-arming switches to make their bombs "hot," there were unexpected results. Someone on board ship had mixed up the wiring between the arming and release circuits—a snafu that caused four bombs to drop free.

Dallas Bergeron, rear gunner for Ensign Milford Austin "Bud" Merrill, felt a sudden jump after the bomb on his SBD was armed. Another gunner in a nearby dive-bomber frantically signaled him that their bomb had dropped. Bergeron called over the intercom to alert Merrill that they had lost their load. Leslie, irate that his own bomb had also been released, broke radio silence to warn his other pilots not to use the electrical release. Positioned farther forward in the VB-3 pack, gunner Fred Bergeron felt relief that his pilot did not toggle their bomb. Although his brother's SBD and three more had lost their bombs, the squadron continued toward the Japanese armada.[6]

Torpedo Three pilot Bill Esders was alarmed by enormous blasts in the water far below from VB-3's errant releases. Flying at fifteen hundred feet, Esders settled into his advance, just below a scattered cloud formation. *Yorktown's* strike group, having the advantage of being last to launch, would prove to be the most efficient. While most squadrons from the *Enterprise* and *Hornet* air groups struggled to locate the Japanese carrier fleet, *Yorktown's* planes flew almost directly toward it.

By 1000, Esders felt anxious. He had been airborne for eighty minutes without any sighting of surface ships. When he reached the distance where the Japanese had been last reported, nothing was there. From his rear seat in 3-T-3, gunner Lloyd Childers was the first to spot something—a column of smoke far to the northwest. He called up to Corl, and his pilot quickly signaled skipper Lem Massey. The time was 1003, as VT-3's skipper swung his squadron to the northwest to investigate the smoke he knew must be the Japanese fleet, still more than twenty miles away.[7]

As *Yorktown's* air group approached the Japanese fleet, it appeared to some of the aviators that the enemy force was already under attack. Being separated from the *Enterprise* and *Hornet* strike groups, they had no idea what had just transpired.

Lieutenant Commander Jack Waldron's *Hornet*-based Torpedo Eight had flown almost directly toward the enemy. Around 0930, VT-8 had commenced its attack on the nearest carrier, *Soryu.* They were swarmed by some two dozen Zeros, which proceeded to steadily hammer the *Hornet* Devastators into the ocean, one by one.

Gone were Waldron and thirteen other TBF crews, all killed in action. Only one plane, piloted by Ensign George "Tex" Gay, survived long enough for him to launch his torpedo. Bullets killed his gunner before Gay was finally shot down. Of thirty VT-8 aviators, he would be the sole survivor of the torpedo-plane aviators launched from his carrier on June 4 to be eventually rescued. Torpedo Six from *Enterprise* fared only slightly better. Only a handful of the Devastators survived long enough to make their drops. No hits were scored and VT-6 suffered ten crews lost. Only four TBDs would return to *Enterprise*, one so badly shot up that it was shoved overboard to help clear the flight deck.

Torpedo Three approached from an altitude of twenty-six hundred feet. More than fifteen miles out, two Japanese fighters met them. The squadron remained in attack formation, but as the fighters began attacking, Massey maneuvered, changing altitude and speed. Above him, the small VF-3 *Yorktown* fighter escort mixed it up with other Zeros.

VT-3 pilots Harry Corl and Bill Esders saw none of it. They were too busy trying to save their own hides. Esders's main focus was in maintaining position on his skipper's wing. The carrier below—later determined to be *Hiryu*—was going into evasive maneuvers, its deck loaded with aircraft. The time was about 1035, and Esders could see smoke rising from two of the Japanese carriers.[8]

Unknown to him, *Enterprise*'s two dive-bombing squadrons had pushed over into dives on the Japanese carriers at 1022 while VT-3 was making its long, slow approach. Due to botched dive-bomber protocol and the heat of the moment, nearly every pilot from the Big E's VS-6 and VB-6 squadrons piled onto the carrier *Kaga*. More than two dozen *Enterprise* SBDs made their drops on *Kaga*, rocking her with at least seven direct hits. The carrier was left blazing, racked with internal explosions.

Only three VB-6 planes, led by squadron commander Lieutenant Dick Best, pushed on to attack another carrier, *Akagi*.

One thousand-pound bomb exploded alongside *Akagi*, while another grazed the flight deck and exploded close enough off the stern to jam her rudder into a constant thirty-degree circle. Best's half-ton bomb crashed through the flight deck and exploded amongst fueled and armed aircraft on the hangar deck. Within minutes, *Akagi* and *Kaga* were staggered by bomb hits that would prove fatal.

Esders cared little who had caused the devastation. He only hoped to contribute to his enemy's destruction. Sister *Yorktown* squadron VB-3 was just commencing its attack on a third Japanese carrier, the undamaged *Soryu*, as VT-3 plowed through intense fighter attacks and antiaircraft (AA) fire toward *Hiryu*.

Skipper Max Leslie had already lost his bomb, but he led his pack from fourteen thousand feet. He fired his .50-caliber wing guns toward the yellowish deck of the carrier below, hoping to draw AA fire away from his pilots who still had payloads. Following close behind him, Leslie's wingman planted his thousand pounder right through the large red meatball painted on *Soryu*'s deck. Four planes back, Texan gunner Fred Bergeron felt heavy g-forces against his body as his pilot, Ensign Bob Benson, pushed their Dauntless into a seventy-degree dive.

Midway down, Bergeron was struck in the back of his head by Benson's goggles and helmet, ripped from the pilot's head as he glanced into their slipstream. Watching the altimeter spiral down, Bergeron called out twenty-five hundred feet just as his pilot toggled their bomb free. *Soryu* was hit in quick succession by three bombs. Despite the sudden eruption of brilliant red flames and aircraft tossed from the flight deck like toys,

Bergeron could not be certain if his SBD's bomb was a hit or a miss.[9]

It didn't matter. *Yorktown's* VB-3 crews had wrecked *Soryu*, igniting fully loaded Kate torpedo planes on her hangar deck. Fred's older brother, Dallas Bergeron, was flying rear seat in one of the squadron's bombless dive-bombers. But his pilot braved the flak to further chew up *Soryu's* topside with .50-caliber slugs. The carrier's destruction was already so certain that four of VB-3's "tail-end Charlie" (rearmost in formation) pilots dropped their bomb loads on a destroyer and a battleship.

In a span of five minutes, thirty-nine dive-bombers from two carriers had knocked out three Japanese aircraft carriers. By morning, *Akagi, Kaga,* and *Soryu* would all be beneath the waves. Though heavily outnumbered, the U.S. Pacific Fleet had already dramatically shifted the course of the Battle of Midway. But as the Dauntless crews were pummeling the IJN carrier fleet, *Yorktown's* torpedo squadron was paying the price for the victory.

Bill Esders was in the fight of his life. It was 1030 as his VT-3 approached *Hiryu*. Esders jinked his plane up and down and right and left, hoping to throw off the aim of both the AA fire and enemy fighters. Large warships fired shells into the water ahead of them, blasting large fountains of water skyward. Torpedo Three steadily dropped altitude until they were just a hundred fifty feet above the wave tops.

About ten miles out, two more Zeros joined the fight. Esders became so focused on maintaining position on skipper Lem

Massey that he had little time to observe the enemy ships. Within minutes, six to eight fighters were firing into the torpedo-laden Devastators.

Two miles from the carrier, Esders could see three Zeros lined up, one behind the other, to starboard. Esders pulled up quickly to dodge their tracers, but one of the Zeros pulled in close and began peppering his plane with hits. One bullet exploded the carbon dioxide bottle located just forward of his rudder pedals. He opened the canopy to clear the choking smoke as the Zeros continued to attack.[10]

From his position on Massey's wing, Esders could see VT-3 torpedo planes burning up and spinning out of control, falling from the sky.

Flying adjacent to Esders in the TBD numbered 3-T-3 was Harry Corl. Childers, his rear gunner, fired back at the Zeros, wishing his plane was equipped with a more potent .50-caliber machine gun instead of his .30-caliber Browning. He did his best to lead his targets, allowing for the natural drop of the slugs over longer distances. But en route to the enemy carrier, his gun jammed. Childers unholstered his .45-caliber sidearm and popped away at the passing Zeros.

Massey's first division was still about one mile out from *Hiryu* when his plane was hit and caught fire. They were now only about two hundred feet above the ocean surface. Massey's Devastator was a blazing fireball as wingman Esders saw the skipper unbuckle himself and stand up in the cockpit. Childers heard his pilot, Corl, suddenly shout, "Look at the skipper!" With one foot on his seat, Massey placed his other out on the wing as he prepared to jump. At such low altitude, he never had a chance. Childers caught a glimpse of Massey's rear gunner, Chief Leo Perry—whose face suddenly changed from disbelief to fear as he saw his pilot climbing out of their blazing Devastator. Their 3-T-1 hit the water, exploding in a mass of churning fire.[11]

Esders wondered for a second if he should join the four planes of Lieutenant Pat Hart's second division that he could see. He decided instead that he would continue to bore in, leading the survivors of the first division. Esders gave the attack signal by rocking his wings. He broke off to port while the other four planes turned to starboard. He intended to make a semicircle around the forward end of the carrier before dropping his torpedo about eight hundred yards out.

But the Zeros were relentless. Corl was amazed to see that no matter how close he was to the water, they still dived under the Devastators upon completion of their firing run. Bullets shot away the elevator controls on Corl's plane, sending it into an immediate steep glide. Just before he crashed into the water, he released his torpedo. Free of the weight, he found that he could bring the nose of his plane up by using tab control.[12]

Esders was still about a thousand yards out when he saw the other four VT-3 TBDs of Hart's division launch their fish. None survived. Within five seconds of dropping their torpedoes, all four splashed into the sea. Only one pilot, Ensign Wesley Osmus, would survive the crash of the four TBDs. Although seriously burned, Osmus inflated his Mae West and bobbed in the ocean until he was fished from the sea by a Japanese destroyer. Fate was cruel to the young ensign, who was beaten, interrogated, and brutally murdered within hours.[13]

Seconds before Esders could make his torpedo drop, bullets ripped into his rear cockpit. His twenty-five-year-old gunner, radioman Robert "Mike" Brazier, said weakly, "I won't be able to be any help to you. I've been hit very badly."

Esders only had time to say, "Very well."

When he figured his distance to be about eight hundred yards from *Hiryu*, Esders released his torpedo. Corl, having also made his drop, turned north to clear the fleet after he saw Esders do the same. Neither of their torpedoes connected with their target carrier. The only two *Yorktown* torpedo planes to survive the attack thus far zoomed past the enemy ships, clawing for altitude through the hailstorm of antiaircraft fire.

Japanese fighter planes continued their assault on the two Devastators. In Corl's rear seat, Childers felt hot stabs of pain as bullets smacked into his left thigh. *The dirty bastard shot me!* he thought. As Corl maneuvered against the slashing fighters, his rear gunner was hit again. Childers grunted loudly as a slug shattered the shinbone in his right leg.[14]

Esders desperately pushed his plane into a dive toward the ocean. At fifty feet above the water, he watched the splashes of Zero slugs in the blue sea beneath him. Each time an enemy fighter bored in close, he threw his TBD into a violent turn toward his aggressor. For almost twenty miles, he dodged four Zeros. Although his *Yorktown* was located to the east, Esders flew north on purpose to avoid giving away the direction back to his fleet. He shouted back to his gravely wounded gunner, Brazier, to help him watch for incoming attackers.

Finally, the last Japanese fighters turned and departed. A few minutes later, Esders noted another TBD-1 approaching him from astern. It was Corl, his plane, 3-T-3, riddled with bullets holes. Black oil streaks were visible down its fuselage, his engine was crippled, his Aldis signal lamp was shattered, his radio was shot out of commission, and his radioman, Childers, was losing blood from three bullet wounds. Corl could manage only to keep his TBD running by setting his engine at twenty-one hundred rpms, with the fuel-mixture control set to rich.[15]

The two planes continued on. Esders's port fuel tank had been pierced by bullets, and he had a leaking fuel line in his cockpit. With only ten gallons left in his port tank, he ran it until it was empty. His engine continued to run satisfactorily, so he leaned his fuel mixture to minimum and throttled back to about eighty-five knots. Seeing no enemy planes, Esders began climbing for the clouds. He called back to Brazier to change coils in the radio receiver so they could pick up *Yorktown*'s YE radio homing signal. Brazier said he was in bad shape and probably unable to do it.

Ten minutes later, Brazier called over the intercom. He said that he had managed to change the coil and asked Esders to change the dial setting to seventy-nine. Esders did so, but could not hear the YE. Corl remained on his wing for some time but finally drifted off on his own course to starboard. Esders continued his climb to fifty-five hundred feet, where he was able to finally pick up the YE signal. He had been off course about ten degrees to port.[16]

Adjusting his course to starboard, he held his altitude, keeping a close watch on his dwindling fuel supply. Around 1140, his fuel gauge read empty. Minutes later, he was much relieved to finally see Task Force 17 ahead. But he almost simultaneously spotted eighteen Japanese dive-bombers to starboard, about four miles away. Esders immediately nosed over and headed for a cloud bank.

He knew that dodging the enemy formation would consume the last of his fuel. There was no making it home now.

CHAPTER EIGHT

BATTERED

E nsign John Lorenz cupped his hands and lit a cigarette. He and his men at quad 1.1-inch Mount 3 had been at their battle stations for hours on the flight deck, aft of *Yorktown*'s island superstructure. They were ready for an enemy attack, and Lorenz trusted their abilities. The crew had been together for the better part of nine months, and he knew each man like a family member. One of his young loaders, Seaman Second Class Richard Worster, joined him to chat, hoping to ease his nerves.[1]

"Sir, do you think we will be attacked today?" Worster asked.

"Hell no," said Lorenz.

"Well, sir, the gunnery officer has a five-dollar bet with the exec that we won't," said Worster. "I sure hope he's right."

"What if they do? We'll knock hell out of them again."

"That's right, sir," said Worster. "But don't you think we'd better warm up the barrels now?"

The comment brought smiles to the entire crew. Perhaps most pleased was the shy and frail second loader, Seaman Second Class Donald Smith—the youngest man on Lorenz's team. Weeks earlier, one of the Mount 3 veterans, a gunner's mate, had asked him, "You know why we run warm water through the cooling system? That keeps the barrels warm, so when we fire our shells, they go faster and easier." Smith had believed him until someone had clued him in.[2]

As the Japanese air attacks on Midway were related over the ship's PA system, the crew had more reason to expect action soon. "We joked and laughed," recalled Lorenz. "It amazed me just how natural our conversation was, despite the fact that every one of us felt the terrible strain of uncertainty."

The talk of upcoming leave and how folks were doing back home died off as *Yorktown* turned into the wind at 1133 to begin launching scout planes. The ship had not conducted flight operations since launching relief CAP fighters two hours prior. Her deck was spotted with ten of Wally Short's VS-5 dive-bombers and a dozen fighter planes. Rear Admiral Jack Fletcher decided it best to send out Short's planes on a two-hundred-mile scout mission to the north and northwest. Seven other SBDs were moved below to the hangar deck for use in a possible secondary strike against the Japanese carriers.

The first returning planes from Task Force 16's morning strike group were beginning to straggle in. Fletcher lacked solid details of the enemy fleet's location, so he launched the ten ready VS-5 SBDs in pairs to bring back fresh intelligence. As the dive-bombers cleared the deck, Murr Arnold's air department flashed word to VF-3's ready room that the deck would also be cleared of the dozen ready F4Fs. *Yorktown's* six airborne CAP Wildcats were low on fuel and needed replacing, since a secondary strike was not needed at the moment.

Scott McCuskey had been waiting in the ready room since returning from his morning CAP mission. He had tuned into the fighter circuit, listening to various reports of enemy snoopers poking around the U.S. task force. His boredom vanished in an instant as Fighting Three was ordered to scramble the available F4Fs to clear the deck. He dashed to his Wildcat, with rookie wingman Ensign Mark Bright on his heels.[3]

By 1150, two VF-3 divisions under Lieutenants (jg) Dick Crommelin and Art Brassfield were off the deck and maneuvering to properly join up in sections. The plan was for the dozen fighters to rendezvous off the port quarter of the ship, but in the confusion of the moment, Bright, who had launched, failed to join. For the time being, McCuskey was left to follow a different section without the protection of a wingman.

Yorktown had scarcely cleared her decks when troubling news arrived. Radio Electrician Vane Bennett, manning the CXAM-1 radar set within the island structure, reported a group of unidentified planes showing up at a distance of thirty-two miles and closing. Fighter director officer Pete Pederson called to Brassfield's freshly launched division at 1152, directing them to investigate the unknown aircraft.[4]

The first SBDs from Max Leslie's VB-3 had returned to Task Force 17 while *Yorktown* was clearing her flight deck. While queued up waiting to land, one of the first dive-bomber pilots took the chance to buzz down *Yorktown*'s port side. As the Dauntless passed, John Lorenz saw both the pilot and the rear-seat gunner clasp their hands above their head and shake them excitedly. Everyone knew what that meant. Without a word spoken, the pilot had conveyed to the *Yorktown* crew that their attack had been successful.

With Lieutenant Short's scouts departed and the CAP refreshed, *Yorktown* began landing the SBDs. First in was a pair of VB-6 pilots from *Enterprise*, both desperately low on fuel. Lieutenant (jg) Bill Roberts made it on board with only four gallons remaining, and Ensign George Goldsmith's plane ran out of gas while deckhands were still extracting his tailhook from the arresting gear. Both SBDs were badly shot up and their rear gunners had been wounded by Japanese bullets.[5]

Lorenz watched *Yorktown* sailors pull radioman Jim Patterson from Goldsmith's rear seat. He had taken two bullets, and Lorenz could see blood on his flight gear as the young man was hustled below to Sick Bay for emergency treatment. Lorenz wondered how the badly damaged dive-bombers had made it back at all.[6]

Yorktown landed another six CAP fighters while Leslie's jubilant VB-3 pilots continued to circle. Behind them came four fighters under Jimmy Thach, who had escorted the strike group to the Japanese carriers. Low on fuel, Thach landed first and hurried to Flag Plot to inform Fletcher of their mission. Behind him came two more VF-3 pilots, including Lieutenant (jg) Brainard Macomber, who in his haste left his leather flight jacket with his plane. Last of his three division mates to enter the landing circle was Machinist Tom Cheek.[7]

As landing signal officer (LSO) Norwood Campbell waved him in, Cheek sensed trouble when his Wildcat settled onto the deck. His tailhook failed to snag one of the arresting wires, and his fighter barreled toward the crash barrier. Among the flight deck personnel witnessing the landing was Lieutenant Joe Pollard, *Yorktown's* newest junior medical officer. He had been called up earlier from Sick Bay to relieve Dr. Nick Dobos as the duty flight deck medical officer.

Bill Roy was on the bridge filming. His videos would later show Cheek's F4F coming in to the right of the center of the flight deck, heading toward the island. Days earlier, VF-3 pilot Don Lovelace had been killed in a horrific crash during landings. As Pollard watched Cheek come in too hot and too high, he feared another fatal pileup was inevitable. As Cheek's F4F careened toward the crash barrier cables, he jammed his control stick full forward and tucked his head down, preparing for the impact. Instead, his propeller grabbed one of the snaring wires and flipped the airplane over, sending it cartwheeling to a screeching halt upside down. Cheek was unhurt, but afraid of being burned in a fire. As he unstrapped himself, he shouted to the flight deck crew, "Get this thing the hell off of me!"[8]

Pollard dived under the wreckage, but Cheek was already out of the cockpit. He headed for his ready room while Chief Boatswain's Mate Chester Briggs and his deckhands repaired the damaged wire barriers. Cheek's battered F-16 was quickly hoisted onto dollies and lowered by an elevator to the hangar deck, where it was left in its upside-down position.

The VB-3 planes still in the air were forced to continue circling while the flight deck was cleared. But Bennett's radar was continuing to track the incoming enemy flight, only twenty-five miles out by 1155. Flight operations were ceased as gunners were called to the ready. A Japanese air strike appeared imminent. For the moment, tense sailors waiting at their battle stations could only pray that the CAP pilots would take care of the incoming enemy aircraft.

Scott McCuskey climbed for altitude as he turned the crank to roll up his landing gear. He had just reached ten thousand feet, and was heading in the direction of the oncoming bogeys. His rookie wingman was nowhere to be seen. Then he spotted a large formation of Japanese dive-bombers.

"My God, what an opportunity!" he mused aloud.[9]

The lead formation of nine Val dive-bombers appeared to his left. Beyond, at a slightly higher altitude, were another nine. McCuskey swung sharply toward them to take on the leading planes, which were at a slightly higher altitude. His first burst was from only hundreds of yards away, and his bullets caused the outside bomber in the left vee to burst into flames. His sights were next filled by the inside Val of the right vee. The range was so close that he had time only to get in a short burst before his plane passed within fifty feet of the enemy dive-bombers.[10]

Seconds after he passed them, he found two other Vals in his path. In the minutes that followed, McCuskey twisted and turned to lock onto fresh targets. The Japanese planes broke formation, creating a swirling melee of action. McCuskey traded short-range head-on shots with as many as four Vals before his machine guns quit functioning. As he fought clear and leveled off, he was frustrated to find that his new F4F-4, carrying a more limited supply than the previous F4F-3s, was out of ammunition.

He was startled by the sound of a bullet striking his left wing. Two Japanese dive-bombers were maneuvering onto his tail. With no ammunition, McCuskey used superior diving speed to plunge for the wave tops. He shook off his pursuers and headed back for *Yorktown* to rearm. The LSO frantically waved him off. The task force was under attack, leaving McCuskey with no recourse other than to clear the curtain of AA flak and wait out the remainder of the attack.

In just minutes, McCuskey had made three Val "kills," plus he had probably shot down or at least damaged another three Japanese planes. In roughly the same span, other VF-3 fighter pilots had also scored. Brassfield chalked up four kills, and other VF-3 pilots knocked down nine more planes. *Yorktown*'s fighters had certainly done their job.[11]

But a few enemy had survived the melee. They began closing on *Yorktown*'s starboard quarter around 1209. The carrier's survival was now in the hands of her own gunnery department, plus the gunners on two nearby heavy cruisers and five escorting destroyers.

Lieutenant John Greenbacker felt optimistic—after all, his ship had succeeded in dodging enemy planes at Coral Sea. The weather was clear and the visibility excellent. From his bridge position as battle stations OOD, he could clearly see enemy dive-bombers approaching at high altitude. Everything was going well as U.S. fighters intercepted them well out.

Greenbacker saw the "burning planes falling like leaves. So many were going down, it seemed to me that surely none would get through."[12]

Captain Buckmaster knew he should remain under protective cover in the bridge conning tower. But he couldn't resist the urge to move out onto the open bridge, both to help conn his ship and to watch the attack. As the planes approached, he shouted maneuvering orders through narrow slits in the forward conning tower. While he was out on the bridge, Buckmaster kept his exec, Dixie Kiefer, under cover in the aft conning tower. That way, Kiefer could take over if something happened to the captain.[13]

Bill Roy once again had free run of the ship to document the attack, thanks to Kiefer. He elected to assume a high perch from Yorktown's signal bridge. At Coral Sea, his visibility had been somewhat limited. Now, on June 4, Roy was more exposed but had an open view spanning the full three hundred sixty degrees. As the first dive-bombers pushed over to attack his carrier, he began filming with no regard for personal safety.

His movie footage would later show some of the dive-bombers coming in, their fuselages tearing apart as shells splintered steel. Through his six-inch telephoto lens, one Val came close enough to nearly fill the frame. Winking bursts from the dive-bombers' wings reminded him of his exposed position. *They are not shooting directly at me*, he thought, *but they're shooting at someone!*[14]

Belowdecks, the sailors manning engineering compartments and standing ready with the emergency repair parties could do nothing but sweat it out. The call to battle stations had motivated Machinist Worth Hare, one of the few survivors from Repair Party Five at Coral Sea. Badly burned by the bomb blast on May 8, Hare had spent weeks recovering in *Yorktown*'s Sick Bay as doctors and pharmacist's mates tended to his healing skin.

As the enemy air attack closed in, one of the doctors asked Hare if he felt well enough to go to his battle station. "We may be needing the space in your bunk before long," he said. After donning protective clothing and additional bandages to protect against further burns, Hare scurried through the main mess hall to report to his revamped party. Lieutenant Oxy Hurlbert, freshly shifted from gunnery to damage control, was now in charge of Repair Three, a new team assembled in the mess hall near Sick Bay to replace the repair group under Milton Ricketts largely wiped out a month prior.[15]

Carpenter Boyd McKenzie's Repair Party Four was nearby, standing ready on the third deck, portside. One of his senior men was Chief Shipfitter Joe Kisela, who was in charge of *Yorktown*'s shipfitter, pipe and plumbing shop. In the dim light, all Kisela could see were the nervous faces of young sailors, "all eagerly wanting to do something, patiently waiting for something to happen and at the same time hoping that nothing would happen."[16]

One deck below, Chief Engineer Jack Delaney was at his battle station in the main engineering control area. He had direct phone communication with the "smoke watch" from the ship's bridge. Talkers kept Delaney continually informed of all plane activities, both friendly CAP fighters and enemy attackers. He breathed a little easier as he received word that *Yorktown*'s fighters were downing the Japanese raiders.[17]

In Sick Bay, Captain Bill Davis ordered his medical team to take cover. In the Coral Sea battle, many men had lost their lives because they were standing when the bomb exploded. As the ship now lurched into its evasive turns, his men duly took to the steel deck and covered their faces to avoid flesh burns. Near misses soon caused the ship to shake and bounce. "We thought each bomb dropped was a hit," remembered Davis.[18]

On the flight deck, aft of the island structure, John Lorenz was as ready as he would ever be. Far out to sea, enemy planes were silhouetted against a large, fluffy white cloud bank like a swarm of bees. He and his crew were ready. "We were glad that the waiting was over," Lorenz remembered.[19]

As the specks on the horizon grew closer, Lorenz saw flames falling seaward as the CAP pilots did their job. By 1209, the larger-caliber guns in the task force were firing at will, and *Yorktown*'s 5-inchers had joined the fray. At one point, he counted four plumes of black smoke trailing down toward the ocean. The sky was steadily darkened as the guns erupted from all quadrants. Then Lorenz saw a distant Wildcat falling like a stone, victim to an enemy gunner.

As he waited for the enemy planes to reach firing range, the ensign glanced at his gun crew. They appeared grim and determined. By this point, he had counted ten smoke puffs on the sea's surface, each marking the final moment of an incoming enemy aircrew.

Frustrating Lorenz was the presence of one large low-hanging cloud nearby. Behind it were Japanese planes approaching *Yorktown*.[20]

He and his men were left unable to see approaching aircraft

until they were well into their dives. Then the escorting destroyer to starboard opened fire into the cloud. The men of Mount 3 were still unable to see the hidden planes.

Two minutes into the firing, gunnery officer Ernie Davis called over the loudspeaker at 1211, "Diving attack starboard beam!"

Lorenz spotted his first Val dive-bomber. As it flew through black bursts of antiaircraft fire, the air seemed aflame with barrels bursts and tracer bullets. In an instant, his mount was alive with action. Shells from their quad 1.1-inchers raced skyward in bright lines toward the first plunging plane.

They hit their mark, but the Japanese pilot managed to release his bomb. Lorenz saw it clear enough to believe its trajectory would carry it far to seaward. His crew immediately shifted their fire to the next plane.

Seaman John Hancock's new battle station was on the island superstructure, facing out from the ship and overlooking the ocean below. As the gun battle erupted, he glanced down to see a number of plane pushers on the flight deck scrambling to take cover. Several climbed the steel rungs to one of the island ladders, where they sat to ride out the attack. They looked like clay pigeons on every rung of the ladder.[21]

Hancock opened up with his machine gun on the Japanese dive-bombers. Farther forward, stationed above the flight deck on the searchlight platform, Seaman George Weise also let loose with his .50-caliber. At Coral Sea, he had been credited with shooting down a Kate torpedo plane. Loader Joel Sledge, sporting his fresh *Yorktown* tattoo, kept the belts of ammunition coming.

Weise was frustrated as the attacks commenced. His Browning could not be raised high enough to bear on the dive-bombers plunging out of the sun. A pipe railing had been installed above his gun to prevent it from being accidentally fired into the ship's stack. Irritated, he slammed his gun against the pipes to get a better shot. That didn't help. But he continued firing, trying to get a line on Vals that dropped into his range.[22]

In concert with Weise and Hancock, ten other .50-caliber gunners poured bullets into the sky toward the next plunging dive-bomber. The sound topside was deafening, with the booming of *Yorktown*'s 5-inch guns, the snapping of .30-calibers, the reports from ten 20mm mounts, and the chattering of four quad 1.1-inchers clustered around the island.

The rain of steel chopped the first dive-bomber into three sections that plunged toward the sea. But the Val pilot's aim was dead-on, and his 242-kilogram high-explosive bomb tumbled free from the wreckage.

John Lorenz never knew what hit him. The ensign had been directing his battery's fire on the first Val. Once the plane broke apart and its bomb appeared to be carrying toward the ocean, he had shifted the aim of his men toward the next aircraft. But the first bomb dropped on *Yorktown* did not miss. It struck the flight deck about fifteen feet inboard, about twenty feet aft of Ensign Charles Broderick's Mount 4. The effects were devastating. A bright red sheet of flame shot more than sixty feet skyward as the bomb ripped a jagged eleven-foot hole in the flight deck. The sweeping blast of fire killed a dozen of Broderick's

USS *Yorktown* (CV-5) viewed in February 1942 as a TBD-1 Devastator torpedo plane launches from her flight deck. Another TBD is beginning its takeoff run near the island superstructure. *(National Archives and Records Administration, 0-G-640553)*

Dauntless dive bombers of Bombing Five (VB-5) warming up on *Yorktown*'s flight deck during 1942 Coral Sea operations. *(U.S. Naval History and Heritage Command Photograph, NH 95571)*

Left to right: Captain Elliott Buckmaster, *Yorktown*'s respected skipper at Coral Sea and Midway *(NHHC, L38-10.03.01)*; Commander Dixie Kiefer, *Yorktown*'s popular executive officer, seen in 1944 *(NHHC, NH 100259)*; Irving Day "Jim" Wiltsie, *Yorktown*'s navigator, took over as acting XO once Dixie Kiefer was injured. Wiltsie perished in 1943 when his carrier *Liscome Bay* was torpedoed. *(U.S. Navy)*

Left to right: Lieutenant John Everett Greenbacker, officer of the deck during the Japanese attacks at Midway, and recipient of the Bronze Star with Valor at Coral Sea *(U.S. Navy)*; Elgin Blaine "Oxy" Hurlbert, seen later as a lieutenant commander. At Coral Sea he was assistant gunnery officer, and at Midway he was assistant damage control officer. *(U.S. Navy)*

Commander Ernest J. Davis, *Yorktown*'s gunnery officer, is pinned with a Purple Heart in Norfolk by his wife for injuries received at Midway. *(NARA, 80-G-42770)*

Lieutenant (jg) Elbert Scott McCuskey was *Yorktown*'s top-scoring fighter pilot at Coral Sea and Midway. Flying with VF-42 and VF-3, he was the top Navy ace of the first six months of the Pacific War with 6.5 kills. He earned two Navy Crosses and the Distinguished Flying Cross. *(U.S. Navy)*

A sailor looks through the large hole amidships through *Yorktown*'s third deck at damage controlmen working on the fourth deck. Photo taken on May 8 of the damage caused by a 250-kilogram bomb. Dozens of men of the ship's engineering repair party were killed or badly injured at Coral Sea in this compartment, C-301-L. *(NHHC, NH 95573)*

Lieutenant Milton Ricketts, of *Yorktown*'s Repair Party Five, was posthumously awarded the Medal of Honor for fighting fires until he died of his wounds on May 8. *(NHHC, NH 95297)*

The Japanese carrier *Shoho* burning and under attack by *Yorktown* and *Lexington* planes on May 7, 1942, in the Battle of the Coral Sea. *(U.S. Navy)*

The Japanese carrier *Shokaku* seen during attack by *Yorktown*'s air group on May 8 at Coral Sea. Her bow is blazing from a direct hit made by Lieutenant John Powers, who perished in his efforts. *(U.S. Navy)*

Pharmacist's Mate Warren Heller, seen during medical training in 1941. *(Warren G. Heller)*

Aviation Machinist's Mate Truxton King "T. K." Ford, seen in World War II flight gear. *(U.S. Navy photo)*

Lieutenant (jg) Edward A. Kearney, *Yorktown*'s junior medical officer. *(Edward A. Kearney)*

Carpenter Boyd McKenzie was in charge of Repair Party 4 at Coral Sea and Midway. He was later awarded the Bronze Star for his lifesaving efforts in these battles. *(Boyd McKenzie Jr.)*

Yorktown in drydock No. 1 at Pearl Harbor Navy Yard on May 29, 1942. She is undergoing emergency 72-hour repairs for her Coral Sea damage in order to make a hasty departure for the Battle of Midway. *(NARA, 80-G-13065)*

Seaman John William Hancock, seen in 1942. *(John Hancock)*

Smoke rises above the after end of *Yorktown*'s island structure during the Battle of Midway on June 4. Seaman John Hancock (circled) as he stands ready at his .50-caliber machine gun. *(NARA, 80-G-21610)*

Brothers Lloyd (*left*) and Wayne Childers both served with *Yorktown*'s Torpedo Squadron Three at Midway. *(U.S. Navy)*

Brothers Dallas (*left*) and Fred Bergeron, fellow VB-3 aviation radiomen, receive decorations for their valor at Midway. *(Fred Bergeron)*

One of VT-3's Devastators, seen about 0840 on June 4 from the cruiser *Portland*. Armed with a Mark XIII aerial torpedo to attack the Japanese carriers, this Torpedo Three TBD did not return to *Yorktown*. *(NARA, 80-G-21668)*

Pilots of *Yorktown*'s VT-3, photographed in late May at NAS Kaneohe. Within weeks of this photo, ten of these pilots would be killed in action at Midway. Machinist Harry Corl (*far left, back row*) and Chief Aviation Pilot Bill Esders (*far right, back row*) were the only two surviving pilots of those launched on June 4, 1942. Lieutenant Commander Lance "Lem" Massey, seated third from left in center row, was among those killed in action. *(NARA, NH 95554)*

Shipfitter Leo Leggins pauses from repairing damage on *Yorktown*'s flight deck to look aft at corpsmen handling two casualties near .50-caliber machine guns. *(NARA, 80-G-312020)*

Fire hoses are stretched across the hangar deck in this fuzzy image taken after the bomb hits at Midway. A TBD Devastator torpedo plane is parked in the distance. *(NARA, 80-G-312023)*

Corpsmen treating casualties on *Yorktown*'s blood-stained flight deck near quad 1.1-inch gun Mount No. 4, following the bombing attack. John Lorenz's 1.1-gun Mount No. 3 is located just to the left. Note the bearded chief petty officer walking by, with his pants tucked into his socks to prevent flash burns. *(NARA, 80-G-312021)*

(Left to right) Ensign John d'arc Lorenz and Seaman First Class Harold Orlando Davies each received the Silver Star for gallantry at Midway. When their 1.1-inch Mount 3 crew was largely wiped out by a bomb hit, the two injured men and two shipmates continued firing their gun at attacking Japanese planes. *(U.S. Navy)*

This still was taken from movie footage shot by photographer Bill Roy on the flight deck after the dive bomber attack at Midway on June 4. *(U.S. Navy)*

A Japanese Type 97 torpedo plane slams into the ocean during the June 4 attack on *Yorktown*. Just left of the camera aiming cross can be seen an F4F Wildcat fighter banking away. *(NARA, 80-G-32250)*

Its tail section shot away, a Val dive bomber (*far left*) is about to crash into the ocean ahead of *Yorktown* on June 4. *(NARA, 80-G-32355)*

The badly shot-up Dauntless dive bomber of Ensign George Goldmsith lands on *Yorktown*'s flight deck shortly after the Japanese bombing attack. *(NHHC, NH 100740)*

Unable to land his Dauntless on *Yorktown*'s battle-damaged flight deck, VB-3 skipper Lieutenant Commander Max Leslie ditches his bomber alongside the cruiser *Astoria*. *(NARA, 80-G-32307)*

Yorktown under torpedo plane attack at Midway. Two *Hiryu* Type 97 Kates can be seen flying among the anti-aircraft bursts. *Yorktown* appears to be heeling to port and may have already suffered one torpedo hit. *(NARA, 80-G-32242)*

Photographer's Mate Bill Roy, seen with his movie camera, captured many dramatic images of *Yorktown*'s final hours at Midway. *(U.S. Navy)*

Yorktown burning and listing after suffering multiple bomb and torpedo hits on June 4 at Midway. Due to fears of the ship capsizing, the crew would soon abandon ship. *(NHHC, NHF-004)*

These two video stills are taken from movie footage shot by Bill Roy from *Yorktown*'s bridge on May 4. Fighter pilot Tom Cheek's F4F veers toward the island about to crash. In second image, Cheek is bent forward an instant before his plane cartwheels. He is directly below where Roy is standing. *(NARA footage)*

Abandon ship! *Yorktown* crewmen can be seen climbing down knotted lines around 1700 on June 4 as her escorting destroyers pick up survivors. The destroyer *Anderson* (DD-411) is at right. *(NARA, 80-G-21694)*

The destroyer *Benham* (DD-397) is seen packed with 720 survivors around 1900 on June 4, as *Yorktown* drifts in the background. *(NHHC, NH 95574)*

Sailors struggle to walk on *Yorktown*'s sloping flight deck after the two torpedo hits as they prepare to abandon ship. Note the F4F Wildcat fighter in the background. *(NARA, 80-G-14384)*

Although water was nearly entering the hangar deck as *Yorktown* lists to port, she remained afloat overnight. Seen at far right is a 26-foot motor whaleboat making a final check for survivors in the water around the ship. *(NARA, 80-G-21643)*

Seaman George Kenneth Weise suffered broken limbs and a fractured skull when a bomb hit tossed him from his .50-caliber gun mount on the smokestack to the flight deck below. Left for dead, he was rescued from his abandoned carrier the next day. *(Carolyn Weise)*

While *Yorktown* sailors fought to save their ship, the carrier's air group handed out revenge to Japanese warships. At left is the blazing carrier *Hiryu* on June 4. Above is the heavy cruiser *Mikuma*, so badly battered by bombs that her gun barrels can be seen dropping toward the water. *Yorktown* SBD dive bombers contributed to the destruction of both vessels. *(U.S. Navy photos)*

During the June 6 salvage attempt, crewmen on the hangar deck prepare to push a TBD-1 Devastator overboard to help correct the list. Photo taken by *Yorktown* photographer Bill Roy. *(NARA, 80-G-32323)*

This historic diorama by artist Norman Bel Geddes depicts the destroyer *Hammann* (DD-412) alongside *Yorktown* assisting her salvage team on June 6, 1942. *(NARA, 80-G-701899)*

In this Bel Geddes diorama, torpedoes from the Japanese submarine *I-168* explode in *Hammann* and *Yorktown*. *(NARA, 80-G-701900)*

In this Bill Roy photo from *Yorktown's* starboard forecastle deck, the destroyer *Hammann* has just disappeared from view minutes after being torpedoed. *(NARA, 80-G-32321)*

In this Bill Roy photo, the stern of the destroyer *Hammann* is about to submerge. Knotted lines from the June 4 abandon ship process are still evident. *(NARA, 80-G-32320)*

Yorktown sinks early on the morning of June 7, as viewed from an escorting destroyer. Photo taken by Bill Roy. *(NHHC, NH 106000)*

Yorktown's sinking was captured well in this series of Bill Roy photos as she capsizes to port, exposing massive torpedo damage to her hull *(NHHC, NH 95576)*; {*bottom*} The ocean surface begins to froth from escaping air bubbles. *Yorktown*'s bow is nearest to camera. *(NHHC, NH 95577)*

Wearing oil-stained life jackets, *Yorktown* survivors are checked in on board the USS *Fulton* (AS-11) on June 6 for transportation back to Pearl Harbor. *(NARA, 80-G-312030)*

Admiral Chester W. Nimitz (*second from left*) and staffers wait on the dock at Pearl Harbor to greet *Yorktown* survivors on June 8. *(NARA, 80-G-312025)*

Carpenter Boyd McKenzie is pinned with a Bronze Star earned at Coral Sea and Midway. *(Boyd McKenzie Jr.)*

gun crew instantly. The men on Lorenz's Mount 3 fared little better.[23]

The explosion slammed Lorenz to the deck, momentarily unconscious. He struggled to regain his senses. His body had been hurled against the mount's splinter shield, tangling his legs beneath him like spaghetti. His clothes were torn open, his helmet and belt pistol blown from his body. It seemed as if fire was all around him. Billowing smoke further added to his confusion.[24]

He stood up, his ears ringing from the explosion. The sight that greeted him was one that would be burned into his brain forever. His crew was devastated. Every last man was down, many moaning and screaming in pain. One man was lying on top of the rest, badly hit.

The first sailor he recognized was gunner's mate Edward Zimmerle. During the past few months, he and Zimmerle had grown closer as they chatted about personal affairs. Only a week before, Zimmerle had shown Lorenz photos of his family and his girlfriend. Now the gunner lay on the deck, his face pale and turned skyward. His eyes were closed.[25]

Zimmerle suddenly opened his eyes and looked at Lorenz. He struggled to form words for a moment. Then his eyes closed again and his head fell limply to one side as he lost consciousness. Nearby lay the body of another Mount 3 loader, Seaman Second Class Pearl Prince, a quiet but efficient young man who had lost his wife and child in an automobile accident only a month before.

Then Lorenz spotted smoke pouring out of the ready service magazine below Mount 3. In the boxlike compartment were thousands of rounds of 1.1-inch shells. He jumped down, flung open the hatch, and climbed inside. Two sailors who had been stationed inside to pass shells through the small opening to the mount had been burned. Bomb fragments had penetrated the magazine and some of the shells, causing them to sizzle and snap as spilled gunpowder burned. The seamen were already in the process of isolating damaged shells, ignoring their pain as they used their hands to beat out the flames on the sizzling shells. Lorenz hoped their efforts would be enough to prevent thousands of rounds of live shells from erupting.

Seaman Pete Montalvo was another loader working the aft 1.1-inch gun mounts. Two months prior, he and his buddy Sid Flum had danced the foxtrot during the *Yorktown* jamboree. Flum had been transferred after suffering severe wounds during the Coral Sea battle. During that action, Montalvo's battle station had been belowdecks in the aerial bomb compartment. But he had since petitioned for a topside station. Now, as Japanese dive-bombers punished his ship, Montalvo had more action than he cared for.[26]

As the enemy planes approached, Montalvo had been chatting about stickball with gunner's mate Walter Maurice, another loader. When the first bomb hit, Montalvo felt a wall of fire engulfing him and a sharp pain on the right side of his head. He came to flat on the deck, calling out for his mother. As he instinctively pulled the steel helmet from his head, blood flowed down and obscured his vision. He wiped it away and looked around. Shipmates were sprawled all about him. Seaman Rupert Gibson, the easygoing young trainer on Mount 3, was gone from the waist up. Only his torso remained in the left-hand seat. Montalvo's buddy Maurice had lost both legs.

The explosion killed seventeen men from the Mounts 3 and 4 gun crews. Another eighteen were seriously wounded. Ensign Broderick felt searing pains as bomb splinters ripped through his back and legs. Around him, twelve of his gunners were killed. Seaman Wendell Thrasher had just bent over to pick up ammunition when the flash occurred near Mount 4. "Everyone was above me, and when the shrapnel hit, they fell on me," he said. "When I came to, they had piled me up with the dead. Someone was washing us with seawater to get the blood off. I was as bloody as they were and not a scratch on me."[27]

Seaman Second Class Terry Dykes caught a glimpse of the bomb before it exploded. The young sailor from Georgia had switched jobs with another Mount 4 sailor, Seaman Second Class Clarence Edwin Hill, just the previous day. Hill stood taller than Dykes and was better able to load the shells into their gun. Fearing for his life this day, Hill had borrowed a complete set of freshly laundered clothes from Dykes the previous evening so he would be clean if he was killed or wounded. The explosion killed Hill instantly as shrapnel sliced into his head. Dykes, standing exposed on the ladder to the turret, had red-hot fragments rip through his legs and back.[28]

Immobilized by his wounds, Dykes tumbled from the ladder. Another 1.1-inch loader, Seaman Eldon Dean, caught him and laid him on the flight deck. Thrasher, dazed but unhurt, dragged Dykes into a compartment below the flight deck and gingerly laid him on an expansion joint. Blood was spurting from wounds in Dykes's upper right leg, so Thrasher used his belt to tighten a tourniquet before leaving him to help others. A short time later, a pharmacist's mate administered morphine to Dykes, assuming the medicine would allow him to die in peace. Dykes slipped into unconsciousness.

Although the dead and dying lay all about them, bloodied survivors on both Mounts 3 and 4 were determined to keep fighting off the Japanese attackers. Ensign Broderick, wounded in his legs and back, got to his feet, helped remove corpses from his mount, and rallied his survivors. Only his gun captain, his trainer, loader Dykes, and he had survived. Broderick persisted with his duty until blood loss prevented him from standing any longer.

Storekeeper First Class Joe Hartlove was manning a 20mm gun directly across the flight deck from the point of explosion. He had fired at the Val all the way down, then watched as its bomb fell free. At Coral Sea, the bomb that damaged *Yorktown* had plunged through her flight deck before exploding deep within. Hartlove expected the same from this one. *Here is the chance of a lifetime,* he thought, *to see a bomb going through a deck.* But this one exploded on impact. For the next few moments, all Hartlove could see was a bright red color with lots of black dots, plus wood splinters blown into his face from the flight deck.[29]

Flight-deck-area casualties quickly overwhelmed surgeon Joe Pollard at nearby Battle Dressing Station No. 1. The lieutenant had been topside, assisting with the removal of Tom Cheek's flipped Wildcat, when the Japanese bombing attack commenced. As *Yorktown's* guns opened fire with a deafening roar, Pollard sprinted across the deck and climbed down the ladder toward his medical station.[30]

Shrapnel from the first bomb sprayed across the flight deck

and into the island superstructure. Boatswain Briggs, who had been working to fix destroyed barrier wires, was hit in his right thigh by a small piece of metal. Pollard's decision to return to Battle Dressing Station No. 1 was lifesaving for him. Normally, he would have been standing on the aft island ladder platform during battle stations. In his place at the moment was Pharmacist's Mate Third Class Stanley Kwapinski. Shrapnel killed him almost instantly. Ironically, corpsman Ed Koslowski had been killed at Coral Sea in the same location.[31]

Without the assistance of Kwapinski, Pollard was overwhelmed with gun crew casualties. Sailors began hauling burned and bleeding men to his station in the midst of the dive-bomber attack. "Some men had one foot or leg off," Pollard recalled. "Others had both off. Everywhere there was need for morphine, tourniquets, blankets, and first aid." Within minutes, his station overflowed into the adjacent passageway, into the parachute loft and other available nearby areas.[32]

John Lorenz, satisfied that the sailors below were subduing the fire in the ready magazine, popped back up through the Mount 3 hatch. To his astonishment, three survivors of his crew were firing their gun again. The least wounded was Seaman First Class Harold Davies, a farm boy from Indiana who had joined *Yorktown* with his brother, Jim, before the war. Shrapnel had zipped into his left knee, but he was oblivious to the fact in the heat of battle. From the pointer's seat, he was busy elevating and firing the four-barreled gun without the normal assistance of a trainer on the right side.[33]

Seaman Second Class Donald Smith's back and legs were bleeding from severe shrapnel wounds, but he continued to load the gun. Chief Gunner's Mate Albert Noland had been hit in both legs and his right arm. Using only his good left hand, Noland was stoically working with Smith to feed ammunition to the gun and make corrections to the mount.[34]

Lorenz helped them continue firing at enemy planes. Davies wondered how much good they were doing, but knew that he had been trained never to leave his battle station. "I felt really guilty that I couldn't get out and help the ones that were wounded," he remembered.[35]

Less than one minute after the first dive-bomber landed a hit on *Yorktown*, another was seen moving in from astern. Its dive was almost as steep as that of the first Val. Once again, *Yorktown* gunners tore the plane apart as it dived. Its bomb also tumbled free, narrowly missing the after flight deck. Pieces of the Val smashed into the carrier's wake and its bomb exploded on impact with the ocean immediately astern of the fantail.

Splinters from this bomb killed or wounded the crews of the .50-caliber machine guns by the after port corner of the flight deck. Other men were hit on the port side of the first superstructure deck aft, and several small fires erupted on *Yorktown*'s fantail. These fires were quickly extinguished.

Seaman Second Class Norman Pichette, manning a fantail 20mm gun, was rendered unconscious by a large piece of shrapnel that ripped his abdomen open. Seaman Ed Cavanaugh was manning a .50-caliber machine gun below the LSO platform on the fantail. Fragments from the near miss ripped the leg off his loader, punctured another man's feet, and hit him in twenty-two places. Dazed and bloody, Cavanaugh stumbled across the flight deck, hoping to get help for his shattered left hand. He was cut down again by three bullets from a strafing Japanese plane. Cavanaugh collapsed until a corpsman raced out to help him toward Sick Bay.[36]

Pete Montalvo wanted to help, but his injuries were severe. A pharmacist's mate assisted him from the devastated Mount 3 area to the landing of a stairwell. The medic administered sulfa powder to burns on Montalvo's right shoulder. He also had shrapnel wounds in both legs. The medic called for two sailors to assist him to an aid station five decks below, where Montalvo was placed in a lower bunk for later treatment.[37]

John Hancock fired his .50-caliber continuously until one of the bomb explosions sprayed shrapnel across the after end of *Yorktown's* island. He crumpled to the deck but was back on his feet almost instantly, bleeding but able. In the heat of battle, he was too keyed up to notice that shrapnel had pierced his neck and right lung. He pushed his uninjured assistant gunner out of the way and resumed firing. When the gunfire finally subsided, Hancock was shocked by the sight of the plane pushers who had elected to ride out the air battle perched on the rungs of an island superstructure ladder. The shrapnel had ripped them apart. One guy sat there, delirious, mumbling, "Texas, beautiful Texas."[38]

Farther forward on the exposed bridge, Captain Buckmaster watched the falling bombs. To him, they looked like small kegs of nails coming down. His battle stations recorder, yeoman Floyd Bennett, ducked at one point as bullets from a diving Japanese plane ripped through the bulkhead inside the bridge.

No one was harmed except Chief Joe Burger, who received a scratch on his shoulder.[39]

Yorktown maneuvered through the water at better than thirty knots as Buckmaster tried to dodge the diving Vals. A bomb struck just astern, tossing water and shrapnel skyward. Another explosion fountained in the carrier's wake as her skipper called for hard turns away from each diving plane.

George Weise, standing on his .50-caliber platform on the side of *Yorktown*'s smokestack, shifted his fire to each new attacker. Another Japanese dive-bomber was diving from eight thousand feet, a bit off-center. For once, Weise felt he had a great target for his gun. Joel Sledge kept the ammunition fed as Weise trained his sights on the incoming Val. It seemed as if this plane was intent on plunging straight down *Yorktown*'s stack.[40]

He continued firing as the bomb detached from the plane. It looked like a bowling ball to Weise. At that instant, Buckmaster threw his carrier into a hard starboard turn. The maneuver was sharp enough that Weise saw the bomb carry past his gun platform by about ten feet and plunge through the flight deck below him.

This, the second bomb to directly strike *Yorktown*, hit the ship at 1214. It passed through the flight deck, the hangar deck, and the second deck and finally exploded in the uptakes of the stack deep inside the ship. The effects were devastating belowdecks. A huge blast of heat immediately swept up *Yorktown*'s smokestack. It set the paint on fire and created such a shudder that everything topside was jarred loose. The explosion slammed Weise's head so hard against the barrel of his

.50-caliber that his skull was fractured. In the same violent motion, his body was pitched skyward, high in the air and over the railing on the side of the ship's stack. His body twisted through space as he plunged down to the pinewood-covered flight deck. The impact knocked him unconscious.

When he regained his senses, he was racked with pain. His left side had taken the brunt of the fall, leaving his left arm and leg shattered. The impact paralyzed the right side of his body. Unable to move and his skull split, Weise lay helpless as machine-gun bullets from a Japanese plane stitched through the wood deck near his body. Then everything went blank.[41]

Near Weise, Signalman William Martin watched the Val all the way down. His job on the searchlight was to challenge incoming planes for the proper response signal. Knowing full well these were Japanese aircraft, he had opened his searchlight shudders wide, hoping in vain to blind one of the pilots and spoil his aim. The shudder that swept over the stacks from the second bomb hit also tossed Martin from his high perch. Fate was kinder to him than to Weise. His downward plunge was arrested two levels below his light when his body slammed into a catwalk rail, leaving him unhurt but dangling from the rail.[42]

The shock waves slammed Vane Bennett's radar room, which abutted the stack near the top of the superstructure. He felt the ship move downward as the massive concussion split the bulkhead seams in his compartment. He was saved from hitting the deck by having one hand clasped against the radar transmitter. His head was cut from striking the gear, but Bennett quickly feared the radar room might become his coffin. Thick black smoke began to fill the compartment through the cracks. The blast wedged the compartment door into the hatch, and he and others had to throw their weight against the door until they managed to burst it open.[43]

The first two bomb hits created fires and casualties throughout the ship. Lying prone on the deck in the mess hall, Machinist Worth Hare felt the ship shudder as the first bombs exploded. Then he felt a tremendous jar as a direct hit exploded inside his carrier. To Hare, *Yorktown* caterpillared through the water from the force of the explosions—ceasing to give way for an instant before thrusting forward again.[44]

The second bomb, weighing two hundred fifty kilograms, penetrated deep into the ship before exploding. At Boiler Emergency Control, boiler division officer Reed Cundiff's men narrowly escaped serious injury. When the dive-bomber attack commenced, he had ordered all of his B Division men to switch on the emergency flashlights he had hung from the overheads. When the chatter of lighter-caliber guns indicated to him that an enemy plane was very close, Cundiff shouted, "Hit the deck!"[45]

The bomb exploded just forward of Cundiff's department in the boiler uptake-intake space. White-hot shrapnel ripped through his compartment and continued on through the aft bulkhead over the men flat on the deck. None of them were even scratched. Cundiff's own office was turned into a pyre—its hatch door welded by the heat into a partially open state—but his men could tackle that blaze later.

The forward-most boiler, No. 1, was under the charge of a short, burly sailor named Charles Kleinsmith. His fuel-burning superheaters boiled water to create steam that powered the ship. The force of the blast knocked him down, damaged the brickwork surrounding his boiler, and extinguished its fire. Cundiff donned a gas mask and thrust a fire hose into the compartment to attack the flames. As he pressed forward into Kleinsmith's compartment, he had no inkling that the interior of the adjacent room was red-hot. He was hit by a blast of steam that knocked him backward and down a ladder. In the process, every part of his face not covered by the gas mask was badly scalded, and his exposed arms were seared. Cundiff retreated just long enough for medics to bandage his arms and tend to his face.

Three of *Yorktown*'s boilers damaged at Coral Sea had not been repaired at Pearl Harbor. Five of the six operational boilers had their fires blown out by the second Japanese bomb. Their loss meant loss of steam and loss of propulsion. The normal vibration of a massive ship underway at full steam began to decrease in intensity. *Yorktown* was virtually powerless, and the ship's speed quickly dropped from thirty knots to about six knots.[46]

Heavy black smoke billowed from amidships, both from her stack and from the two jagged bomb holes in the flight deck. But her punishment was not finished. At about 1215, roughly one minute after the second bomb hit, the ship took another two-hundred-fifty-kilogram semi-armor-piercing bomb hit when a *Hiryu* Val plunged from about seventy-five hundred feet toward her starboard bow. The first to attack from this direction, the pilot caught *Yorktown*'s gunners off guard.[47]

With little AA fire to distract him, the *Hiryu* pilot landed his bomb squarely through the No. 1 elevator forward of *Yorktown*'s island. It exploded fifty feet down, in the rag stowage space. No one was killed, but the entire area erupted into a serious fire that soon threatened nearby gasoline and ammunition stores.

Machinist's Mate Second Class Bill Ogden was stationed with two other sailors in the nearby forward elevator pump room. As smoke and flames engulfed the area, Ogden unselfishly allowed his two shipmates to escape first, and they scrambled upward toward safety. Ogden left, closing each hatch after his exit to preserve watertight integrity and to prevent flames from spreading. As he reached the dark, smoke-filled area where the bomb had exploded, he groped his way forward.[48]

While securing the last hatch, Ogden was overcome by heat and smoke. He collapsed on top of the hatchway. He would later be found still clutching the hatch clamps in his hands. He would be posthumously decorated with a Navy Cross for sacrificing his life to save his two shipmates.

Temperatures soared in the forward magazines. Chief Gunner's Mate Vardie Taylor ordered the compartment flooded with seawater to prevent stacks of 5-inch ammunition from exploding. Topside, *Yorktown*'s gun crews continued to send rounds of high-caliber shells toward the enemy planes at a blistering pace. Seaman Roger Spooner, a husky Georgia farm boy who had joined the carrier only a week after the Pearl Harbor attack, didn't even have time to look up at the plunging Japanese dive-bombers.[49]

Spooner was the first loader on the aft portside 5-inch gun mount. As another sailor lifted each fifty-four-pound shell from the ready locker hoist into the fuse setter, Spooner moved it into its final firing position ahead of a powder charge before both were rammed into the gun. In the midst of bomb explosions and shrapnel that sprayed the stern area, Spooner escaped injury. The last Val's bomb was a near miss off *Yorktown*'s starboard beam. The gun crews didn't cease firing at the retiring planes for several minutes.

Less than five minutes had elapsed since the first Val pushed into its dive on *Yorktown*. On the bridge, battle stations OOD John Greenbacker was stunned. At Coral Sea, the aerial assaults had seemed to last for an eternity. But Captain Buckmaster had twisted and maneuvered his ship with ease, dodging every torpedo and all but one direct bomb hit. To Greenbacker, this dive-bomber attack seemed to have taken but an instant.[50]

The efficient CAP fighters and Task Force 17 gun crews had downed many attackers. But seven *Hiryu* carrier bombers had survived the hailstorm of fire long enough to make their drops on the carrier. Three had scored direct hits and two landed near misses close enough to cause damage and casualties. With her boilers and engineering spaces wrecked, *Yorktown* began to lose way as her speed dropped. Eight minutes after the second bomb hit, the vessel was dead in the water. She belched black smoke from her stacks and from holes in her flight deck, and she was without power for her guns, aircraft elevators, lighting, and steering.

Minutes earlier, Commander Dixie Kiefer had cracked a hatch from Battle II to check the progress of the attack, only to be hit by shrapnel that ripped through the island structure area. Knocked to the deck, Kiefer found that small shards of metal had ripped into his right shoulder and leg. But he decided his wounds were minor as he picked himself up and headed for the bridge. The bloodied XO reported to Buckmaster that the situation on the flight deck looked grim.[51]

Kiefer commenced a damage inspection of the ship. He stopped at his office long enough to retrieve a breathing apparatus, but as he cracked open the door, he nearly suffocated from choking smoke. He decided against retrieving the mask and moved down to the hangar deck, where men were wrestling with fire hoses and jettisoning explosive materials. On the next deck, Kiefer found a fire raging in the ship's photography lab. He located a fire hose, opened the valve, and directed its spray toward the open lab door. Intense heat seared his face and arms, but Kiefer worked the fire hose until several sailors joined him.[52]

The battle to save *Yorktown* had only begun.

CHAPTER NINE

DEAD IN THE WATER

George Weise lay crumpled on the flight deck, unconscious. His skull was fractured, his left arm and leg were useless, and his right side was paralyzed. His forty-plus-foot plunge from the smokestack gun platform was witnessed by yeoman Joseph "Jack" Adams, who was stationed on the port catwalk with the radio repair party. After the Japanese bombers cleared the area, Adams raced out onto the flight deck and found that Weise was not moving. He appeared to be dead, with blood running out of his nose, mouth, and ears.[1]

A pharmacist's mate who joined Adams believed Weise's injuries were fatal. Still, shipmates hustled him into a medical dressing station in the island structure, where he was outfitted with a temporary cast on his left arm and leg. Then he was carried belowdecks to the main Sick Bay. Unable to move, Weise drifted in and out of consciousness.[2]

Just below the flight deck in Battle Dressing Station No. 1, Lieutenant Joe Pollard and his pharmacist's mates worked diligently. They administered morphine, covered patients with blankets, and worked by flashlights in the darkened compartment. Pollard called for stretcher-bearers to begin moving the most seriously wounded—those missing limbs or suffering from severe blood loss—down to the main Sick Bay, where they could receive plasma. The stretcher-bearers quickly found some of the passageways blocked due to bomb-explosion damage.[3]

Pollard climbed up to the flight deck to see what other assistance he could offer. At nearby 1.1-inch Mount No. 4, he saw a pair of legs attached to the hips of a severed body still sitting in the trainer's seat. Portions of other men were scattered about the mount. Blood was everywhere. The firing had ceased, and he noticed that the carrier had gone dead in the water. As he moved aft, Pollard assisted with wounded men in the starboard catwalk and shrapnel victims near the fantail. When they could be spared briefly from Sick Bay, fellow doctors August French, Nick Dobos, and Dewey Jackson and dentist James Lough were called topside to assist with the worst cases.

Chief Jim Wilson's battle station was two decks below the hangar deck. The explosions felled others in his vicinity, but he escaped with only burns on his hands and shrapnel in his knee. Among other shipmates who soon arrived to assist Wilson was Machinist Worth Hare. As the ship slowed to a halt, Hare felt weak. Deciding that his burned body was still not up to par to help Repair Five fight fresh fires, he made his way to Sick Bay to help out. Hare helped swab the wounded just outside Sick Bay and offered water to help others wash blood from their mouths. Senior medical officer Bill Davis found casualties arriving quicker than he could treat them. Many of the first to reach Sick Bay were gunners who had been struck by shrapnel or bullets, but more grievously wounded men from the areas of the direct bomb hits soon began arriving.[4]

Topside, John Lorenz was on the move. As the firing ceased, he worked to help the wounded men from his gun mount down to the nearby Battle Dressing Station No. 1. Among them was his gun captain, Edward Johnson. Lorenz tried lifting him, but the seriously injured man proved to be too heavy. Dragging Johnson to an edge of the gun platform, Lorenz enlisted the aid of another sailor. Lorenz carried Johnson by his legs, while the seaman clutched him around the waist. They struggled along the flight deck toward the dressing station, moving the gunner down a hatch. But by the time they had Johnson to the base of the steel ladder, he had breathed his last.[5]

Lorenz turned back to the flight deck. He realized that the ship was now dead in the water. For the first time, he paused to take in the horrific scene about him. Just opposite the No. 2 aircraft elevator on the starboard side, there was a jagged hole in the flight deck. The nearby island structure was scarred with shrapnel holes. Dead and wounded lay everywhere, and debris was scattered all about.

The battery officer returned to his Mount 3, where he found Seaman Second Class Bill Sullivan, a slender, quiet loader. The eighteen-year-old was lying on his side, his pants caught in some obstruction that had pinned him to the deck. Lorenz and others moved Sullivan to the battle dressing station, then helped administer morphine to the young sailor while his clothing was cut away to get at his wounds. Sullivan's leg, shoulder, and arm were injured. Despite his wounds, he was conscious, chatting about his girl back home in Grand Rapids.

As medics put a tourniquet on his badly wounded leg, Sullivan kept talking. He was propped up with a life jacket and given a cigarette to calm his nerves. Between puffs, he cursed the Japanese in vivid language.

Lorenz returned to help move other wounded men to the dressing station. His fellow Mount 4 officer, Ensign Broderick, had finally collapsed from blood loss and exhaustion. Lorenz helped administer morphine to Broderick and others, and he used his own shirt to make a tourniquet for one sailor. Terry Dykes, a loader whose left leg had been ripped by shrapnel, tried to laugh and joke while smoking a cigarette. Dykes attempted to tease Sullivan about a previous escapade, but he was too wounded to even notice that Sullivan had lapsed into unconsciousness. Another loader, Seaman Walter Walker, lay wounded near Dykes. He told Lorenz he was okay and to help someone else worse off than he was.[6]

Lorenz called for Doc Pollard and other medics to assist his severely wounded gunner's mate, Edward Zimmerle.

"Will he make it?" Lorenz asked.

The doctor shook his head. Lorenz couldn't understand it—his right leg was the only place he was wounded. Pollard administered morphine and wrapped the leg. Lorenz remained with his dying gunner as medics moved on to treat others. Zimmerle asked for water, and Lorenz helped him take a small sip. The gunner locked eyes with his battery officer. His lips were thin and purple as he struggled to speak.[7]

"Tell my folks this isn't the end," Zimmerle gasped. Then he was gone.

Nearby lay Seaman Second Class Edward Thornberg, the first loader on Mount 3. His stomach had been torn open by shrapnel. Thornberg was placed in a comfortable position as medics moved to assist the next man. Lorenz felt a rush of anger at the enemy who had taken so many of his friends.

Carpenter Boyd McKenzie escaped injury at Midway just as narrowly as he had in the Coral Sea battle. This time, a bomb exploded in the compartment above his Repair Party Four, killing a number of sailors. His men went to work even before the Japanese dive-bombers had cleared the scene. Undogging hatches to their compartment, McKenzie's men climbed up to the hangar deck to assist. Twisted metal lay everywhere and dead and wounded were all about. Fire crews attacked the blaze while electricians rigged portable lights to illuminate the dark, smoke-filled holes. Chief Wilburn Wright from McKenzie's team was approached by Seaman Jack Sutter, a wounded young man who hailed from South Dakota.

"What do you want me to do, Wright?" asked Sutter, his face covered with blood. "I'm okay."[8]

Wright took one look and said, "Go to Sick Bay."

"Hell, this is only blood," Sutter said, but he left.

McKenzie's men encountered many other wounded sailors as they advanced through the worst-hit areas. One mortally wounded man was a sailor McKenzie had known for years. The man cried out for McKenzie and another chief to stay with him during his final minutes so they could tell his family his last wishes. McKenzie remained until the young man expired.[9]

On the flight deck, teams attacked the fires burning near the aft 1.1-inch mounts. Medics moved about, treating the wounded and calling for stretchers to haul them below to Sick Bay. Carpenter's mates and shipfitters were already at work, dragging out material to patch the three large holes in the flight deck. Lieutenant Albert Wilson's flight deck repair crews set to work before the dive-bombers were gone. Thick wooden beams were pulled across the twelve-foot hole near the island structure. Repairmen dragged large half-inch-thick steel plates over the beams and drove spikes through the steel into the wooden flight deck to hold them in place. In less than half an hour, Yorktown's deck was sufficiently patched for flight operations.

Bill Roy descended from the bridge with his camera to capture images of the damage control parties and medics in action. With his movie camera, he recorded sailors lugging fire hoses across the deck as black smoke belched from Yorktown's stack. The ship was dead in the water but alive with activity. Roy would not see his footage or stills for a long time, but the images were already burned into his brain. The most grisly scene was the carnage near Broderick and Lorenz's after 1.1-inch mounts, where shipmates labored to remove portions of bodies.[10]

Exec Dixie Kiefer seemed to be everywhere. Still bleeding from his shrapnel wounds, he helped fight the photo lab blaze until it was contained. Then he moved throughout the ship, supervising the damage control efforts and the struggle to help wounded men. Somewhere along the way, a pharmacist's mate bandaged up his wounds. Kiefer inspired each man to continue his fight in his own way. Without power to operate the galley, there was no opportunity to feed the crew, but Kiefer ordered several sailors to go below to the ship's store, where they broke out boxes of candy for anyone who needed a quick bite to eat.[11]

Warrant Gunner Maurice Witting faced a unique challenge. The bomb that passed through the island superstructure had ripped out several electrical cables to the air-armory compartment below. This area contained considerable amounts of ready-to-load ammunition used to rearm Yorktown's aircraft. Noting that these cables were hot, Witting called Commander Aldrich at Central Station and asked him to have his men cut the power before someone could be electrocuted or nearby ordnance could be ignited by the arcing wires. Witting's heated insistence finally worked, although the diagnosis he heard from the sound-powered battle phones was amusing. "That arcing could hurt somebody's eyes pretty bad," a sailor said before the power was finally cut.[12]

Ensign Bryan Crisman descended from his position on an island catwalk once the attack ceased. Moving one deck below the hangar deck to his disbursing office, he decided to retrieve pay records from the ship's safes. He filled three large white canvas packs with the paperwork before securely locking the safes—which held more than $700,000 in cash and coins. Crisman hauled the heavy sacks to his stateroom for safekeeping until they could be transferred elsewhere.[13]

Lieutenant Commander Jack Delaney's engineers had their hands full. Concussions from one of the bomb explosions had damaged many of the ship's boilers and blown out the fires on all but one of the superheaters.

Water Tender Charles Kleinsmith, in charge of Boiler No. 1, had been knocked to the deck by the blast. Despite broken and red-hot boiler casing and fumes from bomb explosions and ruptured uptakes to their boiler, he refused to abandon his post. A half dozen men of his crew—Water Tender Charles Snell and firemen Earl Jansen, Cecil Brooks, James Benton, William Brewer, and Roy Ellison—stayed with him. For the moment, the other boilers were unable to be relit due to choking black smoke pouring into those compartments. But Kleinsmith's team remained in the fight, laboring to ensure that *Yorktown* could soon regain power.

At Boiler Emergency Station, division officer Reed Cundiff ordered two of his men to move up one deck to help with fires on the starboard side. They began tossing overboard lines and tarps that might fuel the fires in *Yorktown*'s uptakes. Cundiff, freshly bandaged for his burns, set to work with his keymen to try to restore power to the ship. It was first necessary to find the source of the damage to the boilers. Kleinsmith's boiler was operational but could not get up sufficient steam to operate the engines. Despite facing noxious gases, the other boiler room crews made repeated attempts to light their boilers but each effort failed.[14]

It was imperative to ascertain the problems and fix them

immediately. Although burned and covered in bandages, Cundiff crawled up into the uptake-intake space. He found that the boiler uptake—the duct carrying the smoke from Kleinsmith's No. 1 boiler—had been ruptured by the blast, as had uptakes from other boilers. As a result, the black smoke was not able to continue on its normal path up toward *Yorktown*'s smokestack. Instead, it was being drawn back down into the other boiler rooms once they started their intake blowers.[15]

Cundiff passed orders to Kleinsmith to reduce his fires to no more than that required to furnish some auxiliary steam. He told the other fireroom chiefs to slowly restart their blowers, light their fires, and slowly bring up the steam pressure. It worked. In short order, the other boilers were brought back online. At that point, Kleinsmith's boiler was secured and his men were moved to other duties. In the after engine room, main propulsion officer Bill Crenshaw, leading chief Nathaniel Poole, and their men worked in complete darkness, fighting fires while helping to reroute the steam necessary to get their carrier moving again.[16]

———

While damage control efforts raged throughout the ship, *Yorktown*'s returning aviators faced their own challenges. Many of the pilots, finding their ship dead in the water, had insufficient fuel to reach another flight deck. Torpedo Three's only two surviving TBD crews had exhausted their fuel even before the first bombs had ripped into *Yorktown*.

Pilot Bill Esders had sighted TF-17 moments before the Japanese air strike. His Devastator had been shot to hell, and rear gunner Mike Brazier narrowly clung to life. Forced to dodge into cloud cover for several minutes to escape nearby Vals, Esders watched three of the enemy dive-bombers crash into the sea as he circled out of harm's way. But at 1203, his engine finally froze up from fuel starvation. Esders radioed *Yorktown* that he was making a water landing about ten miles west of the ship. He put his flaps down and did a full-stall landing. The plane started settling nose down, but Esders tripped the flotation gear and the plane remained afloat.[17]

Brazier called for help. Esders helped him from his bullet-riddled rear cockpit, then inflated their rubber life raft. A bullet had pierced the raft, but it was seaworthy enough to hold Brazier. Esders gave his gunner a drink of water, then patched the holed raft. Minutes later, returning *Yorktown* SBDs—one that Esders could see from its side labeling to be Max Leslie's T-1—swooped low enough to drop float lights. Brazier was suffering terribly, complaining about his back wound. He had also been hit in both legs between the knees and ankles.

At one point, a Japanese dive-bomber passed astern. It turned around and started back toward their raft, apparently intent on strafing. But an F4F suddenly appeared, attacking the Val and driving it back into the clouds. About an hour later, the destroyer *Hammann* arrived to haul Esders—bleeding from a head wound sustained in the landing—on board. By that time, Brazier was dead. *Hammann*'s crew sank the bobbing TBD by piercing its flotation bags with small-arm fire.

Machinist Harry Corl, flying the only other surviving VT-3 Devastator, reached the American task forces around 1225. He circled the carrier twice but saw that there was no chance to land on the powerless *Yorktown*. Rear gunner Lloyd Childers was too weak from blood loss to even raise his head to see the ship. Corl proceeded toward *Enterprise*, some twenty miles away, hoping to land. Lacking tab control for the elevator, he was unable to keep the nose of his plane up. Approaching *Enterprise* from astern at about five hundred feet, he found his oil pressure rapidly dropping.

"Stand by to hit the water!" he called back to Childers.[18]

Corl made a water landing just ahead and to starboard of the carrier. The destroyer *Monaghan* slowed to lower a whaleboat as the pilot helped his wounded gunner into the ocean. Corl helped support Childers until they were hauled into the small boat and carried back to *Monaghan*. Childers was taken down to the wardroom, where the ship's medical officer dressed his bullet wounds and administered plasma. "The doctor told me later that I would have been dead in another thirty minutes without medical help," Childers remembered. He was the only rear gunner of *Yorktown*'s VT-3 to survive the strike against the Japanese carrier fleet.[19]

Bombing Three fared better in its return. Beginning at 1237, fifteen of the seventeen SBDs launched were able to land on *Enterprise*. Their service would be sorely needed to fill in for VB-6 and VS-6: Sixteen *Enterprise* dive-bombers making the strike on the Japanese carriers had been shot down or were forced to ditch. The final two VB-3 planes, piloted by skipper Max Leslie and his wingman, ditched alongside the cruiser *Astoria* after their fuel was exhausted.

Ten other VS-5 SBDs, launched three hours earlier at 1130, were still out on their long-range scouting mission to find the fourth undamaged Japanese carrier. Once *Hornet* and *Enterprise* had recovered all of the morning strike group aircraft that returned, reinforcement CAP fighters were launched to relieve the F4F pilots who had been airborne throughout the Japanese dive-bomber attack. Task force FDOs directed *Yorktown*'s twelve CAP fighters to land on *Hornet* to refuel. Scott McCuskey's errant wingman, Mark Bright, and five other VF-3 pilots were taken on board *Hornet* as directed.[20]

But McCuskey and the balance of the VF-3 fighters independently decided that *Enterprise*'s flight deck looked more welcoming. While his bulletless Wildcat was being rearmed and refueled, McCuskey went below to grab some lunch.

As the remaining fighters and bombers were sorted out between the two undamaged U.S. carriers, Rear Admiral Jack Fletcher struggled with his own dilemma. Choking smoke from the stack had made his Flag Plot and the nearby communication office untenable. Fletcher and his staff assembled on the flight deck as he prepared to shift his flag from the lifeless *Yorktown* to a new flagship, the heavy cruiser *Astoria*. A whaleboat chugged over to retrieve the admiral and half of his staff. By 1342, Fletcher had climbed a Jacob's ladder to *Astoria*'s well deck. Captain Buckmaster's crew was left to continue the damage control battle.

Just a quarter hour after the admiral's departure, things were looking up for *Yorktown*. For more than ninety minutes, she had drifted lifelessly in the breeze. But by 1400, Jack Delaney's engineers achieved a limited success. Much of the smoke had been cleared from her disabled firerooms, and her undamaged boilers were slowly being brought back on the main propulsion steam lines. The carrier began to shudder as her screws dug into the ocean, letting all hands know that their ship was getting underway once again. To mark the event, Buckmaster ordered sailors to break out a huge new American battle ensign to fly aft of the smokestack. Somewhere in the midst of the dive-bomber attack a smaller U.S. flag atop the island had disappeared in the explosions.

Lorenz had done all he could do on the flight deck to help his wounded and dying gunners. When he paused to look toward the island superstructure, he noticed the fresh ensign, which measured fifteen by twenty feet. Although *Yorktown's* engines were just beginning to rumble to life, a light breeze rippled the flag against the sunlight that poked through the blackened battle-seared sky.[21]

For a moment, Lorenz couldn't move. At that critical moment, the new flag gave him renewed hope. "For the first time, I realized what the flag meant," recalled Lorenz. "All of us—a million faces—all our effort—a whisper of encouragement."[22]

As *Yorktown* began to make headway during the next few minutes, signal flags were hoisted up the halyards. To those who understood their symbols, the message was most encouraging: "My speed five."

Cheers sounded throughout the ship and from sailors topside on other TF-17 vessels. A few minutes later, the signal flags were replaced with new ones that indicated *Yorktown* was making ten knots, and flight deck crews began to refuel Wildcat fighters. Jack Delaney sent word that his engineers should be able to soon coax thirteen knots out of their damaged plant. Fighting Three skipper Jimmy Thach was asked if his F4Fs could take off into a thirteen-knot wind. He replied in the affirmative.[23]

The badly damaged carrier would now have a chance against a second attack.

The second attack of the day against *Yorktown* was not long in presenting itself. Japanese search planes had transmitted intelligence of three U.S. carriers, identified as *Yorktown, Enterprise*, and *Hornet*. Confirming this intelligence at 1300 was a report from Destroyer Division Four obtained by a captured VT-3 pilot.[24]

Admiral Nagumo ordered his last undamaged carrier, *Hiryu*, to prepare an immediate counterstrike against the American force. Returning morning strike planes soon reported they had scored bomb hits on an *Enterprise*-type carrier, leaving it burning out of control. By 1331, Nagumo's meager force was on its way: ten torpedo-armed Nakajima carrier attack planes and six escorting Zero fighters. The strike was led by *Hiryu*'s air group commander, Lieutenant Joichi Tomonaga—whose own Kate was forced to depart with a leaking fuel tank. He split his strike group into two *chutai* (divisions) of five planes each. Their distance to *Yorktown*'s Task Group 17 was a mere eighty-three miles.[25]

Less than one hour into their flight, Tomonaga's pilots saw American ships on the horizon. The flight leader soon made out one enemy carrier screened by heavy cruisers and destroyers. His target was underway and appeared undamaged—a testament to the handiwork of *Yorktown*'s crack damage control teams.

At 1432, Tomonaga broke radio silence to order, "Take positions in preparation for attack."[26]

CHAPTER TEN

TOMONAGA'S REVENGE

By 1420, *Yorktown* was making fifteen knots, enough to launch some of the ten fighters being refueled on her deck. But most were nearly void of fuel, less than two dozen gallons in most cases. Only VF-3 skipper Jimmy Thach's F4F, a spare plane, had been fully fueled in the hangar deck. Deck crews began pumping fuel into the Grumman spotted second on the flight deck. As soon as the others could be fueled, Captain Buckmaster was prepared to launch his fighters.[1]

Scott McCuskey had returned to the skies. His F4F had been refueled on *Enterprise* and he had been relaunched at 1340 in command of an ad hoc four-plane division filled out by junior VF-6 pilots. McCuskey's division flew toward *Yorktown*, where they were placed under the direction of FDO Pete Pederson and ordered to circle at ten thousand feet while the dispatching and receiving of various aircraft took place on *Hornet* and *Enterprise*, now some forty miles distant from *Yorktown*'s Task Force 17.[2]

Radar reports soon indicated that trouble was in the making. At 1427, operators on the cruiser *Pensacola* detected unidentified aircraft forty-five miles out. Due to their height, the unknown planes were presumed to be dive-bombers. McCuskey's mixed VF-3/VF-6 division was vectored out to engage them.

Minutes later, Vane Bennett's CXAM radar locked onto the incoming enemy planes, showing as bogeys at thirty-three miles' distance. The refueling activities on deck stopped immediately. Gas lines were purged with carbon dioxide to prevent further fires, leaving two of the topside Wildcats with insufficient fuel to be launched. Thach's fighter was already fully fueled, but others behind him had only enough fuel to safely launch and tangle with enemy aircraft for a few minutes. Beginning at 1440, Thach's eight Wildcats left *Yorktown*'s flight deck to join the CAP fighters already aloft. They departed in intervals of less than fifteen seconds, each pilot cranking his handle twenty-eight turns to raise his landing gear by hand as his Grumman gained altitude.[3]

Tomonaga's *Hiryu* torpedo bombers were already dropping toward attack altitude. Four thousand yards out, he split his group into two divisions and descended to two hundred feet above the ocean to commence torpedo attacks. Tomonaga's first division was met by VF-3 pilots who had scarcely even cleared their flight deck. Thach quickly set one of the Kates aflame, although its pilot managed to release his torpedo before his plane spun into the ocean close off *Yorktown's* port quarter. Other *Yorktown* fighter pilots downed two of the other three planes in the division.[4]

Cloud cover had prevented McCuskey's division from *Enterprise* from intercepting the incoming planes. "Return buster! You have passed them!" Commander Pederson said over the FDO circuit. Understanding "buster" to mean to fly at maximum speed, McCuskey swung his F4F jockeys back toward *Yorktown.*[5]

They returned in time to catch a pair of Zeros at lower altitude working over American F4Fs below them. McCuskey was in excellent position, but he had failed to switch on the light to his N2AN gunsight. He flipped the toggle and had to pull back hard on his control stick, forcing his Wildcat into a zoom climb to stay on his Zero's tail. His bullets began tearing through the plane. In the course of his upward climbing circle, McCuskey's F4F reached the inverted position. Upside down, he continued to pour lead into his opponent until the Zero spun toward the water in flames.

His VF-6 wingman, Ensign Mel Roach, became separated in the process but managed to knock down his own Zero. McCuskey's high-speed zoom caused his engine to stall. He dropped out of the loop and recovered from the spin, then climbed for altitude. He spotted other Zeros closing on American fighters. Diving in, he laced one Zero's windscreen and canopy with .50-caliber slugs. His opponent narrowly regained control of his Mitsubishi and was forced to limp back toward *Hiryu* without having fired a shot.[6]

Thach's eight fighters were credited with downing seven of

the Kates, but VF-3 suffered four planes shot down and one pilot killed. By the time the action with *Hiryu*'s strike force was over, McCuskey had shot down two Zeros. Combined with his earlier score against the Val dive-bombers, they made him the U.S. Navy's second-ever "ace in a day" by achieving five or more aerial kills in a single day.

This distinction was one he now shared with Medal of Honor recipient Edward "Butch" O'Hare, who had become the first "instant ace" in February after shooting down Japanese bombers assailing his carrier *Lexington*. A mere six pilots had become "aces in a day" during World War I, and only sixty-eight U.S. pilots would achieve the feat during World War II. Ironically, the next ace in a day—months later in the Guadalcanal campaign—would be Lieutenant Swede Vejtasa, a member of McCuskey's air group during the Coral Sea battle.

In spite of their valiant intercepts, *Yorktown*'s fighters were unable to prevent some of *Hiryu*'s attack group from pressing home their torpedo attacks.

Joe Pollard had remained on the flight deck to monitor the scramble of *Yorktown*'s fighters as the Japanese planes approached. As the last F4F cleared the deck, and the ship's guns roared into action, he descended the ladder toward Battle Dressing Station No. 1.[7]

To man the after 1.1-inch quad gun mounts, Warrant Gunner Maurice Witting had rounded up a trained reserve gun crew during the past two hours from the flight deck gang. At

Charles Broderick's Mount No. 4, they had to rinse their former shipmates' remains off with fresh water.[8]

John Lorenz's Mount 3 was also largely crewed by replacement sailors. But Seaman Harold Davies, despite the shrapnel in his left knee, remained in the pointer's seat. The sky blackened with smoke as dozens of guns opened up on the low-flying Japanese torpedo planes. Tracers cut bright paths through the air, and Lorenz was pleased to see direct hits slam into enemy planes.[9]

Below deck, pharmacist's mate Warren Heller was still working on victims from the earlier bombing attack. He administered morphine syrettes to bloodied sailors dragged to his first aid station just forward of the No. 1 elevator. "The agony and suffering of the wounded was relieved quickly but the vomiting that ensued from some of the victims made us wonder if the trade-off was worth it," recalled Heller. He was also applying battle dressing to a young sailor who had lost his leg.[10]

The ship's intercom was still working, and it now crackled to life. Chief Pharmacist's Mate Jim Wilson called for a casualty report from the remote aid stations. Medical officer Bill Davis had turned over several bottles of medicinal whiskey to Wilson to dispense to anyone who appeared in need of a soothing swallow of liquor. He also announced to all stretcher-bearers that upon completion of each round-trip, they were entitled to a "short snort" as a reward.[11]

One stretcher-bearer said, "Jesus, what you have to do around here to get a drink!"

Wilson passed word to Heller that he would send a stretcher party to evacuate the most severe cases down to Sick Bay. Heller and pharmacist Ralph Stewart were ordered down there to help move patients one level below to the hangar deck. The two headed toward Sick Bay, leaving a corpsman to man their station.[12]

But their path was blocked by a firefighting party battling blazes on the hangar deck. The pharmacists took a detour to another ladder that led down to the third deck. Their journey aft was slowed due to *Yorktown* being at battle stations. Each compartment door was dogged shut to maintain watertight integrity. To pass through each compartment, they had to spin the dogs to the hatch, swing open the heavy steel door, and step over the six-inch-high sill before closing the heavy door and dogging it down again.

The intercom continued to supply reports of the incoming Japanese air attack. As they neared the center of the ship, the two heard: "Enemy torpedo bombers off the port bow. All hands, hit the deck!"

Heller had just opened another hatch and was stepping through. Behind him, Stewart hit the deck and lay prone, face-down. Heller continued into the next compartment, dogged down the hatch, and also hit the deck. In his confined chamber, he could hear the continuous muffled chatter of antiaircraft guns far above him.

He was in the ship's store compartment on the third deck—only two compartments away from Sick Bay. Separated from Stewart, Heller lay there, silently riding out the torpedo attack alone.[13]

Elliott Buckmaster was in his usual exposed position on the bridge as the torpedo planes approached. At Coral Sea, his carrier had full speed available to help allow him to nimbly maneuver through incoming torpedo wakes. Now his crippled vessel had worked up to only nineteen knots, leaving it with far less ability to dodge the waterborne missiles.

Officer of the deck John Greenbacker yearned for more speed. Torpedo planes were breaking through the furious crescendo of AA fire from *Yorktown* and her supporting warships. "They seemed to keep coming in, miraculously untouched," he recalled. Their determination was both impressive and frightening. These were clearly skilled aviators. But Greenbacker was equally in awe of Jimmy Thach's hastily scrambled F4Fs. He saw the VF-3 pilots fly directly through friendly fire to engage the incoming Kates.[14]

From Lieutenant Tomonaga's first *chutai*, only three aircraft launched torpedoes. Swinging his carrier to starboard, Buckmaster was able to evade their warfish. One torpedo plane burst into flames and slammed into the ocean well short of *Yorktown's* port bow. But the actions of another Japanese aircrew would be remembered by many.

After dropping his torpedo off *Yorktown's* port beam, the pilot continued to fly down the carrier's port side, little more than fifty feet away. Dozens of men on the bridge, flight deck, and hangar deck watched as the Kate roared past. The rear-seat gunner, with his canopy rolled back, stood up and raised a shaking fist.[15]

He was Seaman First Class Giichi Hamada, radioman for the fifth Kate in the second division. Hours earlier, he had seen three of his own carriers burning from American bomb hits. *I'll pay you back for this!* Hamada thought as his pilot, Petty Officer First Class Taisuke Maruyama, bored in.[16]

Many *Yorktown* sailors saw a Kate slam into the water and assumed it was the one with the aggressive radioman. But Hamada's plane escaped the hailstorm of fire, although he was wounded by a bullet from a pursuing Wildcat during his pilot's exodus from the scene. From his exposed position on the bridge, Buckmaster also saw Hamada waving his fist. In contrast to most of his shipmates, Buckmaster correctly believed that this Japanese aircrew "got away with it."[17]

Pilot Maruyama and others would survive to return to *Hiryu*, where they triumphantly reported that they had secured three torpedo hits on a previously undamaged *Yorktown*-type carrier. Indeed, the second *chutai* did achieve results.[18]

Greenbacker, busy shouting to the skipper, saw another Kate drop its torpedo at very close range. He knew instantly there was insufficient time for *Yorktown* to swing out of its path. At 1443, as Greenbacker watched the enemy plane roar past the bow, his gaze was diverted by a column of water shooting skyward. He felt a terrible punch and a great heave of the decks as the first Japanese torpedo to strike CV-5 slammed into her port side.[19]

From his elevated position on the bridge, Bill Roy was filming the attack. He could see white torpedo wakes shimmering through the blue water ahead. Nearby, khaki-uniformed Marines blazed away from a 20mm gun mount as one of the eighteen-foot torpedoes bored in. The torpedo exploded just below the mount, hurled Marines through the air, and knocked Roy flat on his rear. He scrambled back to his feet and resumed filming. As the attack continued, he witnessed a sailor on a nearby .50-caliber machine gun perish as bullets from a strafing plane cut him down.

Joe Hartlove was strapped to his 20mm gun on the port side of the flight deck when a torpedo exploded ahead of his position. A column of seawater fountained two hundred feet into the sky and then crashed down over him. "I thought I might drown right there," Hartlove remembered.[20]

At Battle Dressing Station No. 1, flight surgeon Joe Pollard had taken a seat on the deck. He felt a sickening thud and rumble throughout the ship. The deck under him rose up, trembled, and fell away. Three decks lower, outside of Sick Bay, Machinist Worth Hare had tried to brace himself for a potential impact. But this explosion was unlike the bomb blasts he had previously experienced. Hare was knocked from his feet as *Yorktown* lurched sideways for a brief instant.[21]

Ensign Jack Crawford had ridden out both Japanese air attacks on the hangar deck. As the torpedoes struck home, a heavy tremor ran through the carrier that felt like a bending of the ship's structure. The deck began tilting to port as a purplish brown cloud of smoke erupted. As the list steadily increased, so did his concerns. Having taken a course in naval construction, Crawford knew that when the deck edge began to go under, you started to lose righting.[22]

The torpedo had destroyed two of *Yorktown's* portside firerooms, knocking out power and allowing seawater to rush into the void near her forward generator room. The carrier quickly assumed a six-degree list to port. Chief Water Tender George Vavrek, manning headphones at Central Station, called below to tell men where to transfer oil to help correct the list. But at 1445, less than one minute after the first explosion, a second torpedo slammed into *Yorktown*'s port side fifteen feet below the waterline. The blast killed a number of sailors working in and near the generator room, including the sailor Vavrek was speaking to.[23]

More seawater gushed into the ship, and her list rapidly increased from six to seventeen degrees to port. Roughly sixty-five feet of *Yorktown*'s hull was now ripped wide open. The inrushing water and the concussions from the explosions extinguished the fires to all of her boilers. With her rudder jammed fifteen degrees to port and her propulsion plant knocked out, the carrier once again began coasting to a halt.

Charles Kleinsmith, the water tender who had performed miracles on the boilers after the earlier attack, had paused to catch his breath in the ship's post office compartment while the carrier maneuvered to dodge torpedoes. The first one exploded directly below, instantly killing Kleinsmith and two members of the ship's band.[24]

The back-to-back torpedo hits bracketed the compartment manned by warrant officer Leonard Wingo, in charge of seven electricians stationed in the forward electrical switchboard room. The first explosion blew through the forward generator room, located to the port side of the switchboard room. Concussion and shock momentarily knocked Wingo and his electricians to the deck. Then the second torpedo blasted apart the No. 1 Fireroom directly aft of Wingo's compartment.[25]

The tremendous explosion from the first torpedo tossed Warren Heller, separated from Ralph Stewart by a watertight steel hatch, into the air. Seconds later, a second explosion—louder and much closer—tossed him upward again like being on a trampoline.[26]

In the sudden blackness, he felt the ship quickly canting heavily to port. He jumped to his feet and grabbed the dogs on the next hatch door. There were only two more compartments to pass through to get to Sick Bay. When he reached it, he saw senior surgeon Bill Davis still taking cover beneath a desk in his office. Then he began assisting with the wounded.

The slope of the decks steadily increased, adding to the challenges of dealing with even more wounded men who were soon carried in. It would be some time before Heller learned that one of the torpedo explosion had ripped through the compartment where his buddy Stewart had taken cover, killing him instantly.

———

Carpenter Boyd McKenzie escaped yet another close call. Earlier in the day, a bomb had exploded just above his battle station. During the torpedo attack, his Repair Party Four lay prone on the deck. Now, forward of his position, he felt the rumble of explosions from the two torpedo hits. As *Yorktown* began canting over to the left, McKenzie's crewmen got to their feet and made their way forward to assist.[27]

From Central Station, damage control officer Clarence Aldrich directed other repair parties into action. Lieutenant Oxy Hurlbert, commanding Repair Party Three in the after mess hall, had scattered his men about the large compartment—hoping to prevent mass casualties of a single repair crew, as had happened at Coral Sea. He was lying flat on his belly when the first torpedo hit. The jolt bounced him high and sent him sliding across the slick steel deck as *Yorktown* immediately took on a portside list.[28]

The prodigious effort to relight the boilers after the bomb damage mattered little now. The ship's generator room was destroyed. In Boiler Emergency Control on the third deck, Lieutenant Reed Cundiff's men waited anxiously for orders but received none. One of the chief petty officers finally announced, "We might as well get topside if we're going to abandon ship. If not, we can always return."[29]

As Cundiff's men filed out, they were joined by Machinist's Mate First Class Pressley Holmes and his engineers from the after steering room. But the usual portside passageway route topside was not available. The decks were slick and heavily tilted to port, and the engineers soon encountered a forward compartment that was completely flooded. Holmes worried as they reached each new hatch that bomb damage might have rendered them unable to be opened, but he was lucky. More challenging was the fact that the heavy list forced his crew to ascend ladders leaning in the wrong direction.[30]

Cundiff's engineers could see light streaking in through open portholes on the next deck, but they soon reached another overhead escape hatch. Cundiff helped shove a chief water tender up the badly sloping ladder, then watched him spin the wheel to undog the hatch. A torrent of water cascaded down on them, and Cundiff worried momentarily that his ship might already be underwater. But he and the men fought their way up through the water, the able-bodied taking time to first assist the wounded toward safety.[31]

The flow of water, pooled due to firefighting efforts, quickly ceased. As Cundiff scrambled up the ladder to the next deck, he marveled at how an explosion had peeled back heavy steel deck plates like a banana on either side of the hatch opening. As they made their way past a nearby damage control team, several of Cundiff's engineers were tapped by Oxy Hurlbert to help transport wounded from both the mess hall and the Sick Bay toward the upper decks. "The crossing of personnel traffic at the ladders leading up was like a busy time in the Times Square subway station," Hurlbert recalled.[32]

In the meantime, Lieutenant Commander Delaney led inspection teams into his lower engineering spaces to assess the damage. One of his assistants, Lieutenant (jg) Don Sheu, directed firefighting efforts against the most persistent forward fire, which threatened to detonate the nearby ship's ammunition magazines. Delaney's men risked certain death if their listing ship suddenly completed its roll over to port.

High above on the bridge, Captain Buckmaster monitored the various damage reports coming in from all areas of his ship. Two firerooms were flooded, and two others were taking on seawater. The forward generator room was destroyed. All power had been lost. Nearby, Greenbacker was more alarmed at how rapidly the ship's list increased. The bridge inclinometer had almost immediately tilted to twenty degrees, but it did not stop.

It moved to twenty-three degrees, then to twenty-six. No one was sure that it had gone as far as it would go.[33]

Finally, the first lieutenant, Clarence Aldrich, made his way to the bridge and calmly related the situation to Buckmaster. Without power, there was nothing he could do at the moment to control the increasing list. No one thought to ask him whether the ship was likely to maintain this stability or whether it would continue on over and capsize. Buckmaster was left with the lonely fate of determining what to do for his crew of more than two thousand surviving men. At any moment, weakened bulkheads below might give way, allowing a fatal inrush of seawater that could cause his carrier to roll over onto its side and kill who knew how many men.

Buckmaster paced up and down the starboard catwalk in silence. Minutes passed. Then he muttered, "I hate to give the order to abandon ship."[34]

Greenbacker and others watched for a full minute as their skipper continued reasoning aloud, talking to himself as he weighed his options.

During seven months of wartime service, the skipper had never held an abandon-ship drill, and very little instruction in such procedures had been given. He felt that such drills would be destructive of morale and confidence. Although Buckmaster disliked the idea of doing such a practice, *Yorktown*'s ship's company had made necessary improvements in equipment. Life rafts and whaleboats were packed with provisions, and knotted abandon-ship lines were rigged all about the sides of the carrier.

Finally, around 1455, he stopped and gave the order: "There is nothing else to do. We must abandon ship."

By word of mouth and by sound-powered telephones, the order spread throughout the vessel. Atop the signal hoist, signal flags were raised that visually conveyed the message: "ABANDON SHIP."

CHAPTER ELEVEN

ABANDON SHIP

Lieutenant Joe Pollard was stunned by the order. Lying beside him, a nervous sailor with a serious chest wound and one foot missing asked, "What does this mean for us?" As the number of wounded increased, Pollard and others scrambled to find life jackets, some removed from the dead. Most of the available stretchers in Battle Dressing Station No. 1 had been used earlier to carry casualties down to Sick Bay. Pollard's men carried up the most severely wounded and urged others who could possibly walk to do so. Reaching the flight deck, he and Lieutenant Al Wilson tied lines together and carefully lowered the wounded toward the water.[1]

Knotted lines were hung on both sides of the ship from both the hangar deck and the flight deck. Within fifteen minutes of the second torpedo hit, hundreds of sailors began going over the side, often tossing over life rafts ahead of them. Task Force 17 destroyers began lowering motor whaleboats to assist the masses taking to the sea. An odd phenomenon began to take place. Many sailors stripped to their skivvies, most removing their shoes and placing them along the edges of the deck, as if they expected to use them again later.

Yorktown's list reached twenty-seven degrees, but there it stopped. As the abandonment commenced, some were left to wonder whether Captain Buckmaster's order had been premature. Rear Admiral Fletcher, now commanding TF-17 from the cruiser *Astoria*, fully supported him. He later wrote that *Yorktown's* skipper had "used good judgment in reaching his decision," adding that doing anything otherwise at that moment "would have been extremely unsound."[2]

Damage control officer Clarence Aldrich had just returned to Central Station, five decks below, when he heard the abandon-ship order being relayed. He reluctantly climbed back toward the bridge through an escape trunk. En route, he noted Commander Dixie Kiefer giving his own life jacket to the captain's steward, David Barnes. Aldrich helped release life rafts and coerce young sailors to make their way over the side before he finally did the same. He was soon picked up by a whaleboat from the destroyer *Russell*.[3]

In the absence of abandon-ship drills since the start of the war, many of *Yorktown's* men resorted to carrying out years-old customs. Greenbacker's roommate, Lieutenant (jg) Joe Snyder, and Chaplain Frank Hamilton dutifully proceeded to one of *Yorktown's* stacked motor launches on the hangar deck where sailors were dropping knotted lines over the side, and they clambered into one of the launches. They waited patiently in the boat for several minutes until they sheepishly realized that a powerless vessel could not use its crane to hoist the massive launches.[4]

Greenbacker remained on the bridge through the early stages of the abandon-ship process. He noted many failures on the part of *Yorktown* officers and men, including one that was his own. As officer of the deck, he was required to throw the tactical and signal publications overboard. For this purpose, these books were provided with heavy lead covers. But Greenbacker forgot, and so did others. Only the signal bridge would follow procedure and toss their books into the sea.[5]

Should the Japanese capture the abandoned *Yorktown*, they would have an intelligence field day. Officers also failed to destroy most of the ship's cryptographic publications and coding equipment. In the coding room, during the Coral Sea battle, they immediately returned everything to the safes and locked them. Now coding machines, code lists, code books, and secret message files were all left untouched, and the safe was left open.

On the bridge with Captain Buckmaster, Greenbacker had a bird's-eye view of the scene below. He watched men try to navigate down the knotted lines. The abundance of fuel oil on nearly everything caused many to lose their grip and severely blister their hands as they slid down the lines. Other men had the ties on their life jackets ripped off by the knots. Some of *Yorktown*'s life rafts were launched over the side still bundled together, resulting in stacked piles that left only one usable in each bunch. Wounded men were intended to be placed in these rafts, but dozens of frantic sailors quickly piled onto each bundle.

In some cases, so many men clambered onto the stacked rafts that they submerged below the ocean surface. "It was an odd sight," said Greenbacker. "The ocean was dotted with little islands of tightly packed men in the water. They reminded me of pond lilies floating in an immense pool."

———

Many of *Yorktown*'s engineers were challenged just to reach the upper deck in order to abandon ship. Chief George Vavrek never heard the announcement down in his engine room. As time passed, he heard voices hollering and the sounds of many men shuffling up steel ladders.[6]

Vavrek hollered toward a sailor. "What's everybody doing?"

"Hell, we're abandoning ship," replied the enlisted man. "Didn't you hear the word passed?"

Vavrek secured his engine room and ordered his men topside. There, he helped cut loose rafts from the stern before he jumped overboard. *Yorktown*'s "Oil King" would spend more than ninety minutes in the warm, choppy ocean bobbing in his life vest before he was finally helped onto the deck of a destroyer.

By the time Reed Cundiff's engineers picked their way through flooded compartments and up steel ladders now tilted at crazy angles to the main deck, many of their shipmates were already gone. A strong swimmer, Cundiff gave up his life jacket to a mess attendant who questioned his ability to swim.[7]

One of his men, machinist Dwight Dehaven, was amazed at how many sailors had left their shoes lining the deck edges. As his section chief began removing his, Dehaven told him, "You might need those when you get on the hot steel decks of one of those destroyers." Keeping his shoes on, Dehaven descended a knotted line on the starboard side and swam to a nearby twenty-man life raft. It was soon overflowing with wounded sailors, so he jumped into the sea and swam for a destroyer about seventy feet away.[8]

As he neared its cargo net, general quarters Klaxons sounded. False alarms and snooping Japanese cruiser planes complicated the abandon-ship procedure several times during the first hour. The destroyers *Balch* and *Anderson* temporarily backed clear to assume antiaircraft formation, causing great panic and frustration among many of the men hoping to be rescued. Caught in the propeller backwash of one destroyer, Dehaven was rapidly swept toward its bow. Thanks to the false air-raid alarm, he would spend another hour treading water until he was fished from the sea by *Benham*.[9]

Other engineers faced their own challenges. Upon arriving at the fantail, Lieutenant Bill Crenshaw was ordered overboard by Delaney. Recalling his Naval Academy training, Crenshaw grabbed the line, preparing to go down carefully, hand over hand. His weight and the oily line caused the lieutenant to slip and plunge fifty feet into the Pacific far below.[10]

Crenshaw's roommate, John Wadleigh, twice endured the frustration of destroyers moving away from him due to air-raid alarms. During his second ordeal, Wadleigh grabbed a line hanging below *Russell's* fo'c'scle. He began climbing her slick sides, but *Russell* was already making brisk speed by the time destroyermen helped haul the *Yorktown* officer onto her deck.[11]

Oxy Hurlbert had a similar experience. When he reached

Yorktown's fantail, the lieutenant hung his pistol belt on a 20mm gun mount and placed his shoes on the deck's edge, optimistically thinking he would need them the following day if his repairmen were allowed to return to the ship. He and Lieutenant Vic Wadsworth tossed a life raft over the side and descended knotted lines to the water below. The officers loaded wounded men onto the raft, then helped push it during the next half hour to the side of a destroyer.[12]

Hurlbert and Wadsworth had no sooner helped destroyermen haul the first wounded man up the cargo nets than the warship pulled away in response to an air-raid alarm. This process would be repeated several more times. It wasn't until late afternoon that they managed to off-load all of their wounded shipmates. Only Wadsworth and Hurlbert remained when the destroyer *Benham* came alongside their raft near dusk. Hurlbert ordered Wadsworth up the cargo net first.

As luck would have it, yet another aircraft sighting caused *Benham*'s skipper to sound general quarters. Hurlbert grabbed the bottom of the cargo net as *Benham* got underway. He was soon skipping off the waves as the destroyer increased speed. After a half dozen painful skips off the water, Hurlbert ricocheted high enough that sailors leaning over the sides were able to haul him onto the deck.[13]

Ensign Jack Crawford went over *Yorktown*'s starboard side and clung to a balsa raft until he was picked up by the destroyer *Russell*. He requested permission to visit the bridge to extend his thanks for the rescue. There, he was surprised to find the skipper was Lieutenant Commander Roy Hartwig, his former battalion football coach at the Naval Academy. "Hey, Red!"

Russell's skipper called out. Crawford found Hartwig talking with a rescued *Yorktown* pilot who had played left tackle on their team. Crawford mused on the probability of any combination of them meeting up like that.

As he climbed down from his .50-caliber gun platform, John Hancock was appalled by the carnage on the after end of the island structure. The rungs of the steel ladder and the deck below were slick with blood and gore from the ill-fated plane handlers cut down by the bomb shrapnel.[14]

Reaching the flight deck, Hancock moved forward past the portside 5-inch gun mounts and descended a ladder near the bow to the fo'c'sle deck, his assigned abandon-ship station. After assisting with getting some of the wounded over the side, he decided it was time to save his own hide. Hancock removed his shoes and stripped to his skivvies, stacking his clothes neatly with his cap on top of the pile. Tightening the straps on his kapok life vest, he jumped from the lower port side near the anchor. "The prevailing wind was pushing our high starboard side like a giant sail," Hancock remembered. "Guys who went over the starboard side couldn't get away from the ship because it was sailing down on them." He leaped for an open spot in the water to avoid burning his hands on oily descending lines.

Hancock swam to one of the large life rafts with wooden flooring. He tried to clamber aboard the "biscuit" raft, but was continually pushed away by other sailors. A strong current soon pulled him far astern of *Yorktown*. Hours would pass before the destroyer *Anderson* eased up alongside him. He was covered in fuel oil and so weak that all he could do was grab the screw guard back aft. Sailors had to make a human chain to fish him out.

Buckmaster remained on the bridge to supervise the process, but he began clearing the upper works of nonessential personnel. Greenbacker descended to the steeply slanting flight deck and walked past two F4Fs still parked near the island. He discovered a discarded leather flight jacket inscribed with the name "B. T. MACOMBER," one of VF-42's fighter pilots. Searching through the inner pockets, he found a heavy packet stuffed with what he assumed might be life insurance policies or personal papers. He thought the jacket might come in handy under the circumstances, so he picked it up and put it over his shoulder.[15]

He ran into his communications boss, Jug Ray, and the two discussed their options in going over the side. Greenbacker finally convinced Ray it would be more prudent for them to drop to the hangar deck, where they could climb down lines from the lower port side. When they reached the quarterdeck area of the hangar, Clarence Aldrich was in the process of inflating a small life raft retrieved from a spare aircraft strapped to the hangar deck's overhead space. Greenbacker thought this a grand idea, so he climbed up into the storage area and found his own.

He tossed his raft overboard and descended one of the knotted lines. When he reached the water, Greenbacker was amazed at how well his kapok life jacket held his head above the water, despite his heavy load—he was still wearing his shoes and his pistol belt and had his binoculars and even Lieutenant Macomber's flight jacket draped around his neck. But other

Yorktown survivors overloaded his raft before he could reach it. Greenbacker struggled to catch the group, finally passing them his waterlogged gun, binoculars, and flight jacket to place in the raft.

He and others helped kick and push the loaded raft toward the nearby destroyer *Russell.* Just as a whaleboat was preparing to take their raft in tow, the destroyer's Klaxons sounded another air alarm. Greenbacker panicked. He abandoned the raft, and all his personal belongings, to board the whaleboat before it chugged back to the *Russell.*

Ship's cook Tom Saxon from Mississippi went over the side clutching his pet white rabbit. During the battle, his rabbit had been hopping around the galley. He scooped up the animal, carefully placed it in his battle helmet, and stuffed the helmet in a gas mask bag so it would float. When he reached the water, Saxon held the bag aloft to keep his pet dry. But Saxon was badly injured when another sailor slipped from the lines and landed on his back.[16]

Saxon and his rabbit were both hauled on board a destroyer. Ultimately hospitalized for many months, he passed his pet rabbit to the care of Chief Cal Callaway. Nicknamed "Midway," the animal would outlive his former master, as Saxon later died from his back injuries on February 9, 1944, in a California naval hospital.

Transporting wounded sailors over the carrier's side was a special challenge. Chief Phil Dahlquist encountered one young sailor on the fo'c'sle who had been wounded by a bomb blast near his gun mount. His head was so heavily wrapped in bandages that he had to be led along the deck like a blind man. Dahlquist helped tie a heavy line around the sailor and lowered him to a waiting raft.[17]

Warren Heller was assisting in Sick Bay when the abandon-ship order came over the loudspeakers. Chief Jim Wilson asked him to help evacuate the wounded topside. Assembling a group of ship's musicians, Heller and the medics loaded the severely wounded onto stretchers as the carrier's list to port increased. Tensions mounted as the large group reached the wildly angled ladder leading up to the hangar deck. "The passageway was a mass of terrified humanity, all pushing and shoving, struggling to get to and up the ladder," recalled Heller.[18]

He shouted, "Gangway! Gangway! Make room for the stretchers!"

Men stood aside. Moving to the foot of the ladder, he repeated his command. Those on the ladder peered down at him. The terror in their eyes was shocking to Heller. They were, he thought, "behaving like rats fleeing a sinking ship."

Heller shouted again, "Give us a hand with these stretchers!"

The panic-stricken crowd suddenly calmed. Eager hands grabbed the sides of stretchers and gently began passing them up to the hangar deck in orderly fashion. Heller found the hangar-deck surface so covered with oil that walking was nearly impossible with the sharp list. But he and his comrades eventually moved most of the wounded to safety.

Some of the other injured men were not so fortunate. Among them was Terry Dykes, a survivor from the after 1.1-inch gun mounts. After the bombing attack, he had been given morphine and taken below, where he lapsed in and out of consciousness during the torpedo strikes. When Dykes next awoke, someone was nudging the tourniquet still strapped around his right leg. Another man said, "He's not going to survive. Let's just leave him."[19]

Dykes clamped his arms around an officer's legs to demonstrate his will to live. Two men hauled his tattered body topside and gingerly placed him in a lifeboat fastened to the bulkhead, where Dykes fell into unconsciousness again. When he awoke, he was alone in the powerless motor launch. His legs were useless, but he used his remaining strength to muscle his body over the side of the boat. Naked except for one sock, he dragged his bloodied body down the steeply sloping deck toward the lower port side. When he tried to navigate down a knotted line, he lost his grip and plunged into the sea. Sailors on a nearby raft of wounded hauled Dykes on board. He was soon being lifted up onto a destroyer's deck.

The last two doctors to leave Sick Bay were Captain Bill Davis and his chief of surgery, Lieutenant Commander August French. They worked with handheld flashlights and the dim blue emergency lantern as they treated a patient. When the surgery was complete, Davis stepped out of the operating room and called for a stretcher-bearer to move their patient into the recovery ward.[20]

There was no reply. Davis spotted a sailor in the corner manning the battle phones and asked him where the corpsmen had gone.

"Oh, they passed the word some time ago for all hands to abandon ship," the sailor said. "They just told me to secure the telephone and abandon ship."

Davis and French struggled to move their final patient up the steel ladders to the slanting hangar deck. By the time they had secured him into a lifeboat, most of the ship's company had already gone over the side.

After they departed Sick Bay, two pharmacist's mates— Robert Harned and Ray Cook—made a hasty pass through the medical department beds before departing. A number of the dead lay crumpled near Sick Bay and in bunks where they had expired. No one appeared to be living.

But two men were. Seaman Norman Pichette, a gunner whose stomach had been ripped wide open by bomb shrapnel, was unconscious in one bunk. Several bunks away, .50-caliber gunner George Weise was also alive. His skull was fractured, and his left arm and left leg were immobilized in temporary casts. The right side of his body was paralyzed from his fall off the smokestack platform to the flight deck. He had regained consciousness only for brief stretches since the Japanese bombs had landed. Following the torpedo plane attack, Weise awoke briefly to hear the broadcast to abandon ship. When he next regained his senses, Harned and Cook were about to leave the nearly dark compartment.

Cook put his arm around Weise, attempting to hold him up. "What about him?" he asked the first-class pharmacist's mate.[21]

"Leave him and let's go," said Harned. "He's going to die anyway."

The young pharmacist's mate broke down, crying at the

thought of leaving a dying man behind, but he and Harned headed topside. Weise lapsed back into unconsciousness.

He woke sometime later, swearing a blue streak. He sat up in the bunk with only the dim blue battle lantern to illuminate the empty Sick Bay around him. He was all alone, save the bodies of dead shipmates. *I don't want to be left on board a sinking ship*, he thought.

His fear turned to anger. During his training days, he had been taught to help others. Now he couldn't fathom the fact that trained medical personnel had left him to his fate.[22]

His fractured skull swimming with pain and anger, Weise once more faded into unconsciousness.

David Pattison was stuck in own personal hell. The eighteen-year-old Iowan had been firing a hastily rigged .30-caliber machine gun at the Japanese torpedo planes until the second torpedo exploded below his port catwalk, ripping catwalk meshing loose from its weldings. Amid the tangled mass of metal, Pattison was pinned by angle iron—an iron cleat for joining parts of a structure at an angle—that had punctured his thigh.[23]

The VF-42 aviation ordnanceman remained as his fellow sailors began to abandon ship. Warrant officer Chester Briggs, also wounded during the earlier attacks, led a rescue party onto the precariously hanging catwalk to attempt Pattison's rescue. He and Marine Corporal Peter Kikos used an airplane jack to force the twisted metal away from the wounded man's body. Throughout the effort, Pattison pleaded with Kikos and the other men to forget about him, as the ship might roll over at any moment.[24]

Another man who came to Pattison's aid was Ensign Bryan Crisman. Once released from the signal bridge, the ship's disbursing officer had dashed down to his stateroom to retrieve the three canvas bags of pay records he had stashed there earlier. In the end, he was too concerned over the ship capsizing to make any more trips topside with the heavy bags. Crisman instead donned a pair of gray leather gloves and grabbed the long line he had used earlier to haul the bags. Both items seemed likely to come in handy.[25]

Reaching the flight deck, Crisman spotted Kikos, Briggs, and other prying the mangled catwalk back with the aviation jack to free Pattison. Once the angled iron rod was extracted from his leg, a pilot's white scarf was used as an emergency tourniquet. Pattison's rescue team was determined to move him to the high starboard side, where he could be lowered to a waiting lifeboat. But they had not taken into account the precarious cant of the flight deck, now slick as butter with fuel oil and firefighting foam.

Crisman lashed his long line to the starboard-side railing. Working with Ensign Richard O'Brien, they tied their line around Pattison and carefully dragged him up the sloping eighty-five-foot-wide flight deck to the starboard side. Then he was lowered to the raft of wounded and eventually lifted on board one of the task force destroyers.[26]

Bill Roy had moved down from the island to document some of the abandon-ship process. With his movie camera, he filmed the wounded being lowered to the water, where hundreds of sailors bobbed about. The ship's photography lab had been gutted by fire, but Roy still had three cans of film with him. He carefully taped them up and stuffed them in his life jacket to protect them. From the starboard side of the hangar deck, he prepared to go over the side, still wearing an expensive pair of boots. He figured he could hold the line with one hand, and with the other continue to document his descent down *Yorktown*'s hull.[27]

"Please hand me the movie camera," an officer said. "It'll drown you."

Roy reluctantly agreed. His motion picture camera was left on the hangar's starboard deck edge as he carefully worked his way down the hull toward the water's edge. When his nonregulation boots reached *Yorktown*'s exposed armor belt, he paused to assist a mess attendant tangled in several of the lines. He was clearly panicked, hollering, "Please help me!"[28]

Once freed, the steward and Roy continued their descent with their feet against the ship's side. But the abandon-ship lines had been cut too short to factor in the carrier's severe list. Fifteen feet above the water, the lines came to an end. Although the mess attendant was wearing a life jacket, he cried, "I can't swim!" Roy gave him a shove and then pushed off the hull to land nearby.[29]

Both men bobbed to the surface in the oily water. Roy used one hand to assist the terrified steward and began stroking toward a life raft with the other. By the time he got the man onto the raft, he was exhausted. Bunker oil fumes made it difficult to breathe. His eyes, nose, and mouth burned. Others around him were throwing up. Roy still hoped to protect the wrapped film in his life jacket, but there were simply too many men clinging to one raft. *Yorktown*'s drift added to the chaos by keeping the vessel pinned against the hull, where rust and sharp barnacles tore at their exposed skin. Frustrated, Roy kicked away from the group, resolving to work his way around *Yorktown*'s stern.[30]

Far above on the island structure, Captain Buckmaster finally decided it was time for him to leave as well. He made his way down steel ladders to the flight deck, then walked along the high starboard side near the 5-inch guns in the outer catwalk. When he reached the No. 1 crane, he returned to the flight deck. In keeping with the ancient maritime tradition of the captain being last to leave his stricken vessel, Buckmaster made his rounds, urging everyone still remaining to abandon ship.

He encountered flight surgeon Joe Pollard aft of the island on the starboard side of the flight deck. "What are you waiting for?" Buckmaster asked.[31]

"I'm waiting to get off all the wounded," Pollard said. "We searched the topside structure and the catwalks. I'm sure we have every man still alive in this area on life rafts now."

Buckmaster explained that as skipper, he must be last to leave the ship. "I'm ready to go now," he said. "Would you leave?"

Pollard worked his way carefully down the high side, pausing twenty feet above the water on the armored belt—a layer of heavy metal plating on the outer hull designed to absorb the impact of torpedoes or bomb near misses. He carefully scuttled sideways across the belt to a position above a life raft. But as he resumed his descent, the oily line caused him to slip, as so many had before him. He plummeted into the ocean, burning his hands on the line in the process, but began swimming toward rescue boats.

Buckmaster had to order others to go over the side. Many of the ship's ninety-five Marines had helped man guns during the battle. Now they were reluctant to leave until all others were safe. Sergeant Perry Canton and Corporal Pete Kikos were later cited for helping wounded men and for freeing others pinned in wreckage. While floating in the ocean, Private First Class Charles Kozloski supported a wounded man until they were both rescued.[32]

"Thank you, Marines, for the magnificent fight you made," Buckmaster said to a dozen of them. "But you must abandon the ship now. We did our best—may God be with you all."

His greatest desire was to ensure no living man was left on board. Buckmaster climbed down from the flight deck to Dressing Station No. 1 and moved forward through Flag Country to his own little-used captain's cabin. From the port side, he descended a ladder to the cavernous hangar deck, now void of crewmen. A Marine orderly offered Buckmaster a life jacket, but he refused. His attempts to penetrate deeper into the bowels of his carrier were in vain. Someone had swiped his emergency flashlight long ago.

There were emergency lights in the superstructure, but the lower decks were another story. Groping his way through a myriad of labyrinth-like passageways, the captain found nothing but darkness as he slipped on the oily, sloping decks.

Buckmaster called out frequently but heard no human responses. The only sounds were belching gasps of air rushing from compartments as water rushed in.[33]

John Lorenz was not ready to leave yet. Once the abandon-ship orders were passed, he told his 1.1-inch Mount 3 gunners—largely replacement men—to save themselves.[34]

Trainer Harold Davies, one of the injured men who had stayed for the second air battle, now worried about his brother, Jim, who was stationed on a .50-caliber gun near the stern. It would be some time before he learned that his sibling had also survived the attacks. Davies climbed down a starboard-side line and spent more than an hour clinging to a line from a raft of wounded men before he was hauled on board the destroyer *Balch*.[35]

Lorenz decided to make a hasty dash below to his cabin. There, he retrieved a photo of his girlfriend, Delight McHale. Stashing it in his cap, he returned to the flight deck. He contemplated whether to risk burning his hands slipping down an oily line or whether simply to leap overboard from the lower port side.[36]

But a sudden inclination swept over him to bid farewell to his fallen gun crew before leaving them forever. Once again, he descended into the darkened ship toward the aid station where their bodies had been moved. En route, he encountered Captain Buckmaster, busy making his final inspection of his stricken vessel.

"Get off immediately, Ensign," he said. "She's going to roll over."

Lorenz explained his desire to say his goodbyes to his fallen gunners.

"Very well," Buckmaster said. "Do it quickly. Then get off the ship!"

Lorenz descended to the aid station, one deck below the flight deck and now engulfed in darkness. He unsnapped a battle lantern from the bulkhead and began playing its bright beam over several bodies in search of his men. They were just as he had left them earlier. Then Lorenz spotted an eye twitching on one of the prone figures. It was Bill Sullivan, one of the wounded loaders he had helped after the dive-bomber attack. *He's alive!* thought Lorenz. Wounded by shrapnel in multiple places, Sullivan had been injected with morphine and carried below for treatment.[37]

Lorenz now found himself in a quandary. He had been ordered off the ship, which might roll over at any time. But he knew he could not leave a wounded comrade behind to drown. Sullivan was too husky for Lorenz to move by himself, and he was too sedated to get to his feet. His face was gray and his breathing shallow. Frantic, Lorenz hurried topside again in search of assistance.

On the flight deck, he spotted ensigns O'Brien and Crisman, who had just finished moving wounded ordnanceman Pattison toward safety. Lorenz explained that he needed their assistance in moving a wounded, sedated gunner from a lower deck. The trio hurried down to where Sullivan lay and began the arduous task of manhandling him to the flight deck.

Once there, they made their way to the aft end of the ship. O'Brien climbed below to the fantail. There he found a wooden sled used by the dive-bomber pilots for target practice when towed behind *Yorktown*. It measured roughly ten feet in length and was constructed of two-inch-by-twelve-inch timbers. He tossed it overboard and descended a line to hold the sled in place for Sullivan.[38]

Lorenz and Crisman lashed their line around the unconscious sailor's legs and under his arms to make a type of boatswain's seat to lower him. The officers each wore a kapok life vest, but they couldn't find a jacket for Sullivan. They carefully lowered him over the stern down to O'Brien, who lashed Sullivan to the dive-bomber sled. Lorenz climbed over the side and down into the warm water.

O'Brien and Lorenz held to the raft, holding Sullivan's face carefully above the waves. Crisman watched from the ship's stern as they slowly moved out from the carrier, pushing the raft toward the closest rescue destroyer about a thousand yards away. Crisman dropped into the water but struggled to swim against heavy waves. It would be hours before he was finally hauled up onto the destroyer *Anderson*, his skin, eyes, mouth, and throat burning from fuel oil and exposure.

O'Brien, Lorenz, and Sullivan would spend almost three hours struggling in the water on their small wooden raft. The prevailing current steadily pulled them away from the cluster of rescue boats. As they drifted farther from the main group, Lorenz feared that they would be left behind. Sullivan was in bad shape but Lorenz continued talking to him, trying to keep his spirits alive. He talked about his beautiful girlfriend, Delight, whom he planned to marry one day. Lorenz promised Sullivan that if he survived, he would name one of his sons after him.[39]

Lorenz had shucked his pistol belt and Colt .45 automatic pistol before abandoning ship, but O'Brien still had his on.[40]

"Fire your .45 into the air three times," Lorenz told him.

O'Brien pulled back the slide, chambered a round, and pointed his Colt skyward. As their dive-bomber sled rose to the top of the next swell, he fired. On the open sea, the round made a mere popping sound, but the trio remained hopeful. O'Brien fired two more rounds, each at the top of a swell.

Lorenz spotted a distant whaleboat turn and chug toward them. By this point, he was thoroughly exhausted, both mentally and physically. His heart grew heavy as he glanced at the ghostly hulk of his ship on the horizon. Events of the past eighteen months flashed through his mind. Closing his eyes, Lorenz could still see his brave crew firing at Japanese dive-bombers. Then strong arms were hauling him and the other two men onto the whaleboat.[41]

Pete Montalvo, a wounded survivor from Lorenz's Mount 3, helped get wounded men overboard before he moved toward the stern to follow suit. One of his 1941 boot camp comrades, Seaman John Pallay, helped him in transiting the oily lines to the water below.[42]

"Do you need help swimming?" asked Pallay.

"If I had to, I'd swim to New York!" Montalvo yelled. The two laughed, wished each other luck, and struck out for the nearest destroyer.

Carpenter Boyd McKenzie swam through the ocean toward his rescue destroyer, *Russell*. As the destroyer *Gwin* moved past him, some of its sailors dived overboard to rescue an unconscious *Yorktown* sailor drifting in a life jacket. McKenzie was amused at the sight of an officer swimming in a life vest while taking great care to keep his ball cap above the water with one hand. The officer later told McKenzie that his wife had gone to great efforts to buy him the "scrambled eggs" cap, and he was damned well not going to let the Japanese ruin it.[43]

Machinist Worth Hare prepared to abandon ship near the bow on the high side. Although he was wearing a life jacket, Hare had no idea how to swim. Next to him, the ship's junior doctor, Ed Kearney, said, "You go first." Steeling his nerve and kicking off his brand-new shoes, Hare began sliding down a line toward a loaded life raft far below. But he lost his grip and began sliding fast. Hare tightened his grip on the line but seriously friction-burned his hands in the process. He reached the life raft, so loaded with wounded men that it was nearly swamped. By the time Hare was helped on board the destroyer *Benham*, his hands were covered with blisters as large as fifty-cent pieces.[44]

Pharmacist's mate Warren Heller wanted to make sure all of the wounded were helped over the side. Once all the stretchers reached the hangar deck, he and others helped lift the wounded and slipped life jackets around them. After the most severe cases had been gently lowered to waiting life rafts, Heller encountered one last patient. It was the water tender whose appendix he had helped remove days before the Midway battle. By this time, all life jackets had been issued and most of the men had gone over the side.[45]

The sailor lay on the deck, unable to move. Heller and a

chief petty officer inflated inner tubes the chief found in a storage locker. The appendicitis patient meekly admitted that he was unable to swim. Heller tried to soothe his fears. The chief rigged a makeshift boatswain's chair from the lifelines and arranged them about the patient, and Heller promised to take care of him in the water.

Heller took a last look about his beloved ship. Then he slowly worked his way down the side, holding on to a knotted line. Halfway down, one of the knots flipped his wedding ring off his finger. Reflexively reaching for it, he lost his grip on the rope and plunged feetfirst into the sea some forty feet below. When his head cleared the surface, he gulped in lungfuls of air and looked up.

High above him, the water tender was dangling from the rigging the chief had fashioned. Heller swam beneath the sailor and helped ease his entry into the water. Heller released him from his harness and began pushing him through the thick, oily slime on the surface. The inner tube beneath the man helped support his weight as Heller moved him away from *Yorktown*.[46]

Heller and his patient drifted leisurely toward the circling destroyers. In short order, they were hauled on board the destroyer *Russell*. On the main deck, Heller was struck with three concerns. The first was the hot deck, followed by the oil in his bushy beard. Finally, he mourned the loss of his wedding ring.

He was able to fashion some slats from an orange crate into wooden sandals to protect the soles of his feet from the hot steel deck, and a hot shower later helped remove some of the oil. *Russell* was soon cruising away from *Yorktown*, Heller and his companion being among the last picked up by the warship. As he finally relaxed long enough to reflect, Heller's greatest relief was the recovery of his appendectomy patient.

Senior medical officer Bill Davis believed he was one of the last to abandon *Yorktown*. He hung his gun on a lifeline and carefully placed his shoes under the gun before descending toward the water. Like others, he was frustrated when one potential rescue destroyer got underway for an air-raid alarm before he could reach it. As he turned to swim back toward the carrier, he spotted something bobbing up and down nearby. It looked like the snout of a fish. He swam away, but it followed him. He made a nervous grab toward it and came up with his own wallet.[47]

Buckmaster completed his tour of the ship at the aft end of the hangar deck. He found a few officers there.

Radar officer Vane Bennett was among them. Earlier, after making his way down to the hangar deck, he had been confronted by boatswain's mate Bill Kelso. The young sailor confessed that he had always dreamed of diving off the ship and requested permission to do so.[48]

Bennett looked over the side. The surface of the water was about seventy-five feet below. "Be my guest," he said.

The sailor carefully folded his clothing, placed his shoes on top, and neatly dived off the high starboard side. Bennett's last view of Kelso was of him swimming strongly toward a nearby destroyer. Bennett made a tour of lower compartments to search for men left behind. When he returned topside, Buckmaster ordered him down one of the knotted lines.[49]

Dixie Kiefer, the popular overweight executive officer, finally went over the starboard side. The oily line caused him to slip and friction-burn his hands while trying to check his swift descent. Kiefer caromed off the heavy armor belt, breaking his lower right leg and ankle in the process. Despite one useless leg, he would spend an hour and twenty minutes in the water before he was picked up by the destroyer *Russell*.[50]

Content that he was the last to leave, Buckmaster took a final look at his carrier before he swung himself over the stern. After making his way down a line and dropping to the ocean, he swam toward the life raft loaded with wounded that Lieutenant Pollard was helping to steer. Buckmaster refused to come on board and displace any of his wounded sailors. He swam to another raft and hung on to the side of it until a passing whaleboat from the *Russell* tossed the men a line. But the whaleboat's coxswain proceeded at such a fast clip that one of *Yorktown*'s mess attendants, William Fentress, was knocked overboard.[51]

Fentress began flailing about, screaming that he couldn't swim. Buckmaster turned loose of his raft and stroked over to him. He clung to Fentress and tried to coach him through an impromptu swimming lesson. Lieutenant Oxy Hurlbert, pushing a nearby life raft of wounded men, thought his captain resembled "a great walrus," swimming along and holding the man's head out of the water.[52]

When he became exhausted, Buckmaster yelled for help. Another able sailor—who had been on the University of California swim team—swam over to assist and eased Fentress back onto another raft. Buckmaster continued swimming on his own until he was brought on board the destroyer *Hammann*.[53]

Task Force 17 destroyers and cruisers spent nearly two hours fishing exhausted *Yorktown* sailors from the sea. When Jug Ray climbed on board the destroyer *Russell*, he heard a sailor say, "My God, mister, you look like a one-man invasion force!" The oil-soaked commander was still wearing all of his gear, including a pair of binoculars around his neck and a .45-caliber pistol strapped to his waist. Clinched in Ray's teeth was his ever-present corncob pipe.[54]

Roger Spooner, first loader from the after portside 5-inch gun, was one of the last sailors to be rescued. He had abandoned ship from the fantail, only to spend hours floundering through thick fuel oil. When he was finally tossed a line, he was too exhausted to attempt to pull himself up. "I took it and threw a half hitch around my right leg," recalled Spooner. "When they pulled me up onto the deck, I couldn't even get up on my all fours. I was that tired."[55]

At 1646, rescue operations were called off for the evening. Some 2,270 men had been rescued, an astonishing ninety-four percent survival rate. *Hammann* had recovered eighty-five men, *Hughes* two dozen, and *Morris* 193 officers and men. The other lifeguard destroyers were more crowded: *Anderson* with 204, *Russell* with 499, and *Balch* with 544. But Lieutenant Commander Joe Worthington's *Benham* claimed top honors with 721 men picked up from *Yorktown*.[56]

On board his new flagship *Astoria*, Rear Admiral Fletcher believed that *Yorktown*'s list had stabilized. By 1615, he had already radioed Admiral Nimitz in Hawaii to send tugboats to assist with salvaging his carrier. His combat air patrol fighters had tangled with snooper planes launched from Japanese cruisers, so he decided that trying to tow the crippled flattop during the night was too risky. Instead, Fletcher determined it best for his task force to retire for the night. He ordered a small salvage party organized and sent back in the morning.[57]

Shortly after the warships headed east at 1715, *Astoria* slowed to let the destroyer *Hammann* nestle alongside. Buckmaster came aboard soaking wet and without a hat, a coat, or a necktie. Buckmaster met with Fletcher and began laying out plans to gather essential personnel from the various destroyers who would be needed to form the salvage party.[58]

Fletcher selected Lieutenant Commander Donald J. Ramsey's destroyer *Hughes*—which had the fewest survivors on board—for watchdog duty. While the other warships moved on, *Hughes* was assigned the unenviable task of standing by the derelict *Yorktown* until she sank, the Japanese found her, or the TF-17 salvage party returned. Buckmaster clung to the belief that his beloved carrier could still be saved.

Earlier that afternoon, while *Yorktown* endured its torpedo attacks, its air group did its part to further Japanese losses. At 1445—as two *Hiryu* Kates ripped *Yorktown*'s port side with torpedoes—Lieutenant Sam Adams located the last undamaged enemy carrier.

He and his VS-5 wingman were among the teams dispatched before Japanese dive-bombers found *Yorktown*. About a hundred ten miles from his launch point, Adams sent the much-desired contact report that firmly located *Hiryu*'s force. The true distance was perhaps thirty miles farther than Adams figured, but such details mattered little to Rear Admiral Ray Spruance. He was eager to knock out the last Japanese flattop, and preparations began immediately to launch a strike group.

Starting around 1530, *Enterprise* sent off a mixed bag of VS-6 and VB-6 dive-bombers, plus all fourteen *Yorktown* VB-3 planes that had landed on her deck after the morning bomb strike. With Max Leslie out of commission on board the cruiser *Astoria*, acting command of VB-3 fell on its XO, Lieutenant Dave Shumway. The two dozen SBDs made a quick departure toward *Hiryu* without any fighter escort. Wildcats were deemed too valuable and were needed to protect their own carriers. Communications snafus caused a smaller SBD group launched from *Hornet* to depart a half hour later.

Shortly after the strike groups departed, Wally Short's ten VS-5 scout bombers were taken on board TF-16 carriers. Bill Christie and his wingman, Hank McDowell, had made no contact other than a Japanese scout plane on their way out. But on their return, they encountered the ragged formation of Japanese strike planes that had survived their torpedo attack on *Yorktown*. Outnumbered and facing the potential of Zero attacks, they moved on to find their own carrier listing and being abandoned. They were directed to land on *Enterprise*, and eight of Short's flight did so. But the flight deck was suddenly fouled by a crash. Low on fuel, Christie signaled McDowell to follow him. They landed on *Hornet* a few minutes later.[59]

Hornet had taken severe losses. Christie and McDowell were temporarily assigned to Scouting Eight, and were provided with the essentials of survival and a place to sleep. There were plenty of empty bunks, since many pilots had not returned. Christie was made a division leader and McDowell a section leader for the rest of the Midway battle.

By 1645, less than an hour after departing TF-16, the mixed *Yorktown/Enterprise* strike group made its approach on the *Hiryu* task group under perfect weather conditions. The fourteen Zero fighters on station in the area did not respond until 1701, when the first *Enterprise* SBDs were already into their dives on the carrier. Several of the first VS-6 pilots to attack missed with their bombs. An alert Dave Shumway quickly shifted his VB-3 planes from an assigned battleship target to the carrier.

The AA fire from *Hiryu* and her escorts was brutal. Black puffs of smoke filled the sky, and the concussion of bursting shells rocked the American dive-bombers as their crews pushed over from nineteen thousand feet. The AA fire forced Shumway to release at four thousand feet, but those following him stayed in their dives closer to two thousand feet before toggling their thousand-pound bombs.[60]

Japanese fighters and antiaircraft fire destroyed three of the SBDs: one from VB-6 and two from *Yorktown*'s VB-3. But *Hiryu* was slammed by at least four thousand-pound bombs that ignited parked aircraft on her flight deck and hangar. The carrier was blazing and exploding by the time the SBDs were chased from the scene by Zeros. *Hiryu* was so wrecked that the last two VB-3 pilots in line shifted their attack back to the battleship *Haruna*. Fred Bergeron, rear gunner for Ensign Bob Benson, was in awe of the firepower erupting from the battleship, but he fired back with his .30-caliber machine gun as their SBD pulled out of its dive.

The *Yorktown* SBDs were assailed for eight minutes as they tried to clear the area. Several planes were hit by 7.7mm slugs and 20mm shells, injuring three rear-seat gunners. Fred Bergeron's brother, Dallas, was among them. Ensign Bud Merrill's 3-B-17 was engaged by two Zeros that landed 20mm hits just aft of Bergeron's rear cockpit. Explosions frayed the plane's control cables and sent shrapnel ripping into the young Texan's left leg and right ankle.[61]

Next on the scene were sixteen SBDs from *Hornet*, but they achieved only near misses on the blazing *Hiryu* and heavy cruiser *Tone*. The surviving *Yorktown* and *Enterprise* dive-bombers made their return to TF-16 by 1820, just as sunset was approaching. Upon landing, two of the wounded VB-3 rear-seat gunners were hustled below to *Enterprise*'s Sick Bay for treatment. Once Benson landed his 3-B-6, Fred Bergeron hung around the flight deck, anxious to see how his brother had fared.

Bud Merrill's battered Dauntless was the last to land. Bergeron counted dozens of bullet holes in his brother's dive-bomber as deck crews swarmed over it. When Dallas Bergeron was extracted from his rear cockpit, his flight suit was covered with blood. He was taken below for surgery. His brother busied himself with gathering personal grooming supplies for VB-3's wounded gunners, since all of their possessions were on *Yorktown*.[62]

Fred Bergeron and his fellow *Yorktown* aviators were blended into the *Enterprise* air group, and they rightfully felt pride in having knocked out *Hiryu*—the Japanese carrier that had destroyed their own ship.

The *Yorktown* orphans were assigned empty bunks vacated

by aviators lost in action. Rear gunner Lynn Forshee of VS-5 crawled into one in the enlisted area and noted the name stenciled on the mattress cover to be "Red Durawa" of Torpedo Six. Gregory Durawa, a young gunner with whom Forshee had attended radio school in San Diego, was among the many VT-6 men who had lost their lives that day.[63]

CHAPTER TWELVE

GHOST SHIP SAILORS

Lieutenant John Greenbacker worked through the night. With his yeomen in the destroyer *Russell's* office, they made out a muster roll of the 499 officers and men taken on board from *Yorktown*. A pleasant surprise awaited Greenbacker when a shipmate returned the pistol and binoculars he had left in the lifeboat. To his disappointment, the leather flight jacket didn't appear.[1]

Bill Roy awoke on the morning of June 5 in a spud locker. Exhausted and covered with oil after more than an hour in the ocean, he had sought a quiet place to sleep after being hauled onto *Russell's* deck. He had passed off his carefully wrapped cans of film, images he would not see developed for quite some time. Once awake, his body was scrubbed of the fuel and he was given a new shirt, dungarees, and shoes. As he happened past the fo'c'sle, he looked down and noticed a distinctive pair of boots on the deck. He bent and flipped the tongue down. The name "ROY" was stenciled on the inside.[2]

"Where'd you get those boots?" he asked a sailor nearby. The man explained that he had found them before abandoning *Yorktown* and had brought them on his swim to safety.

"You want your shoes?" the sailor asked.

"No, you brought them on," said Roy. "Keep them."

On board the cruiser *Astoria*, Captain Buckmaster's vision of saving his carrier was becoming a reality. With Rear Admiral Fletcher's support and the approval of Admiral Nimitz in Hawaii, the submarine tender *Fulton* and a tugboat were already en route to assist. The process of assembling Buckmaster's handpicked salvage crew commenced shortly after daybreak.

At 0600, the first salvage team members began transferring via highline from the destroyer *Benham* to *Astoria*. During the next six hours, survivors from *Hammann*, *Balch*, and *Anderson* were moved to *Portland*. The cruiser, in company with destroyers *Morris* and *Russell*, had orders to move their full loads of *Yorktown* survivors southeast to rendezvous with the inbound *Fulton*.[3]

Amid the shuffling of nearly two thousand survivors, keymen needed for the salvage operation were culled out and moved to *Astoria*. Among them was machinist Dwight Dehaven. As he swung above the wave tops in a buoy basket from *Benham*, he saw comrades from his boiler emergency repair team moving about shoeless. As the morning temperature increased, the sailors sought shade to protect their bare feet from the warm steel decks. Dehaven was pleased that he had retained his own shoes.[4]

When *Russell* nestled alongside *Astoria* at 0912, she transferred over a number of key officers for the salvage party: first lieutenant Clarence Aldrich, communications officer Jug Ray, navigator Jim Wiltsie, supply officer Ralph Arnold, as well as warrant officers Chester Briggs and Boyd McKenzie. As John Greenbacker waited his turn to climb into the transfer basket, he noted a strong desire among his shipmates to help save *Yorktown*. "Everyone wanted to go, and finally guards had to be placed at the highlines to keep additional personnel from coming over in their determination to go back to their ship," Greenbacker remembered. "The dedication to the 'Old Lady' was most impressive."[5]

Chief Joe Kisela, in charge of *Yorktown*'s shipfitters and piping and plumbing shop sailors, found Chief Carpenter's Mate Thomas Coleman among those eager to volunteer. Retired at age sixty-two, Coleman had rejoined the ship in January nearly forty years after his initial enlistment. Because of his advanced age, he was told by Buckmaster that it was too hazardous to take him along on this mission. He wept so unashamedly that he was allowed to accompany them.[6]

Black mess attendant David Barnes had no plans to reboard his abandoned vessel. But when an officer loudly read Captain Buckmaster's list of volunteers, he was stunned to hear his name called. He had enlisted from Huntington, Alabama, in 1939, and had since worked his way up in the segregated Navy to become the skipper's steward on *Yorktown*. Although Barnes thought highly of Buckmaster, he assumed there must be some mistake. He headed up to *Astoria*'s flag bridge and received permission to speak with his skipper.[7]

As he entered the compartment, he found Buckmaster in conference with Admiral Fletcher. "Captain, I'm sorry to interrupt," said Barnes. "But I did not volunteer."

Buckmaster merely smiled at his favored assistant and said, "I volunteered you to go with me."

After Commander Ray highlined to *Astoria*, he also made his way to the bridge, where he found Fletcher and Buckmaster discussing their salvage plans. He strolled in, puffing on his trademark pipe, which was freshly cleaned from the oil it had collected in the ocean the previous afternoon.[8]

Fletcher and Buckmaster erupted into laughter.

Unfazed by protocol that might be expected before his superiors, Ray said, "What the hell are you two guys laughing about?"

Fletcher replied, "I might have known that if they pulled you out of the Pacific, you'd come up with that goddamned pipe in your mouth!"

Monitoring the numerous ship-to-ship personnel transfers, Greenbacker was suddenly hailed from *Astoria* by Lieutenant Macomber. "When you return to the *Yorktown*, would you be so kind as to look for my flight jacket?" the pilot asked.

Macomber explained that the jacket contained $1,500 of Fighting 42's welfare fund. Greenbacker confessed that he had carried the jacket partway to the destroyer but had left it behind when the air-raid alarm sounded. Greenbacker never saw Macomber again nor heard anything of the money. He was left to wonder if the caring individual who had returned his binoculars and gun might have pinched the VF-42 funds.[9]

After the various transfers of key personnel had been completed, the destroyer *Hammann* nudged alongside *Astoria* at 1235. Her skipper, Lieutenant Commander Arnold True, had orders to transfer the *Yorktown* salvage team back to their ship. This further shuffling of men would consume another hour as thirty officers and more than a hundred forty enlisted men boarded the smaller destroyer. Bill Roy was observing the process but his name had not been listed. Buckmaster spotted the young photographer he had come to recognize from his recent time spent on the bridge. The skipper called out, "Roy, come with me!" Wrangled into the team of repair experts, Roy hoped he could contribute in some way, even if it was only to document yet another important chapter in *Yorktown*'s battle to survive.[10]

Once the men were properly assembled on *Hammann*, Fletcher decided it was necessary to refuel the destroyers that would escort the salvage team. The balance of the afternoon was spent transferring fuel from *Portland* to these ships. It was nearly sundown before Fletcher departed the scene with his two cruisers and three destroyers to head for the incoming *Fulton*. The destroyer *Hammann*, transporting Buckmaster and his salvage experts, headed northwest in company with *Balch* and *Benham*. The abandoned hulk of *Yorktown* was drifting roughly a hundred fifty miles away—a voyage that would consume the entire night.[11]

Don Ramsey's destroyer, *Hughes*, had maintained a lonely vigil through the night after the carrier was abandoned. At daybreak on June 5, his warship was still circling *Yorktown*. The early-morning hours had been uneventful, save one radar contact that proved to be a snooping Japanese cruiser floatplane. The morning found the carrier drooping so far to port that the edge of her hangar deck was nearly awash. But she had remained stubbornly afloat.

Unbeknownst to anyone, two sailors were still clinging to life in the abandoned ghost ship. George Weise was still prone on a bunk in Sick Bay. The seaman's right side was paralyzed. His left arm and leg were fractured. More disabling was his fractured skull, which left him unconscious for long periods. His moments of lucidity were brief, but Weise had finally comprehended his perilous situation. He had been left for dead on a sinking ship. At one point, in a foggy state, he thought he heard someone calling out to him. He believed he was hallucinating.[12]

Moments later, he heard the voice again.

"Weise!"

Straining to see in the dim blue light, Weise finally made out the form of another man lying four bunks away. It was Seaman Norm Pichette, a sailor he knew from the 3rd Division.

"What can we do?" Pichette asked.

Weise said he was unable to move, much less climb out of his bunk to try to walk. Pichette told him that his stomach was ripped wide open from bomb shrapnel and that he had lost a lot of blood. But it became obvious that if anything was to be done, it would have to be done by him.[13]

Weise suggested that Pichette should wrap a bedsheet tightly around his abdomen to hold his intestines in place. Weise urged him to make it topside and try to fire a machine gun. *Yorktown* was still afloat, so escort warships must be nearby. "Someone will know that we are still on board," Weise told him.

Around 0925, Pichette secured sheets around his midsection, then began the painful ascent from the third-deck Sick Bay. Total darkness did little to ease his challenging journey, but the young sailor somehow struggled up the steel ladders to reach the empty, sloping hangar deck. There, he found a jury-rigged .50-caliber machine gun still pointing out toward the open ocean.

Pichette took his position behind the gun and opened fire, spraying bullets in the direction of a destroyer that was slowly circling the listing carrier. At 0941, a lookout on the destroyer *Hughes* shouted an alert to the officer of the deck: Bullets were hitting the water from a gun being fired from *Yorktown*'s hangar deck. Lieutenant Commander Ramsey eased his warship up alongside the carrier's port side. His crew spotted a sailor clutching a sheet and frantically waving from the hangar deck.

Ramsey slowed his destroyer long enough to lower a motor whaleboat with an inspection team. *Hughes* resumed circling the carrier while her boat churned over and a team scrambled up lines onto the hangar deck. Two sailors found Pichette slumped over, unconscious, near the .50-caliber he had been firing. They carefully lowered him down to the whaleboat, which returned alongside *Hughes* at 1035.[14]

Pichette was carried to the destroyer's Sick Bay, where he regained consciousness only momentarily. He was in critical condition and suffering from shock. As the ship's medical officer examined him, Pichette told him that he had been hit by shrapnel while manning his stern 20mm gun. Then he mumbled something more shocking: "There's another man alive in *Yorktown*'s sickbay."[15]

Ramsey immediately ordered his whaleboat back over to *Yorktown* for a rescue crew to perform a more thorough search. They found George Weise in Sick Bay, lying semiconscious in his bunk and swearing a blue streak. When one of the *Hughes* sailors touched his hand, Weise passed out. The destroyermen hauled his body topside and returned him to their warship at 1117. "I remember coming to on the *Hughes*, lying on a mess table," Weise recalled. "The doctor was giving me a transfusion of blood, his own."[16]

Ramsey sent his inspection team back to *Yorktown* a third time to look for men and to investigate strange tapping noises heard on their previous trip belowdecks forward and aft. During this time, lookouts spotted a life raft and maneuvered to pick up VF-3 pilot Ensign Harry Gibbs. Downed by Japanese aircraft the previous day, Gibbs had paddled his raft six miles to reach the circling *Hughes*. The rescue team found no more survivors, but did return with many classified papers and three electronic coding machines. They were confident that no one else was alive on *Yorktown* and that the carrier did not appear to be sinking.[17]

Weise's slow road to recovery was only just beginning. His savior, Norm Pichette, was given blood transfusions but his wounds were grave. He died the following day and was buried at sea. It was not until 1967 that Pichette was posthumously awarded the Navy Commendation Medal with Combat Distinguishing Device for saving a fellow shipmate.

While salvage efforts were organized on June 5, orphaned members of *Yorktown*'s air group participated in mop-up efforts against the Japanese task forces near Midway. Based on morning PBY reports of the burning carrier *Hiryu* still being afloat, strikes groups were launched from both *Hornet* and *Enterprise* in the afternoon. But *Hiryu* had slipped below the waves at 0900, the last of four Japanese carriers lost due to American dive-bombers at Midway.

Gunner Fred Bergeron's dive-bomber failed to start, leaving him marooned on *Enterprise* for the day. But thirty-two other SBDs crews were launched, including ten from *Yorktown*'s VB-3 and seven from VS-5. Instead of an enemy carrier, the TF-16 strike groups located only the Japanese destroyer *Tanikaze*. Her skipper maneuvered his warship like a speedboat, successfully dodging fifty-eight bombs. Furthering the frustration of the *Yorktown* pilots was the fact that one of their own—Lieutenant Sam Adams of VS-5—was shot down and killed by *Tanikaze*'s efficient gunners. The luckless *Hornet* and *Enterprise* dive-bombers returned to the task force after dark, desperately low on fuel.

The efforts to save the crippled *Yorktown* continued throughout the day. Three vessels dispatched by Admiral Nimitz— the ocean tug *Vireo* (AT-144) and the destroyers *Gwin* and

Monaghan—joined Don Ramsey's *Hughes* on June 5. *Vireo* took the massive carrier under tow toward the east, although *Yorktown*'s jammed rudder prevented the tug from making more than three knots of headway. A salvage party from *Gwin* boarded *Yorktown* during the afternoon and began to jettison topside weight to help correct the twenty-six-degree list. The destroyermen were recalled to their ship at dusk as *Vireo* slowly chugged toward Pearl Harbor with *Yorktown* in tow.[18]

Just before dawn on June 6, further hope arrived as Captain Buckmaster's salvage team on *Hammann* reached the scene with escorting destroyers *Balch* and *Benham*. *Hammann*'s skipper carefully edged his destroyer alongside *Yorktown*'s high starboard side as *Vireo* continued to tug the flattop slowly east. Buckmaster's trusted XO Dixie Kiefer was sidelined with a broken leg, so Commander Jim Wiltsie joined the repair group, serving as acting executive officer.

Around 0615, the salvage team began boarding *Yorktown*. It was as simple as stepping across to her hangar deck. Buckmaster's steward, David Barnes, noted that the sea was as calm as a glass of water as he did so. Finding the canted deck slick with fuel oil, he removed his shoes to avoid slipping in the darkness. With no motors running on the powerless ship, the stillness was eerie. "I realized we were on a ghost ship," Barnes recalled.[19]

Barnes was one of only four black sailors tapped to accompany the salvage team. His fellow officer's cooks and mess attendants—Augustus Wilson, Andy Mills, and Spencer Sledge—had rarely mingled with the carpenters, machinists, and electricians who boarded *Yorktown* with them this day. But they would each contribute equally to the efforts to save their proud ship.

Oldest of the quartet was twenty-seven-year old Mills, who had joined the segregated Navy from Tuscaloosa, Alabama, in 1934, and would be one of the first blacks to achieve the rank of chief petty officer. Unlike Barnes, he had volunteered. After nearly two years of service on *Yorktown*, he had hated to abandon ship. When the salvage volunteer list was being compiled, he had not hesitated.[20]

Damage control officer Clarence Aldrich and assistant Oxy Hurlbert made a quick appraisal of the ship's condition and reported their findings to Captain Buckmaster. A fire was still raging in the forward rag stowage locker, but they thought it could be quenched with proper fire hoses. They also found that the torpedo hits had flooded three firerooms on the port side, including a superheater fireroom. The trunk leading to the gasoline pump room was also flooded, along with the generator room. Two mess halls and berthing compartments immediately above these engineering spaces were destroyed and flooded to a height of eight feet. With many compartments on the port side open to the sea, and with a list they estimated to be about twenty-seven degrees, Aldrich and Hurlbert reported that little could be done to correct the flooding until the ship's list was reduced.[21]

Despite the seriousness of the job, there were moments of humor. Among the hundred forty-nine enlisted men coming aboard were Chief Cal Callaway and four of his ship's cooks. Prior to the first air attack on June 4, one of the cooks had broken out several cases of chicken to thaw. As he hustled from *Hammann* down toward the galley, Aldrich heard him remark that he needed to get the chicken back in the refrigerator before it spoiled.[22]

Chief Yeoman Floyd Bennett was amazed to see hundreds of shoes still neatly lined along the hangar and flight decks, each pair facing out to sea. Beneath the shoes were carefully stacked piles of clothing, knives, service revolvers, cigarette lighters, and other personal effects. To Jack Delaney, the scene on the hangar deck reminded him of a parlor car on a train where shoes were left neatly lined up for a porter to "turn to" on them with polish.[23]

Delaney's engineers huddled quickly to hand out assignments. Machinist George Bateman found the pile of clothing he had left on the deck on June 4. Retrieving his flashlight and gloves, he headed below to begin repairing pumps, hoping to use power from the adjacent *Hammann*. Once they were functional, he set to work pumping water from the after engine room into empty tanks on *Yorktown's* starboard side. Boiler officer Reed Cundiff, still recovering from his burns, led a team of men deep into the ship. As they entered one of the boiler rooms, he realized how quickly it had been abandoned. Halfway up the ladder, a pair of headphones once used by a battle talker hung from the rungs of the ladder.[24]

Carpenter Boyd McKenzie directed the firefighting efforts against the blaze raging near the gasoline tanks. Four of his keymen—first-class shipfitters Clyde Upchurch, Vance Brazile, Norris Hook, and Paul Vander—entered holes cut in the deck and took hoses down to the third deck to battle the persistent fire. Greenbacker spent his first hour back on *Yorktown* helping to set up the fire hoses. Many of the remaining hoses strewn about the hangar deck had to be discarded due to holes that fires had burned through them. But enough solid hose sections and sufficient water pressure from *Hammann* finally allowed McKenzie's firefighting team to attack the blaze. Directed by carpenter's mate Glyn Dillard, the shipfitters eventually succeeded in extinguishing it.[25]

McKenzie surveyed the ship, searching each damaged area for any survivors and for bodies of fallen shipmates. He had heard that two men escaped from the elevator pump room on June 4, but their senior man, machinist Bill Ogden, had not been seen since. Taking a group of sailors with him, McKenzie inspected the area adjacent to and below the elevator pit. They found access to the forward elevator pump room blocked by the body of Ogden. McKenzie ordered two sailors to move the body up to the hangar deck.[26]

McKenzie and another sailor continued to descend. He checked the pump room first and found it empty. He kept a safety man above him as he descended to each lower deck, checking the area before calling the other man to follow him down. They found no other victims and returned to the hangar deck. There he found that Chief Pharmacist's Mate Fred Epstein—working with junior medical officer Ed Kearney—had identified Ogden's body by the dog tag still around his neck.

After assisting with the fire hoses, Greenbacker began fixing the careless mess created during *Yorktown*'s hasty abandonment. In the four squadron ready rooms, he was stunned to find some seventy sets of classified aviator's contact codes lying about. He transported the confidential papers to the ship's vault, still loaded with four unopened sacks of cryptographic publications.[27]

Chief Pharmacist's Mate Jim Wilson and his assistant moved

to the sharply canted flight deck to deal with the deceased still lying topside near gun mounts. As they began preparing bodies for burial at sea, Captain Buckmaster appeared, silencing them with a wave of his hand. The skipper removed his cap and began praying. He thanked the Lord for allowing his comrades to win the battle for free men, then recited the eloquent but seldom-used service for Burial of the Dead at Sea.[28]

Bill Roy roamed the ship, pitching in with salvage efforts while continuing his documentary work. He had left his 35mm Bell and Howell movie camera on the starboard deck near the ship's photo lab when he abandoned ship on June 4. Now it was nowhere to be seen.[29]

Roy ducked into the burned-out lab to retrieve a still camera and some film. He had left two cameras in the right corner, although one was now covered with burned paint. He passed the K-20 aerial camera and its expensive Zeiss lens over to *Hammann* for safekeeping, and proceeded with his photo work, using a more portable 4x5 Graflex Speed Graphic folding camera.

Topside, he found gunnery officer Ernie Davis supervising a crew working on the portside 5-inch guns. By removing some of the massive weight on *Yorktown*'s lower side, Davis hoped to help in any way possible to correct the heavy list. Roy snapped one photo of the men cutting through the massive steel barrel. Once it was free, he set down his camera to help other sailors jack up the gun barrel and push it overboard. Cheers rang out but there was more work to be done. Davis, Gunner Maurice

Witting, and their shipfitters turned their attention to cutting away the next 5-inch barrel.

Roy was asked to assist below in the hangar deck. Other sailors like David Barnes were busy jettisoning extra weight to help reduce the list. The two spare F4Fs on the flight deck had already been pushed overboard. Now the men turned their attention to spare TBDs on the hangar deck. Without a flash, Roy used his Graflex to capture a picture of one of the Devastators as sailors pushed it through a portside hangar opening. He playfully called out to Buckmaster, asking if he could keep the plane for himself. "You've got it, Roy," the skipper kidded as the TBD-1 tumbled over the side.[30]

Chief Pharmacist's Mate Epstein enlisted the photographer's help in preparing bodies for burial at sea. Roy moved to each corpse, carefully removing watches, dog tags, and personal effects, which were placed in envelopes labeled with each man's name. As Epstein turned one victim over, Roy noted that the man's chest had been penetrated by a large-caliber shell, and his legs were peppered with shrapnel wounds. Below the starboard catwalk, in a radio cubbyhole, they found another sailor who had crawled into the space before expiring from his wounds. Roy said a prayer for each shipmate before the body was rolled over the side.

Throughout the morning, Buckmaster maintained lookouts on *Yorktown*'s bridge. Should enemy planes or submarine torpedoes be spotted, they had orders to fire one of the bridge guns as a warning signal for the men working below.[31]

Supply officer Ralph Arnold moved the ship's pay records over to *Hammann*. Then he headed below with mess attendants

Andy Mills and Spencer Sledge to retrieve large amounts of payroll cash locked in the ship's safe. Although Arnold knew the combination, he couldn't get the vault door to open. He asked one of his assistants to give it a try. "I went up there and turned it," recalled Mills. "Click! Money fell all out of it."[32]

So many coins spilled out that they literally covered Mills's shoes. "Don't bother with the silver," Arnold said. "Get the green stuff and let's get out of here." Mills and Sledge stuffed a satchel with what they estimated to be close to a half million dollars. They carried the load of cash up to the hangar deck, where it was hauled across to the destroyer snugged alongside.[33]

By midday, Buckmaster had reason for confidence. The fire raging below had been quenched. The pump work below was moving water into empty starboard-side tanks to help settle the ship. Besides jettisoning excess weight, his salvage team had decreased the portside list to twenty-two degrees.

While the fight to save *Yorktown* carried into the early afternoon of June 6, her aviators were still engaged with the retiring Japanese invasion fleet. SBD scouts from *Enterprise* located a force of two heavy cruisers and two destroyers roughly a hundred thirty-three miles away. *Hornet* was first to launch a strike of twenty-five dive-bombers, escorted by eight VF-8 Wildcats.

They arrived over the Japanese warships at 0950 and commenced attacks on the cruisers *Mogami* and *Mikuma*. Lieutenant Bill Christie, flying as a section leader with VS-8, carefully lined up on *Mogami* as he dived through intense antiaircraft fire and released. He felt certain his bomb was a direct hit amidships. Two planes were lost in the attack, but the *Hornet* group had plastered both cruisers with damaging bomb hits.

By 1045, *Enterprise* had launched her own strike group of thirty-two SBDs, twelve VF-6 escort fighters, and Torpedo Six's last three TBDs. In the hurry to man planes, radioman Fred Bergeron was tapped to fill in for Ensign Bob Campbell's sick gunner. Searching for a replacement, Campbell waved freshly made ham sandwiches toward Bergeron. "I'll give you these if you'll fly with me," he said.[34]

Bergeron kidded the pilot, telling him his wife would be ashamed of him coercing a nineteen-year-old kid into combat with ham sandwiches. Although he greatly preferred the real ham over mess hall spam, Bergeron was eager for revenge. The ham sandwiches weren't necessary.

The *Enterprise* group reached the Japanese cruiser force at 1235 and commenced its attack. Mixed in with VS-6 and VB-6 were a dozen *Yorktown* aircrews: seven from Lieutenant Wally Short's VS-5 and ten from VB-3 under Lieutenant Dave Shumway. Short was credited with a direct hit on *Mikuma*. Two planes back, gunner Lynn Forshee braced himself as Lieutenant Carl Horenburger plunged their SBD into its dive. Seconds later, Forshee turned and looked back. He hollered to his pilot that he had made a good attack, landing their bomb directly behind the cruiser's smokestack amidships.[35]

Short's VS-5 crew claimed five direct hits. Shumway estimated that his Bombing Three pilots scored four direct hits and five near misses on their target, *Mikuma*. His last pilot, Ensign Roy Isaman, switched his dive at the last moment to the less damaged cruiser *Mogami* and was credited with a direct hit aft. The airwaves were filled with expletives and joyous cheers as TF-16's strikers departed, leaving *Mikuma* dead in the water and *Mogami* blazing from numerous hits.

A second *Hornet* strike group began launching at 1330. Flying as section leader with VS-8 on his second warship attack of the day was VS-5's Bill Christie, with *Yorktown* squadron mate Hank McDowell on his wing. The *Hornet* dive-bombers further plastered both cruisers and landed damaging near misses alongside the pair of nimble Japanese destroyers. McDowell claimed a direct hit on *Mikuma* while Christie bore in through the AA fire on the *Mogami*—the larger target, but not the one emitting the most smoke.[36]

Mikuma absorbed so many thousand-pound-bomb hits during the day that she slipped under the waves that evening with the loss of more than six hundred fifty lives. *Mogami* was badly battered, but managed to limp away during the night with her two destroyers. The final action in the Battle of Midway was complete, and *Yorktown*'s planes had contributed heavily to avenge the damage to their own ship. Four Japanese carriers from the IJN strike force had been sunk, along with two heavy cruisers knocked out, one of them fatally holed. At the cost of *Yorktown* drifting abandoned, along with heavy aircrew losses, the U.S. Navy off Midway had achieved its most significant victory of World War II thus far.

Pilot Bill Christie was elated as he flew back toward his temporary home carrier, *Enterprise. Two bombing runs, two hits,* he thought. *That made up for missing out on the CVs on June 4.*[37]

CHAPTER THIRTEEN

"TORPEDOES TO STARBOARD!"

Lieutenant Commander Yahachi Tanabe finally had a reason to celebrate. On the bridge of his submarine, *I-168*, one of his able lookouts had spotted the American aircraft carrier. It was shortly before dawn on June 6, and the black shape on the horizon was eleven miles distant. "It was the easiest intercept a submarine commander ever made," Tanabe recalled.[1]

He was eager for revenge. Two days earlier, American divebombers had wiped out four Imperial Japanese Navy carriers—frightening news that had quickly spread through the sub. The following morning, *I-168* had briefly shelled Midway Island, but Tanabe had been forced to dive when searchlights from the atoll illuminated his deck gunners. Later that day, when Japanese scout planes located the crippled *Yorktown*, Tanabe was ordered to locate and destroy the U.S. carrier.

He submerged *I-168* at daybreak and commenced a slow approach to *Yorktown*. She was under tow from *Vireo*, making about three knots, and a destroyer was tied up along her starboard side. The presence of five other watchguard destroyers necessitated caution in Tanabe's approach. He knew his sub might get sunk. Before that happened, he meant to do the maximum possible damage to the carrier.[2]

I-168 eased closer, with the sound of echo ranging ever present throughout the sub, emanating from the U.S. destroyers. But as the noon hour approached, they ceased emitting detection signals. Tanabe quietly told his crew that the Americans had interrupted their war for lunch. There were jokes made about what to give them for dessert. But on his next periscope observation, *Yorktown* and her hugging destroyer were too close, literally filling his lens. His torpedoes—older-variant models—would not have the distance to arm themselves. They required more than three hundred yards of running distance in order to properly stabilize and to activate their detonators—a built-in safety feature to prevent torpedoes from exploding at a dangerously close range to the submarine that fired them.

Tanabe chose to ease *I-168* into a right-hand circle out to one mile before turning back in for his next approach. He passed orders that all four bow tubes would be fired, in groups of two, tightly bunched to ensure maximum damage amidships on his target. Peering through his periscope, Tanabe waited until the range was down to twelve hundred yards before giving the order at 1331. His *I-168* belched out four torpedoes, each seen clearly speeding through the calm blue ocean.[3]

Tanabe refused to dive until he saw the results of his efforts.

If *I-168* was going to die, he at least wanted the satisfaction of seeing whether their torpedoes hit home.

———

More than six hours into the salvage work, Captain Buckmaster decided his men needed a break. It was around 1300 when Cal Callaway's cooks broke out corned beef sandwiches, tomato juice, and warm Coca-Cola for the late lunch.

Lieutenant Commander Delaney grabbed a snack on the hangar deck. Then he moved across to the port side, opposite from *Hammann*, to take a cigarette break with fellow officers Ernie Davis and Jim Wiltsie. The smoking lamp was out, but a large acetylene torch was cutting away a gun mount a few feet from them, so they figured they could grab a few puffs during a break.[4]

John Greenbacker had just reached the quarterdeck. He had been tapped by communications officer Jug Ray to assist with gathering Admiral Fletcher's message files from the safe in Flag Plot. Ray and Greenbacker stuffed the documents in a mailbag and headed below to pass them over to *Hammann*. En route, Greenbacker spotted several cases of Coca-Cola. Dropping his mailbag, he paused to enjoy a bottle.[5]

Supply officer Ralph Arnold had gone below on a new mission. Members of the repair party recalled that two portable army gasoline stoves had been brought on board ship after the Coral Sea battle. Deciding these could be of use, Arnold and two of his storekeepers—Russell Lainson and Charles Wood— headed below to search for them. He kept his assistants strung out on ladders below the hangar deck, listening for any alarm from topside. Arnold had searched one storeroom and was about to try a second when Lainson and Wood began shouting that a machine gun was firing topside. Arnold made flank speed up the ladders.[6]

Shipfitter Earl "Ed" Fogarty, having spent the morning using his torch to help cut away the 5-inch guns, was eating lunch on the starboard side of *Yorktown's* hangar deck, near the No. 1 aircraft elevator. From his vantage point, he and his fellow repairmen could see over *Hammann's* bridge out to the open water. Chief Joe Kisela, glancing out beyond *Hammann*, suddenly announced that he could see blackfish (black porpoises) playfully jumping out of the water. Looking to where Kisela was pointing, shipfitter Clyde Upchurch shouted, "Blackfish, hell! Those are torpedoes!"[7]

Seconds later, at 1336, lookouts on both *Yorktown* and *Hammann* spotted the white wakes of four torpedoes. They were approaching from the starboard beam, beyond the destroyer screen. The 20mm signal gun on *Yorktown's* bridge began chattering as sailors opened fire. *Hammann's* gunnery officer also ordered two bridge 20mm gunners, Willie Allison and Roy Nelson, to open fire on the torpedoes in hopes that their machine-gun bullets might detonate one or more warheads before they arrived.[8]

Belowdecks, boiler division officer Reed Cundiff heard the guns firing. He shouted, "Let's get out of here!" Scrambling up the steel ladders in mere seconds, Cundiff and a comrade, Water Tender William "Pinky" Davis, raced over to the starboard side near *Hammann* to determine the cause of the shooting. Spotting the approaching torpedo wakes, Cundiff cursed his luck. An avid photographer, he realized he was missing what could have been a once-in-a-lifetime shot.[9]

On the hangar deck, Lieutenant Commander Ray spotted Lieutenant Commander Arnold True on the bridge of his adjacent destroyer, *Hammann*. As the torpedoes approached, he urged True to cut the lines and cast off to save his ship. "No, never mind!" True shouted back. "There's no time!"[10]

Ray's assistant, Greenbacker, was still enjoying his Coke when he heard 20mm gunfire, the raucous buzzing of *Hammann*'s general quarters alarm, and shouts of "Torpedoes!" He snatched up his bag of confidential papers and raced to the lower port side. Then an ominous thought struck him: *What if torpedoes are coming from this side too? I'm awfully close to the water here.*[11]

Greenbacker secured the mailbag to the ship's structure and seized one of the lines sprawled across the canted hangar deck. Deciding to take his chances on the higher starboard side, the lieutenant furiously worked his way back up the slanting deck like a mountain climber.

Standing near Captain Buckmaster on the hangar deck, Lieutenant Oxy Hurlbert thought the torpedo wakes resembled two pairs of streetcar tracks he had once seen on San Francisco's Market Street. Photographer Bill Roy was watching shipfitters finish cutting away their second 5-inch gun barrel on the port side of the flight deck when the 20mms began firing. He raced to a high starboard-side catwalk to look.[12]

Roy had just enough time to swing his Graflex into action and snap a photo of a *Hammann* boatswain's mate chopping at mooring lines with a fire ax. Then the first torpedo slammed into *Hammann*. The resulting explosions tossed the boatswain's mate through the air over the destroyer's bow. Roy was dazed as his head and left shoulder were slammed into *Yorktown*'s bulkhead. Two more torpedoes exploded into his carrier, slamming him into the bulkhead again and onto the steel-grating deck of a catwalk perched above the ocean.

Warrant officer Leonard Wingo had just come topside for a smoke. As he gazed out on the quiet beauty of the Pacific, he spotted the white wakes approaching and shouted toward *Hammann*'s lookouts, "Torpedoes to starboard!"[13]

With no place to go, he braced himself against the deckhouse. One of his electricians, Chief Bill Wright, also saw the torpedoes approaching. Wright turned, ran a short distance, and made a wild leap from the flight deck down to the destroyer's deck, hoping for a safer refuge. He had no sooner regained his footing than one of the torpedoes exploded in *Hammann* and blew Wright high into the air and out into the water. By some strange twist of fate, the *Yorktown* electrician would be rescued uninjured.

Seaman First Class Mallory Hill, on the carrier's hangar deck, began to run when he saw the torpedoes, but found it did no good. There was no place to go, so he stopped and stood there to watch them hit. The force of the explosions threw Hill over the side of the ship and into the ocean. He swam back toward *Yorktown*'s low side and worked his way back up to the hangar deck, using one of the knotted abandon-ship lines.[14]

The first torpedo exploded in *Hammann*'s after fireroom, breaking her keel. The next two torpedoes hit *Yorktown* just below the turn of her bilge at the after end of the island structure. The resulting explosions ripped open compartments on her starboard side and further devastated the destroyer with their concussions. *Hammann*'s bow momentarily rose up like a stricken animal before she began quickly settling, her bow nosing under the water first.

On *Yorktown*'s hangar deck, there was a tremendous heave upward. Commander Aldrich was slammed to the deck with such force that his left arm was broken. Boyd McKenzie was thrown into the open elevator shaft, where he lay stunned, his back badly injured. Rivets holding the base of *Yorktown*'s mast were sheared off and the ship's bell was knocked off, crashing to the deck and shattering to pieces. Buckmaster paused long enough to pick up a piece of the bell and stick it in his pocket as a keepsake.[15]

Jug Ray, clutching a lifeline rail, nearly bit the stem off his pipe. The explosion in *Hammann* was violent enough to toss gunnery officer Ernie Davis overboard. Ray saw Davis flailing about in the water as the next two blasts rocked *Yorktown*. When Greenbacker picked himself up from the deck, he heard cries for help coming from Boatswain Chester Briggs. Lieutenant Albert Wilson was just climbing up through a hangar-deck hatch from the lower deck when the explosions released the heavy steel hatch. Wilson was pinned, his left arm badly broken. From below him Briggs wrestled with the hatch while Greenbacker lifted from above until Wilson's crushed arm was freed.[16]

Had Greenbacker not paused to enjoy a Coke, he would have been on board *Hammann* with Fletcher's confidential papers. Moving back to the quarterdeck, he watched in awe as

Hammann settled in the water on an even keel with her stern slowly rising upward. She gave him the impression of a ship dropped from a great height, upright but broken.[17]

Hammann sank in less than four minutes, but during that time more than two hundred of her crew got off the ship. As she went down, her stern section lifted high in the air. Boilermaker Ray Fitzgibbon and Torpedoman First Class Berlyn Kimbrel remained on the stern, passing out life jackets. Once they ran out, Fitzgibbon dived over the side. But Kimbrel, as witnessed by dozens of his fellow shipmates and *Yorktown* men, remained on the rising stern, feverishly attempting to make sure all of the depth charges were set to safe. He was last seen still at this task when *Hammann*'s stern submerged. Her screws were still turning, and her propellers chewed noisily against *Yorktown*'s keel, reminding one sailor of a playing card slapping against the spokes of a bicycle tire.[18]

Bill Roy, knocked down twice, used his Graflex to capture the last minute of *Hammann*. His images of her stern rising up and then plunging below the surface would be among the most famous of a ship's loss during World War II.

Despite Kimbrel's efforts to set all of the depth charges to safe, some of her antisubmarine explosives detonated as *Hammann* sank to greater depths. Massive shock waves swept through some two hundred sailors in the ocean. Jug Ray had just reached *Yorktown*'s flight deck when the charges erupted. Heads that he had seen bobbing on the surface suddenly disappeared like droplets of water removed by a wiper from a windshield.[19]

Cundiff dived onto the deck just before the torpedoes

exploded. His companion, Pinky Davis, had swung down to *Hammann*'s deck just before the destroyer was hit. The resulting explosion blew him into the sea, where he was still struggling when her depth charges exploded. Although he was later pulled from the sea, Davis had suffered mortal internal injuries from the concussions.[20]

Ernie Davis, blown overboard by the torpedo blasts, had just made it to *Yorktown*'s side. Grabbing an abandon-ship line, he was pulling his body from the water when the depth charges erupted. The severe concussion broke his back and perforated his intestines in hundreds of places. Machinist Pressley Holmes, also blown off *Yorktown* by the explosions, had scrambled up onto a large plank floating in the water, which probably saved him from severe internal injuries. Holmes assisted Davis to the plank until the pair could be fished from the water.[21]

Jim Wilson found himself in the ocean for the second time in two days. He escaped without serious injury, but had to tread water for a half hour before climbing onto the minesweeper *Vireo*. Carpenter Glyn Dillard, who had led the firefighting efforts for hours, dived overboard and helped keep two *Hammann* sailors afloat until they could be rescued by a whaleboat.[22]

Many of *Hammann*'s sailors were killed or gravely injured. Eighteen-year-old James Cunningham, blown from the deck when the torpedo exploded and hanging on to a raft, was now lifted from the water by the concussion from the depth charges. The shipmate clinging to the raft to his right was killed instantly while the man to his left was virtually uninjured. Cunningham felt pains in his chest, but crawled onto another raft filled with wounded. By the time he was hauled on board the destroyer *Benham*, he was coughing up blood. Ship's cook Robert Schaefer lost all feeling from this waist down and believed his legs were gone. As he was pulled onto another destroyer, he finally glanced down and was greatly relieved to see his legs still intact.[23]

John Greenbacker was stunned by the rapid demise of *Hammann*. He and others were roused into action by Commander Ralph Arnold shouting orders. Arnold called for *Yorktown* men to obtain mattresses from the officers' staterooms to serve as substitute life rafts, since they would float. The closer staterooms seemed safe enough to venture into. But as the mattress supply became short, volunteers had to navigate deeper into the darkened carrier to find more.[24]

The mattress working party dwindled until only Greenbacker and mess attendant Augustus Wilson remained. Greenbacker later recommended Wilson for a commendation for hauling six more mattresses topside from deep inside the ship. Each offered a wounded man a chance to survive in the water.

The two new torpedo hits had opened *Yorktown*'s starboard side, and the flooding that ensued served to shave five degrees off her portside list. *Vireo*'s captain immediately separated his towing line and maneuvered his tug to help retrieve wounded men from the ocean. Sailors on *Yorktown* used the abandon-ship lines to pull men onto the carrier. Fireman Adam Bartel was suffering from several internal injuries from the depth charges. His buddy George Bateman tried to comfort him as

Bartel moaned that he wanted to die. Afraid *Yorktown* might sink also, Bateman worked a life jacket around Bartel and helped lower him over the side again. Together, they bobbed in the water until recovered by sailors on *Vireo*.[25]

Jack Delaney decided to head below with Lieutenant Al Emerson and warrant officer Phil McDonald to secure any engineering spaces that might have been opened up by the torpedo hits. Emerson announced that he would check the air department's spaces. Delaney believed his buddy planned to pass by Sick Bay to salvage some medicinal whiskey they could enjoy later on a rescue destroyer. But he asked Emerson to make sure *Vireo* did not leave without him. The tug skipper was nudging his small ship alongside *Yorktown* to retrieve salvage team members who had not jumped overboard.[26]

As Delaney and McDonald disappeared below, *Yorktown* salvage members began jumping across to *Vireo*. Lieutenant Greenbacker was amazed by the audacity of some: "The tug's people were not pleased to receive suitcases which some of the officers of the salvage party were thoughtful enough to pack during the period they were on board."[27]

Boyd McKenzie was helped from the elevator shaft, suffering from back injuries. He joined Lieutenant Ed Kearney and others on the fantail, where they urged shipmates to jump onto *Vireo*. The doctor finally turned to McKenzie and said, "It's your turn."[28]

"No, it's your turn, Doctor," replied McKenzie.

"What do you mean?" said Kearney. "I am the senior officer here."

McKenzie was aware by naval regulations that a warrant officer ranked higher in succession than a medical corps specialist. "But I am the senior line officer," he said.

Kearney and McKenzie made a compromise: They would jump across to *Vireo* together, and they did.

Buckmaster remained near the forward fo'c'scle deck, wanting to be the last to leave *Yorktown* once again. He moved aft toward the tug, again calling out for anyone left behind. He heard nothing but the sound of the sea crashing into empty compartments. He finally grabbed a line and swung down to *Vireo*'s deck. At that moment, Delaney and McDonald returned to the hangar deck. On the tug's deck, Emerson spotted them and raced forward, waving up toward *Vireo*'s captain, Lieutenant James Legg, that two men were still on board *Yorktown*. Delaney and his companion dashed across the hangar deck, shouting at the tug to wait.[29]

McDonald and then Delaney swung down lines to *Vireo* at the last instant. Greenbacker noticed that Buckmaster was "tremendously upset," deprived of being the last to leave his ship. Grabbing a knotted line, the skipper tried to swing himself back over the water to touch *Yorktown* one last time, hoping to fulfill an ancient maritime tradition of the captain being the last to touch a dying vessel. *Vireo*'s skipper had little patience. His tug had been nestled alongside the carrier for more than a half hour in the same position recently vacated by the sinking of the destroyer *Hammann*. Legg shouted at Buckmaster to hurry up.[30]

Buckmaster's efforts were in vain. Legg cast off from his precarious position and backed the tug away. Climbing back onto *Vireo*'s superstructure, Buckmaster spotted his acting executive officer, Jim Wiltsie. "Why didn't you tell me there was someone else left aboard?" he shouted.

During this time, destroyers *Gwin*, *Monaghan*, and *Hughes* were aggressively conducting depth-charge attacks against the Japanese submarine. *Benham* and *Balch* moved about, using their whaleboats to help scoop injured *Yorktown* and *Hammann* survivors from the water. By late afternoon, around 1628, Jug Ray on *Vireo* noticed only three heads still bobbing in the water. *Balch* sailors soon fished out the last survivor—*Hammann*'s skipper, Arnold True. The torpedo explosion had thrown him into his chart desk, breaking two of his ribs. He had then struggled in the water for three hours, trying to keep two dying shipmates afloat.[31]

Vireo transferred many *Yorktown* survivors to task force destroyers that evening. Commander Ray was moved as one mortally injured *Hammann* sailor wrestled with his final moments. He desired extreme unction, as he was about to die. "I was not a Roman [Catholic] but I thought that it wouldn't send me to hell any faster if I became one for the moment," Ray recalled. He sent for a Roman Catholic prayer book and gave the dying sailor his last rites.[32]

Of *Hammann*'s 239-man crew, ninety-one were killed, missing, or mortally wounded. Another sixty men had been injured to varying degrees, some in critical condition. A number of *Yorktown* sailors were injured, some with broken limbs and others with massive internal injuries from the exploding depth charges. One salvage team member, water tender Pinky Davis, would perish from his.

As evening approached, Buckmaster still clung to hopes of saving his carrier. *Yorktown* had settled but did not appear to be sinking. Plans were made to return to the ship at first light with a smaller salvage party, just large enough to help with towing. Greenbacker's feelings matched that of many of his fellow salvage team members: He would go back if he had to, but he saw little that they could do to repair the latest torpedo damage.[33]

Those faint hopes faded with daybreak on June 7. Weakened bulkheads allowed more flooding on the port side. At 0635, *Yorktown* began slowing rolling over, and in the process, the vast torpedo damage to her starboard side was finally exposed. *Yorktown* survivors were nudged from their bunks. In *Gwin*'s wardroom, Lieutenant Oxy Hurlbert was awakened by a destroyer officer. "You'd better get topside if you want to get a last look at your big silver baby," he said. "She's about to go over."[34]

Buckmaster could see his ship was going down fast. On the destroyer *Balch*, Bill Roy was startled to hear an announcement for the photographer to come to the bridge. Grabbing his aerial camera, he arrived in time to take a half dozen photos of *Yorktown* as her shattered stern section slowly sank from sight.[35]

Jug Ray and others saluted their carrier as she disappeared around 0658. "I'm sure that the tears that came from Captain Buckmaster's eyes were no more salty than those from mine," Ray recalled. Yeoman Bill Lancaster was equally moved: "I shall never forget the unabashed and shameless tears that streamed down the faces, my own included. It was if we had just witnessed the death of a close friend."[36]

Buckmaster asked *Balch's* skipper to take him through the flotsam that marked *Yorktown's* departure. *Balch* circled two more times before the destroyer skipper finally said it was time to head for Pearl Harbor. It was Sunday morning, the seventh of June—six months to the day since the Japanese had made their surprise attack on the Hawaiian Islands.

Yorktown was gone, but her fighting spirit, and her contributions to the Coral Sea and Midway victories, would be permanently etched in the annals of American history.

AFTERWORD

Yorktown's survivors were moved from ship to ship en route to Pearl Harbor. On June 7, the majority were transferred to the newly arrived submarine tender *Fulton*. Gunner John Hancock was among them. Picked up by the destroyer *Anderson*, he had been scrubbed of oil and given fresh dungarees and a new shirt before being highlined to the cruiser *Astoria* the next day. By the time he finally swung across to the more spacious *Fulton*, Hancock was pleased to trade two nights of sleeping on steel decks for a comfortable cot.

Assisted by tugs, *Fulton* was nestled into a berth on June 8 at Pearl Harbor's submarine base. In addition to waiting ambulances, Admiral Chester Nimitz and his staff were on hand to congratulate the heroes of the Battle of Midway. Salvage party volunteer Bill Lancaster was impressed that the admiral greeted them individually, shook their hands, and thanked them for the efforts they had made. "I think every man after that incident would have followed him anywhere," Lancaster remembered.[1]

As Ensign Jack Crawford stepped onto the dock, he realized that his tenure on his new carrier had lasted less than one week. Standing with Nimitz was the captain who had reluctantly signed his transfer papers at the last minute. Crawford saluted him and said, "Captain, I guess your were sorta prophetic. You said I was headed for trouble, but the trouble came a little faster than either of us thought it would!"[2]

The initial pleasure at seeing Nimitz greet them was replaced by shock and anger for many *Yorktown* sailors. The loss of the carrier was deemed classified, and fears that the news might leak out created an initial desire to prevent the survivors from spreading the news. *Yorktown's* survivors were trucked to Camp Catlin, a Marine Corps base on Oahu, where they would spend weeks in seclusion.

While there, Jack Crawford was surprised one day when Ensign Mo Slater strolled into his tent. Tossing a familiar pair of Bausch & Lomb binoculars onto Crawford's bunk, he said, "Here you go, Red." Slater had recovered the binoculars while part of the salvage party. Hoping to liberate a GI pair, Slater had been a bit unhappy when he found his comrade's name engraved onto the prism cover plate. But he felt honor bound to give them back to Crawford.

Yorktown's crew was eventually released from the camp for liberty back home before moving on to new assignments. Many of the wounded men faced long roads to recovery. Seaman George Weise, left for dead in *Yorktown's* Sick Bay, would spend months in naval hospitals recovering from his fractured skull. He refused offers to take a medical discharge. After returning to active duty, he advanced in rank to boatswain's mate first class in charge of a shore patrol and later served on the attack cargo ship USS *Merrick*. Weise was honorably discharged from the Navy on August 8, 1946. The sailor once written off as unsavable ultimately outlived the majority of his shipmates. Weise passed away in his home state of North Carolina at age ninety-seven in March 2019.

Elliott Buckmaster, the deeply respected final skipper of *Yorktown*, was advanced to flag rank soon after the Midway battle. Two weeks after the historic June 1942 victory, he wrote that he could not "praise too highly the aggressive fighting spirit of the entire complement of the *Yorktown* and her Air Group, not only in the Battle of Midway but in all the actions in which they have participated." His wishes that the fighting spirit be preserved by more than just memory would soon be realized when the United States renamed a new carrier then under construction as *Yorktown* (CV-10). The announcement was made on September 26, the same day the Navy officially announced the loss of CV-5. It was only fitting that Rear Admiral Buckmaster and his wife were present months later on January 3, 1943, when First Lady Eleanor Roosevelt christened the new *Yorktown*.[3]

Bill Roy turned in his dramatic photos at Pearl Harbor and eventually rode the attack transport *Henderson* back to San Francisco. While walking in uniform along Market Street after his arrival, he was stunned to see the front of the Telenews Theatre. One of the feature films shown on a poster was titled

Yorktown *Sunk*. Realizing that his dream of making a movie had come true, Roy persuaded the theater manager to offer him a private screening. As he watched the narrated wartime footage, he eagerly pointed out to the manager which scenes he had filmed during *Yorktown*'s final battle.[4]

Following leave, Roy was assigned to the Naval School of Photography in Pensacola as an instructor. He advanced to chief petty officer and later was promoted to lieutenant before he retired from the Navy. After a long civilian career, Roy passed away in Florida in 2015 at the age of ninety-five.

Jack Crawford, who served on *Yorktown* less than one week, returned to the war as assistant gunnery officer on the escort carrier *Santee*. He retired from the Navy as a captain in 1963 and went on to a long career in nuclear energy. As of 2021, the 101-year-old veteran was the last living officer of CV-5—and in his Rockville, Maryland, home were the Annapolis binoculars retrieved from *Yorktown* that bear his name.

Officer John Lorenz would receive the Navy Cross for his actions at Midway. The memories of his fallen gun-crew mates was almost more than he could stand. During his first month of recovery in the Hawaiian camp, he turned to alcohol to help ease his suffering. When he was able to return home on leave in August 1942, he immediately married his fiancée, Delight McHale. Due to *Yorktown*'s damage at Coral Sea and loss at Midway, none of John's letters had reached her. She had nearly given up hope until one day her mother announced that a naval officer was walking up the front sidewalk.[5]

Lorenz later served as gunnery officer to the escort carrier *Bogue*. He retired from the Navy in 1945 with the rank of lieutenant commander. John and Delight raised three sons while he pursued a career as an insurance claims manager. During the Midway battle, he had helped inspire wounded gunner Bill Sullivan to cling to life until he was safely moved to a rescue destroyer. Lorenz had promised Sullivan that if he survived, he would name a son after him. True to his word, William Sullivan Lorenz was so christened in 1965. Unknown to John Lorenz, Sullivan's wounds were severe enough that he was discharged from the Navy after Midway and was sent back home to Grand Rapids, Michigan. Sullivan passed away at the early age of thirty-eight.

Gunner John Hancock's injuries caught up with him during the crew's detainment in Hawaii. The shrapnel wounds to his neck had been treated during his return to Pearl Harbor. But the shard that had punctured his lung had gone undiagnosed. He was on cleanup duty at Camp Catlin one afternoon when a shipmate suddenly asked, "What the hell's the matter with you, Hancock?"[6]

"Nothing," Hancock snapped. "What the hell's the matter with you?"

"Your lips are purple," his buddy said. "What have you been eating?"

Hancock then noted that even his fingertips had darkened under his nails. The base corpsman assessed the sailor and hauled him by jeep to the armory on Oahu. They found that his lung had collapsed. Hancock was taken by ambulance to the hospital at Pearl Harbor, where he spent weeks in recovery before returning home for liberty with his family in Georgia. Hancock returned to combat in World War II on a tank transport ship for amphibious campaigns that stretched from Cape Gloucester to Iwo Jima and Okinawa. His childhood dreams of learning to fly were realized later that year when he was accepted for flight training to become a fighter pilot. In later years, he transitioned from active duty to the Reserves, retiring with the rank of captain.

He and his wife, Ruth Anne, still live in Georgia, where he is the father of three sons and has "an army" of grandchildren. Hancock has since participated in numerous reunions and military programs as a special guest. In 2012, he spoke at the seventieth Battle of Midway reunion from the deck of the USS *Yorktown* (CV-10) in the Patriots Point Naval and Maritime Museum in Mt. Pleasant, South Carolina. "Battle at sea is like a thunderstorm," he said. "It's as if everything is crashing around you and there is no break. But then, all of a sudden, it is over and you realize you are still alive."[7]

During the commemorative ceremony, speakers reminded the crowd how crucial the Battle of Midway had been toward the overall success of America in World War II. The men of Hancock's carrier *Yorktown* had given their all at Coral Sea and Midway.

In his closing remarks, Captain Hancock summed up the meaning of the victory of Midway. "We hold these ceremonies," he said, "to remind not just those who were around during the time of the battle, but the youth as well. They need to know what we did to preserve this great nation's freedom."

★ ACKNOWLEDGMENTS ★

The story of *Yorktown*'s valiant final fights at Coral Sea and Midway has fascinated me since I was a youth. So I must thank my longtime agent, Jim Donovan, and Penguin editor Brent Howard for encouraging me to bring this story to print. Fortunately, the *Yorktown* story and the Battle of Midway have long garnered the attention of American historians, ensuring that hundreds of veterans' accounts have been captured over the last several decades.

Some of these personal stories were offered by historians who had known these veterans well. Don Bourgeois of Oregon, a close friend of battery officer John Lorenz, was kind enough to share numerous articles and biographical sketches he had compiled of Lorenz's service. Allan Gehring likewise provided his 2009 interview with gunner Terry Dykes.

Many other museums and historians offered advice, articles, oral histories, transcripts, and videos for my review. The list of those to whom I am indebted include: Jeremy Collins and Joey Balfour of the National WWII Museum in New Orleans for reviewing their oral history collection; Laura Waayers, Rick Stone, and Timothy Francis from the Naval History Heritage Center in Washington for procuring 1960s interviews conducted by historian Walter Lord; Associate Director of Communications Jackie Furton from the U.S. Naval Academy Alumni Association and Foundation in Annapolis; Bonnie Towne from the National Naval Aviation Museum in Pensacola for copying articles from *The Hook*; Colonel Don Patton of the World War II History Roundtable; historians James Sawruk, Mark Horan, and James Scott; Thom Walla of the Midway Roundtable Forum; author David Rocco; and Megan Harris from the Veterans History Project in Washington.

From the *Yorktown* CV-5 Association there were Sandra Yost Muse, Warren G. Heller, and Mike Leggins. Mike was kind enough to take me into his Texas home to review boxes of *Yorktown* papers, newsletters, and previously published articles and books. I am also grateful to many children of *Yorktown* veterans who offered articles, memoirs, and photos of their loved ones. They include Sheri Flum, Thomas Good, Edward A. Kearney III, Joy Neal Kidney, Boyd McKenzie Jr., Jacklyn Richels, and Carolyn Weise.

Finally, I am honored to have talked with some of the *Yorktown* veterans who shared their stories: Fred Bergeron, John Crawford, Eugene Domienik, T. K. Ford, John Hancock, Roger Spooner, and Stanley Vejtasa. Their respective battle stations were on the ship's guns, with damage control teams belowdecks, and in the cockpits of *Yorktown*'s aircraft. Each man contributed valiantly to their ship's final thirty days of action in historic carrier conflicts that forever changed the course of this great nation.

★ NOTES ★

CHAPTER ONE: CARRIER DOWN

1. Stanley Vejtasa, interview with author.
2. Ted Edwards, *Seven at Santa Cruz: The Life of Fighter Ace Stanley "Swede" Vejtasa* (Annapolis, MD: Naval Institute Press, 2018), 47.
3. William F. Christie, correspondence with Mark Horan, 1986, 3–4.
4. Ibid., 6.
5. Lynn Forshee, *Standby! Mark!*, chapter 10.
6. John B. Lundstrom, *The First Team: Pacific Naval Air Combat from Pearl Harbor to Midway* (Annapolis, MD: Naval Institute Press, 1984), 210–13.
7. Pat Frank and Joseph D. Harrington, *Rendezvous at Midway: The U.S.S. Yorktown and the Japanese Carrier Fleet* (New York: The John Day Company, 1967), 35–36.
8. John Hancock, interview with author, October 19, 2020.
9. John Hancock, email to author, December 31, 2020.
10. George K. Weise, "I Was Left On Board," *Yorktown* (VA) *Crier*, May 1988, 3–4.
11. Ibid., 5; Jeff Nesmith, *No Higher Honor: The U.S.S.* Yorktown *at the Battle of Midway* (Atlanta: Longstreet, Inc., 1999), 170.
12. Lundstrom, *The First Team*, 210–11.
13. Ibid., 80.
14. Ibid., 179.

15. Stanley Johnston, *The Grim Reapers* (New York: E. P. Dutton & Co., Inc., 1943), 29.
16. Lundstrom, *The First Team*, 211.
17. Vejtasa, interview with author.
18. Frank and Harrington, *Rendezvous at Midway*, 104; Stuart D. Ludlum, *They Turned the War Around at Coral Sea and Midway: Going to War with* Yorktown*'s Air Group Five* (Bennington, VT: Merriam Press, 1991), 90.
19. Hancock, email to author, March 3, 2021.

CHAPTER TWO: "DON'T GET IN MY WAY"

1. Vejtasa, interview with author.
2. Ibid., 138.
3. "Conneautville Man Tells of *Yorktown*'s Sinking," *Greenville* (PA) *Record*, December 11, 1942, 1–2.
4. Warren Heller, "Stories for My Family" (unpublished memoir, circa 1980s), 142–44.
5. Warren G. Heller, interview with author.
6. Heller, "Stories for My Family," 97–102.
7. Ibid., 105–6.
8. Heller, interview with author.
9. Heller, "Stories for My Family," 138, 144.
10. Ibid., 139, 142.
11. Ibid., 143.
12. William G. Roy, Veterans History Project oral history interview; William G. Roy, National Museum of the Pacific War oral history, September 18, 2004, 2.
13. William G. Roy, National WWII Museum interview, September 18, 2004.
14. Don Keith with David Rocco, *The Indestructible Man: The True Story of World War II Hero "Captain Dixie"* (Indian Springs Village, AL: Erin Press, 2017), 58–59.
15. Roy, National WWII Museum interview.
16. Admiral Elliott Buckmaster, interview with Walter Lord, April 18, 1966.
17. John B. Lundstrom, *Black Shoe Carrier Admiral: Frank Jack Fletcher at Coral Sea, Midway, and Guadalcanal* (Annapolis, MD: Naval Institute Press, 2006), 53–54.
18. Frank and Harrington, *Rendezvous at Midway*, 73.
19. Lundstrom, *Black Shoe Carrier Admiral*, 7.
20. Ibid., 183.
21. Ibid., 185.
22. Lundstrom, *The First Team*, 225.
23. Robert Cressman, *That Gallant Ship: USS* Yorktown *(CV-5)* (Missoula, MT: Pictorial Histories Publishing Company, 1985), 99.
24. Christie to Horan, 7.
25. Lundstrom, *The First Team*, 90–91.

26. Nesmith, *No Higher Honor*, 105.
27. Lundstrom, *The First Team*, 243–44.
28. Ibid., 244.
29. Rear Adm. Clarence C. Ray to Walter Lord, 1966.
30. Rear Adm. Clarence C. Ray, "Saga of the *Yorktown* (CV-5) Part I, April 1941–May 1942," *Shipmate* (May 1982), 36.
31. Ray to Lord.
32. Lundstrom, *The First Team*, 245.
33. Christie to Horan, 7.
34. Lundstrom, *The First Team*, 232–33.
35. Ibid., 234–35; Elbert Scott McCuskey interview with Eric M. Hammell, June 22, 1990, American Fighter Aces Association, Museum of Flight, Seattle, WA, 8.

CHAPTER THREE: "MAN YOUR GUNS!"

1. E. H. Domienik, *I Remember the* Yorktown (privately published, 2006), 118–22.
2. 1935 *Lucky Bag*, Naval Academy yearbook.
3. William Kowalczewski, radio interview with Dave Eddy of WBCK AM 930, June 2, 1994, at Battle Creek, MI, CV-5 reunion.
4. Domienik, *I Remember the* Yorktown, 122.
5. John Field, "Life and Death of the U.S.S. *Yorktown*," *Life*, November 16, 1942, 133; Domienik, *I Remember the* Yorktown, 123.
6. Captain Stanford E. Linzey, USN (Ret.), *God Was at Midway: The Sinking of the USS* Yorktown *(CV-5) and the Battles of the Coral Sea and Midway*, second edition (San Diego: Black Forest Press, 1999), 65.
7. Captain John E. Greenbacker, oral history interview with Donald R. Lennon, November 8, 1995, East Carolina University Manuscript Collection, 1–2.
8. Ibid., 3–8.
9. Ibid., 18–19.
10. Ibid., 18.
11. Cressman, *That Gallant Ship*, 105.
12. Lundstrom, *The First Team*, 270.
13. Edwards, *Seven at Santa Cruz*, 55.
14. Vejtasa, interview with author.
15. John d'Arc Lorenz to Walter Lord, 1966.
16. John d'Arc Lorenz, "I Was on the *Yorktown*," *Sea Power*, May 1943, 11–12.
17. Hancock, interview with author, October 19, 2020.
18. Hancock, email to author, January 12, 2021.
19. Cressman, *That Gallant Ship*, 105.
20. Roy, National WWII Museum interview.
21. Weise, "I Was Left On Board," 5.
22. Ibid., 5; Lundstrom, *The First Team*, 252; George K. Weise to Walter Lord.

23. Roy, National WWII Museum interview; Roy, National Museum of the Pacific War oral history, 5; Capt. Elliott Buckmaster, "Report of Action of *Yorktown* and *Yorktown* Air Group on May 8, 1942," 6.

CHAPTER FOUR: DEVASTATION BELOW

1. Hancock, email to author, January 12, 2021.
2. Buckmaster, "Report of Action of *Yorktown* and *Yorktown* Air Group on May 8, 1942," 6.
3. Roy, National WWII Museum interview; Greenbacker, oral history, 19.
4. Judson M. Brodie, National Museum of the Pacific War oral history, March 12, 2007, 31–32.
5. Buckmaster, "Report of Action of *Yorktown* and *Yorktown* Air Group on May 8, 1942": "Enclosure H, War Damage Report"; "Enclosure A: Direct Hit by Bomb," 1.
6. Frank and Harrington, *Rendezvous at Midway*, 127.
7. Ibid., 127–28; "Purple Heart Award to Air Station Chief," *Ottumwa* (IA) *Daily Courier*, July 10, 1943, 1–2.
8. "Battle of Midway Celebration 2015 Veterans' Biographies," 25.
9. ENCS Worth E. Hare correspondence with Walter Lord, March 3, 1966.
10. Nesmith, *No Higher Honor*, 113–15.
11. Ibid., 122.
12. Buckmaster, "Report of Action of *Yorktown* and *Yorktown* Air Group on May 8, 1942," 46.
13. Linzey, *God Was at Midway*, 68.
14. Field, "Life and Death of the U.S.S. *Yorktown*," 133.
15. Frank and Harrington, *Rendezvous at Midway*, 129.
16. CWO Raymond C. Davis to Walter Lord.
17. Nesmith, *No Higher Honor*, 254, 123.
18. Buckmaster, "Report of Action of *Yorktown* and *Yorktown* Air Group on May 8, 1942," 45–46; Nesmith, *No Higher Honor*, 124.
19. Ibid., 124.
20. Dixie Kiefer, "Noteworthy Incident Occurring During Engagement on May 8, 1942, and in the Operations Leading Up Thereto Involving Individual Instances of Personnel Deserving of Praise—Report of" (May 19, 1942), 9, 11.
21. Lundstrom, *The First Team*, 258.
22. Buckmaster, "Report of Action of *Yorktown* and *Yorktown* Air Group on May 8, 1942," 37–38.
23. Dwight Dehaven, National Museum of the Pacific War oral history, June 13, 2000, 1–10.
24. Donald Wilson letter, *Yorktown* (VA) *Crier*, undated.
25. Kiefer, "Noteworthy Incident," 9.
26. Buckmaster, "Report of Action of *Yorktown* and *Yorktown* Air Group on May 8, 1942," 7.
27. Domienik, *I Remember the* Yorktown, 127–28.

28. Ibid., 128.
29. Frank and Harrington, *Rendezvous at Midway,* 129.
30. Buckmaster, "Report of Action of *Yorktown* and *Yorktown* Air Group on May 8, 1942," 45–46.
31. Ibid., 45.
32. Heller, "Stories for My Family," 145.
33. Ibid., 146.
34. Ibid., 146.
35. Hancock, email to author, January 12, 2021.
36. Lorenz, "I Was on the *Yorktown,*" 12.
37. Frank and Harrington, *Rendezvous at Midway,* 130.
38. Truxton K. Ford, interview with author.
39. Edwards, *Seven at Santa Cruz,* 59.
40. Robert Hodgens to Peter Montavlo, *Yorktown* (VA) *Crier,* February 1982, 4.
41. Lundstrom, *The First Team,* 273.
42. Ibid., 273.
43. McKelvey, Wallace. "Ocean City Survivor of Midway Abandoned *Yorktown* Under Torpedo Fire," *The Press of Atlantic City,* June 6, 2012, 1.
44. Lundstrom, *The First Team,* 277.
45. Ibid., 279.
46. Rear Adm. Ralph J. Arnold to Walter Lord, 1966.
47. Roy, National WWII Museum interview.
48. Lundstrom, *The First Team,* 282.
49. Heller, "Stories for My Family," 146.
50. Ibid., 146–47.
51. Buckmaster, "Report of Action of *Yorktown* and *Yorktown* Air Group on May 8, 1942," 46.
52. Heller, "Stories for My Family," 147.

CHAPTER FIVE: SEVENTY-TWO HOURS

1. Ray, "Saga of the *Yorktown* (CV-5) Part I," 38.
2. Rear Adm. John R. Wadleigh, "Memories of Midway Thirty Years Ago," *Shipmate,* June 1972, 5.
3. Frank and Harrington, *Rendezvous at Midway,* 142.
4. Forshee, *Standby! Mark!*
5. Wadleigh, "Memories of Midway Thirty Years Ago," 5.
6. Frank and Harrington, *Rendezvous at Midway,* 136; Don Bourgeois email to author, January 13, 2021.
7. McCuskey with Hammell, 8.
8. Buckmaster, "Report of Action of *Yorktown* and *Yorktown* Air Group on May 8, 1942," 48–55.
9. Cressman, *That Gallant Ship,* 115.
10. Walter Lord, *Incredible Victory* (New York: Harper & Row, 1967), 33.
11. Capt. John E. Greenbacker to Lord, 2.

12. Ibid., 3.
13. Lord, *Incredible Victory*, 36–37.
14. Cressman, *That Gallant Ship*, 116; Lt. Cdr. Boyd M. McKenzie to Lord, March 31, 1966.
15. Nesmith, *No Higher Honor*, 170.
16. Hancock, interview with author, October 24, 2020.
17. McCuskey with Hammell, 10.
18. Wilhelm George Esders, American Airpower Heritage Foundation, Commemorative Air Force oral history memoir, March 19, 1991, 1–7.
19. Ibid., 9.
20. Barrett Tillman, *The Dauntless Dive Bomber of World War II* (Annapolis, MD: Naval Institute Press, 1976), 59.
21. Christie to Horan, 11.
22. Capt. Elgin B. Hurlbert to Walter Lord, May 3, 1966, 1.
23. Maurice E. Witting to Walter Lord, 1966.
24. Arnold to Lord.
25. Frank and Harrington, *Rendezvous at Midway*, 144.
26. Ensign (SC) USNR Bryan Crisman, *"Intervention" Won the Battle of Midway* (Privately published, 2002), 19.
27. Wadleigh, "Memories of Midway Thirty Years Ago," 5–6.
28. Lt. Joseph P. Pollard, "Recollections of the Battle of Midway," oral history from the Historian, Bureau of Medicine and Surgery, Naval History Heritage Command.
29. "A *Yorktown* Veteran Remembers," John Crawford oral history video, "Part I: The Academy."
30. John Crawford, interview with author.
31. Ibid.
32. Wadleigh, "Memories of Midway Thirty Years Ago," 6.
33. Ibid., 6.

CHAPTER SIX: "MAY GOD KEEP US SAFE TOMORROW"

1. Hancock, email to author, October 19, 2020.
2. Roy, National WWII Museum interview.
3. Pollard, "Recollections of the Battle of Midway."
4. McCuskey with Hammell, 10.
5. Lundstrom, *The First Team*, 322.
6. Crawford, interview with author; John Crawford, "Seven Days at Midway," *Proceedings*, June 2017.
7. Lorenz to Lord, 1966.
8. Pollard, "Recollections of the Battle of Midway."
9. Lundstrom, *The First Team*, 322–23.
10. Heller, "Stories for My Family," 52.
11. Ibid., 52–53.
12. Frank and Harrington, *Rendezvous at Midway*, 153.

13. Rear Adm. Charles R. Cundiff to Lord.
14. Crawford, "Seven Days at Midway."
15. Lorenz, "I Was on the *Yorktown*," 12.
16. Bourgeois email to author, January 13, 2021.
17. Lloyd F. Childers, "Midway from the Backseat of a TBD," *The Hook*, Vol. 18, August 1990, 36.
18. Ian W. Toll, "Rear-Seat Gunners at Midway," *Naval History* 27, no. 3 (May 2013).
19. McCuskey with Hammell, 10.
20. Crawford, interview with author; Crawford, "Seven Days at Midway."
21. Lundstrom, *The First Team*, 332.
22. Ibid., 336.
23. McCuskey with Hammell, 11.

CHAPTER SEVEN: THE PRICE FOR GLORY

1. Lundstrom, *The First Team*, 337.
2. Greenbacker to Lord, 3–4.
3. Lundstrom, *The First Team*, 339.
4. Toll, "Rear-Seat Gunners at Midway," usni.org.
5. Lorenz, "I Was on the *Yorktown*," 13.
6. Milford Austin Merrill, National WWII Museum.
7. Wilhelm George Esders, CAP, Report of June 6, 1942, 1; Esders, American Airpower Heritage Foundation, Commemorative Air Force oral history memoir, 10–11; Toll, "Rear-Seat Gunners at Midway," usni.org.
8. Esders, Report of June 6, 1942, 1; Esders, American Airpower Heritage Foundation, Commemorative Air Force oral history memoir, 11.
9. Frederick P. Bergeron, interview with author, February 4, 2011.
10. Esders, Report of June 6, 1942, 1; Esders, American Airpower Heritage Foundation, Commemorative Air Force oral history memoir, 13.
11. Esders, American Airpower Heritage Foundation, Commemorative Air Force oral history memoir, 11; Toll, "Rear-Seat Gunners at Midway," usni .org.
12. Mach. H. L. Corl, statement, June 15, 1942, 1–2.
13. Esders, American Airpower Heritage Foundation, Commemorative Air Force oral history memoir, 12–13.
14. Childers, "Midway from the Backseat of a TBD," 37.
15. Esders and Corl statements, June 6, 1942, 2.
16. Esders, statement, June 6, 1942, 2.

CHAPTER EIGHT: BATTERED

1. Lorenz, "I Was on the *Yorktown*," 12.
2. Ibid., 12.
3. McCuskey with Hammell, 11.

NOTES

4. Lundstrom, *The First Team*, 374.
5. Stephen L. Moore, *Pacific Payback: The Carrier Aviators Who Avenged Pearl Harbor at the Battle of Midway* (New York: NAL Caliber, 2014), 257–58.
6. Lorenz, "I Was on the *Yorktown*," 13.
7. Lundstrom, *The First Team*, 373.
8. Pollard, "Recollections of the Battle of Midway"; Lundstrom, *The First Team*, 373.
9. McCuskey with Hammell, 13.
10. Lundstrom, *The First Team*, 377.
11. Ibid., 383, 390.
12. Greenbacker to Lord, 4.
13. Buckmaster to Lord.
14. Roy, National WWII Museum interview.
15. Hare to Lord.
16. Cdr. Joseph Kisela to Walter Lord, 1966.
17. Rear Adm. John F. Delaney to Walter Lord, 1966.
18. Davis to Lord.
19. Lorenz, "I Was on the *Yorktown*," 13.
20. Ibid., 13.
21. Hancock, interview with author, October 19, 2020.
22. Weise, "I Was Left On Board," 5.
23. Lundstrom, *The First Team*, 383.
24. Lorenz, "I Was on the *Yorktown*," 13.
25. Ibid., 11, 13.
26. Peter Montalvo, "Memories of the Battle of Midway," *Yorktown* (VA) *Crier*, Spring 2015, 23.
27. Clyde L. Stancil, "Graduating Grandpa. Moulton Man, 81, Receives Diploma After Leaving High School to Serve in WWII," *The Decatur* (AL) *Daily News*, May 26, 2006, 1.
28. Terry Dykes, interview with Gehring, June 6, 2009.
29. Joe Hartlove, recollections, *Yorktown* (VA) *Crier*, Spring 2002, 15.
30. Pollard, "Recollections of the Battle of Midway."
31. Capt. Chester E. Briggs Jr. to Walter Lord, 1966.
32. Pollard, "Recollections of the Battle of Midway."
33. Harold Davies, Veterans History Project oral history interview.
34. Lorenz, "I Was on the *Yorktown*," 13–14.
35. Davies, Veterans History Project oral history interview.
36. Frank and Harrington, *Rendezvous at Midway*, 191.
37. Montalvo, "Memories of the Battle of Midway," 23.
38. Hancock, interview with author, October 19, 2020.
39. Buckmaster to Lord; Capt. Vane M. Bennett to Walter Lord, 1966.
40. Weise to Lord; Weise, "I Was Left On Board," 5.
41. Weise to Lord; Weise, "I Was Left On Board," 5.
42. Master CQM William C. Martin to Walter Lord, 1966.

NOTES

43. Robert D. Ballard and Rick Archbold, *Return to Midway: The Quest to Find the Yorktown and the Other Ships from the Pivotal Battle of the Pacific War* (Washington, DC: National Geographic/Madison Press, 1999), 95–97.
44. Hare to Lord.
45. Cundiff to Lord.
46. Frank and Harrington, *Rendezvous at Midway*, 196.
47. Lundstrom, *The First Team*, 385.
48. William Stephen Ogden Navy Cross citation.
49. Roger Spooner, interview with author.
50. Greenbacker to Lord, 5.
51. Keith with Rocco, *The Indestructible Man*, 91; Greenbacker to Lord, 5.
52. Keith with Rocco, *The Indestructible Man*, 92.

CHAPTER NINE: DEAD IN THE WATER

1. Roger Steinway, "Pearl Harbor to Midway," *Military History*, June 2001, 46–47.
2. Weise to Lord; Weise, "I Was Left On Board," 5.
3. Pollard, "Recollections of the Battle of Midway."
4. "Conneautville Man Tells of *Yorktown*'s Sinking," 1–2; Hare to Lord; Davis to Lord.
5. Lorenz, "I Was on the *Yorktown*," 14.
6. Ibid., 14.
7. Ibid., 15.
8. Field, "Life and Death of the U.S.S. *Yorktown*," 136.
9. McKenzie to Lord.
10. Roy, National WWII Museum interview.
11. Ibid; Keith with Rocco, *The Indestructible Man*, 93.
12. Witting to Lord.
13. Crisman, *"Intervention" Won the Battle of Midway*, 44.
14. Davis to Lord.
15. Cundiff to Lord.
16. Capt. William R. Crenshaw to Walter Lord, 1966.
17. Esders, statement, 3.
18. Corl statement, 3.
19. Childers, "Midway from the Backseat of a TBD," 38.
20. Lundstrom, *The First Team*, 389.
21. Lorenz, "I Was on the *Yorktown*," 15.
22. Ibid., 14; Lorenz to Lord, 1966.
23. Cressman, *That Gallant Ship*, 148.
24. Lundstrom, *The First Team*, 394.
25. Ibid., 394–95.
26. Ibid., 398.

CHAPTER TEN: TOMONAGA'S REVENGE

1. Lundstrom, *The First Team*, 397.
2. Ibid., 397.
3. Ibid., 400.
4. Ibid., 400–3.
5. Ibid., 399, 403–4.
6. Ibid., 404.
7. Pollard, "Recollections of the Battle of Midway."
8. Witting to Lord.
9. Lorenz, "I Was on the *Yorktown*," 15.
10. Heller, "Stories for My Family," 148.
11. Lt. James E. Wilson to Walter Lord, 1966.
12. Heller, "Stories for My Family," 148.
13. Ibid., 148.
14. Greenbacker to Lord, 5–6.
15. Crisman, "*Intervention*" *Won the Battle of Midway*, 44–45.
16. Nesmith, *No Higher Honor*, 226.
17. Buckmaster to Lord.
18. Lundstrom, *The First Team*, 410–12.
19. Greenbacker to Lord, 6.
20. Joe Hartlove recollections, 15.
21. Pollard, "Recollections of the Battle of Midway"; Hare to Lord.
22. "A *Yorktown* Veteran Remembers," John Crawford oral history video, "Part V: Abandon Ship." Naval Historical Foundation, YouTube video, June 2, 2017.
23. Lord, *Incredible Victory*, 219–20.
24. Frank and Harrington, *Rendezvous at Midway*, 208.
25. Leonard A. Wingo to Walter Lord, 1966.
26. Heller, "Stories for My Family," 148.
27. McKenzie to Lord.
28. Hurlbert to Lord, 2.
29. Dehaven, National Museum of the Pacific War oral history, 17.
30. Lt. (jg) Pressley E. Holmes to Walter Lord, 1966.
31. Cundiff to Lord; Lt. Oliver C. Thore to Walter Lord, 1966.
32. Hurlbert to Lord, 2.
33. Greenbacker to Lord, 6–7.
34. Ibid., 7.

CHAPTER ELEVEN: ABANDON SHIP

1. Pollard, "Recollections of the Battle of Midway."
2. Lundstrom, *Black Shoe Carrier Admiral*, 274.
3. Rear Adm. Clarence E. Aldrich to Walter Lord, January 31, 1966.
4. Greenbacker to Lord, 8.
5. Ibid., 8–9.
6. "Courage of *Yorktown* Men Told by Survivors," *Endicott* (NY) *Daily Bulletin*, September 17, 1942, 8.

7. Cundiff to Lord.
8. Dehaven, National Museum of the Pacific War oral history, 19.
9. Lundstrom, *Black Shoe Carrier Admiral*, 275; Dehaven, National Museum of the Pacific War oral history, 20–21.
10. Crenshaw to Lord.
11. Wadleigh, "Memories of Midway Thirty Years Ago," 7–8.
12. Hurlbert to Lord, 3–4.
13. Ibid., 4.
14. Hancock, interview with author, October 24, 2020.
15. Greenbacker to Lord, 9–10.
16. "Crew of *Yorktown* Wrote Epic of Heroism; Story of Doomed Plane Ship's Final Hours," *The Gazette* (Cedar Rapids, IA), September 2, 1942, 1–2; "Veteran Mascot of Navy Battle Gets Discharge," *Berkeley Daily Gazette*, April 10, 1943, 9; "Rabbit Is Tucked in Gas Mask Bag, Saved by Sailor," *Ames* (IA) *Daily Tribune*, July 24, 1942, 8.
17. Sophie Ruth Meranski, "Red Headed Stepchild: The Barrett Family Memoir of Navy Life."
18. Heller, "Stories for My Family," 54.
19. Dykes interview with Gehring.
20. Davis to Lord.
21. *Yorktown* (VA) *Crier*, June 4, 1992, 36–37; Weise to Lord.
22. Weise to Lord.
23. Nesmith, *No Higher Honor*, 228–29.
24. Ibid., 241–42; Briggs to Lord.
25. Crisman, *"Intervention" Won the Battle of Midway*, 46.
26. Ibid., 46.
27. Roy, National WWII Museum interview.
28. Roy, National Museum of the Pacific War oral history, 9.
29. Ibid., 9.
30. Roy, National WWII Museum interview.
31. Pollard, "Recollections of the Battle of Midway."
32. "Illinois Marines Describe Leaving Mighty *Yorktown,*" *Dixon* (IL) *Evening Telegraph*, October 12, 1942, 2.
33. Buckmaster to Lord.
34. Lorenz, "I Was on the *Yorktown,*" 30.
35. Davies, Veterans History Project oral history interview.
36. Don Bourgeois, "Ens. John d'Arc Lorenz at Midway, June 4, 1942."
37. Ibid.
38. Crisman, *"Intervention" Won the Battle of Midway*, 46.
39. Admiral Mike Mullen, "Why Midway Matters," *Naval History*, June 2002, 15.
40. Bourgeois, "Ens. John d'Arc Lorenz at Midway, June 4, 1942."
41. Lorenz, "I Was on the *Yorktown,*" 31.
42. Montalvo, "Memories of the Battle of Midway," 24.
43. McKenzie to Lord.
44. Hare to Lord.

45. Heller, "Stories for My Family," 54–55.
46. Ibid., 55.
47. Davis to Lord.
48. Frank and Harrington, *Rendezvous at Midway*, 212.
49. Bennett to Lord; Ballard and Archbold, *Return to Midway*, 107.
50. "Cmdr. Kiefer Has High Praise for Sailors of Today," *Kingston* (NY) *Daily Freeman*, October 24, 1942, 13.
51. Pollard, "Recollections of the Battle of Midway."
52. Frank and Harrington, *Rendezvous at Midway*, 213.
53. Buckmaster to Lord; Roy, National WWII Museum interview.
54. Ray to Lord.
55. Spooner, interview with author.
56. Lundstrom, *Black Shoe Carrier Admiral*, 275; Cressman, *That Gallant Ship*, 157–58.
57. Lundstrom, *Black Shoe Carrier Admiral*, 275–76.
58. Ibid., 276.
59. Christie to Horan, 12–13.
60. Tillman, *The Dauntless Dive Bomber of World War II*, 85–86.
61. Moore, *Pacific Payback*, 292–93.
62. Bergeron, interview with author; Fred P. Bergeron, oral history interview, April 29, 2004.
63. Forshee, *Standby! Mark!*, chapter 13.

CHAPTER TWELVE: GHOST SHIP SAILORS

1. Greenbacker to Lord, 12.
2. Roy, National WWII Museum interview; Roy, National Museum of the Pacific War oral history, 10–11.
3. Lundstrom, *Black Shoe Carrier Admiral*, 287.
4. War diaries of USS *Russell, Benham, Morris, Astoria,* and *Balch,* June 5, 1942; Dehaven, National Museum of the Pacific War oral history, 23–24.
5. Greenbacker to Lord, 12.
6. Kisela to Lord.
7. David Parker Barnes Jr., Veterans History Project oral history interview, Washington, DC.
8. Ray to Lord.
9. Greenbacker to Lord, 13.
10. Roy, National WWII Museum interview.
11. Lundstrom, *Black Shoe Carrier Admiral*, 287–88.
12. *Yorktown* (VA) *Crier*, June 4, 1992, 36–37.
13. Weise, "I Was Left On Board," 6.
14. Lt. Cdr. D. J. Ramsey, "Operations in Connection with USS *Yorktown* from Time of Abandonment About 0301, GCT, June 5, 1942, Until Sinking at 1659, GCT, June 7, 1942" from USS *Hughes* war diary, June 1942.
15. Weise, "I Was Left On Board," 6.
16. Ibid., 7.

17. Ramsey, "Operations in Connection with USS *Yorktown*."
18. Cressman, *That Gallant Ship*, 164–65.
19. Barnes, Veteran History Project oral history interview.
20. Peter Rowe, "The Battle of Midway's Unsinkable San Diegan," *Growth Spotter*, June 2, 2012.
21. Frank and Harrington, *Rendezvous at Midway*, 228.
22. Aldrich to Lord.
23. Bennett to Lord; Delaney to Lord.
24. CWO George Edward Bateman to Walter Lord, 1966; Cundiff to Lord.
25. Greenbacker to Lord, 14.
26. McKenzie to Lord.
27. Greenbacker to Lord, 14.
28. Wilson to Lord.
29. Roy, National WWII Museum interview.
30. Ibid.
31. Ray to Lord.
32. James Clark, "102-Year-Old Trailblazing World War II Vet Receives Extremely Rare Navy Honor," Task & Purpose, August 11, 2017.
33. John Wilken, "Andy Mills, Battle of Midway Survivor, Dies at 103," *San Diego Union-Tribune*, May 24, 2018.
34. Bergeron, oral history interview; Bergeron, interview with author.
35. Forshee, *Standby! Mark!*, chapter 14.
36. Christie to Horan, 13.
37. Ibid., 13.

CHAPTER THIRTEEN: "TORPEDOES TO STARBOARD!"

1. Yahachi Tanabe, "I Sank the *Yorktown* at Midway," *Proceedings*, May 1963, 61.
2. Ibid., 62.
3. Ibid., 63.
4. Delaney to Lord.
5. Greenbacker to Lord, 15.
6. Arnold to Lord.
7. Earl "Ed" Fogarty, radio interview with Dave Eddy of WBCK AM 930, June 2, 1994, at Battle Creek, MI, CV-5 reunion; Kisela to Lord.
8. Ens. Norman W. Shaw, USN (Ret.), *Screened Her Going Down* (Albany, NY: Fort Orange Press, Inc., 1984), 337.
9. Cundiff to Lord.
10. Ray to Lord.
11. Greenbacker to Lord, 15.
12. Frank and Harrington, *Rendezvous at Midway*, 234; Roy, National World War II Museum interview.
13. Wingo to Lord.
14. "Crew of *Yorktown* Wrote Epic of Heroism; Story of Doomed Plane Ship's Final Hours," 1–2.
15. Buckmaster to Lord.

16. Ray to Lord; Greenbacker to Lord, 16.
17. Greenbacker to Lord, 16.
18. Shaw, *Screened Her Going Down*, 340; Dehaven, National Museum of the Pacific War oral history, 31–34.
19. Ray to Lord.
20. Frank and Harrington, *Rendezvous at Midway*, 234.
21. Ray to Lord; Holmes to Lord.
22. "Conneautville Man Tells of *Yorktown*'s Sinking," 2.
23. Frank Geary, "Midway Sailor Recounts Events, Puzzles over His Seemingly Miraculous Survival Among 165 Dead," *Jax Air News*, November 4, 1999, 7; Shaw, *Screened Her Going Down*, 339; "Describes Sinking of Destroyer on Which Co. Lad Lost His Life," *Lebanon* (PA) *Daily News*, August 14, 1942, 1, 19.
24. Greenbacker to Lord, 17.
25. Bateman to Lord.
26. Delaney to Lord.
27. Greenbacker to Lord, 18.
28. Nesmith, *No Higher Honor*, 255. Nesmith's text references this person to likely be chief petty officer Thomas Coleman but McKenzie was the only warrant carpenter on board with the *Yorktown* salvage party.
29. Delaney to Lord.
30. Greenbacker to Lord, 18.
31. Shaw, *Screened Her Going Down*, 342.
32. Ray to Lord.
33. Greenbacker to Lord, 19.
34. Frank and Harrington, *Rendezvous at Midway*, 237.
35. Buckmaster to Lord; Roy, National World War II Museum interview.
36. Ray to Lord; Cdr. William W. Lancaster to Walter Lord, 5.

AFTERWORD

1. Lancaster to Lord, 5.
2. Crawford, interview with author.
3. Cressman, *That Gallant Ship*, 176, 179.
4. Roy, National Museum of the Pacific War oral history, 10–11.
5. Bourgeois, "Ens. John d'Arc Lorenz at Midway, June 4, 1942."
6. Hancock, interviews with author, October 19 and 24, 2020.
7. Senior Airman Dennis Sloan, "War Hero Relives Battle 70 Years Later," Joint Base Charleston Public Affairs, June 4, 2012.

★ BIBLIOGRAPHY ★

ORAL HISTORIES / PERSONAL INTERVIEWS

Bergeron, Frederick P. Oral history interview, April 29, 2004, and telephone interview with author, February 4, 2011; subsequent follow-up conversations and emails.

Crawford, John W. Telephone interview with author, October 24, 2020.

Domienik, Eugene. Telephone interview with author, October 28, 2020.

Flum, Sheri (daughter of veteran Sidney Flum). Telephone interview with author, December 12, 2020.

Fogarty, Earl "Ed." Radio interview with Dave Eddy of WBCK AM 930, June 2, 1994, at Battle Creek, MI, CV-5 reunion.

Ford, Truxton K. Telephone interview with author, October 26, 2020.

Hancock, John W. Telephone interviews with author, October 19 and 26, 2020. Email correspondence from October 2020 to March 2021.

Heller, Warren G. Telephone interview with author, November 4, 2020.

Kearney, Edward A., III. Telephone interview with author, November 17, 2020.

Kowalczewski, William. Radio interview with Dave Eddy of WBCK AM 930, June 2, 1994, at Battle Creek, MI, CV-5 reunion.

McKenzie, Boyd M., Jr. Telephone interviews with author of November 17 and November 28, 2020. Email correspondence through April 2021.

Richels, Jacklyn (daughter of veteran Sidney Flum). Telephone interview with author, December 12, 2020.

BIBLIOGRAPHY

Spooner, Roger. Telephone interview with author, October 24, 2020.
Vejtasa, Stanley W. Telephone interview with author, January 7, 2011.
Weise, Carolyn (daughter of veteran George Weise). Email correspondence from November 24 to December 4, 2020, including papers and photos.

ARTICLES / LETTERS / MEMOIRS / OFFICIAL STATEMENTS

Barnes, David Parker, Jr. Veterans History Project oral history interview. Washington, DC.
"Battle of Midway Celebration 2015 Veterans' Biographies." Privately published reunion program.
Bourgeois, Don. Memoirs, articles, and interview notes with John D. Lorenz, provided to author, including "Ens. John d'Arc Lorenz at Midway, June 4, 1942."
Brodie, Judson M. National Museum of the Pacific War oral history, March 13, 2007. Fredericksburg, TX.
Buckmaster, Capt. Elliott. "Report of Action of *Yorktown* and *Yorktown* Air Group on May 8, 1942."
Childers, Lloyd F. National WWII Museum interview. New Orleans.
Childers, Lt. Col. Lloyd F. "Midway from the Backseat of a TBD," *The Hook*, Vol. 18, August 1990, 36–38.
Christie, William F. Correspondence with Mark Horan, 1986.
Clark, James. "102-Year-Old Trailblazing World War II Vet Receives Extremely Rare Navy Honor," Task & Purpose, August 11, 2017.
"Cmdr. Kiefer Has High Praise for Sailors of Today." *Kingston* (NY) *Daily Freeman*, October 24, 1942.
"Conneautville Man Tells of *Yorktown*'s Sinking." *Greenville* (PA) *Record*, December 11, 1942.
Corl, Mach. H. L. Statement. June 15, 1942.
"Courage of *Yorktown* Men Told by Survivors." *Endicott* (NY) *Daily Bulletin*, September 17, 1942.
Crawford, John. "Seven Days at Midway," *Proceedings*, June 2017.
"A *Yorktown* Veteran Remembers," John Crawford oral history video, "Part V: Abandon Ship." Naval Historical Foundation, published on YouTube June 2, 2017.
"Crew of *Yorktown* Wrote Epic of Heroism; Story of Doomed Plane Ship's Final Hours." *The Gazette* (Cedar Rapids, IA), September 2, 1942.
Davies, Harold. Veterans History Project oral history interview, Washington, DC.
Dehaven, Dwight. National Museum of the Pacific War oral history, June 13, 2000. Fredericksburg, TX.
"Describes Sinking of Destroyer on Which Co. Lad Lost His Life." *Lebanon* (PA) *Daily News*, August 14, 1942.
Dykes, Terry. Interview with Allan Gehring, June 6, 2009.
Esders, Wilhelm George. American Airpower Heritage Foundation, Commemorative Air Force oral history memoir, March 19, 1991.

Esders, Wilhelm George, CAP. Report of June 6, 1942.

Fentress, William. Veterans History Project oral history interview, Washington, DC.

Field, John. "Life and Death of the U.S.S. *Yorktown.*" *Life*, November 16, 1942.

Forshee, Lynn. *Standby! Mark!*, privately published memoirs.

Geary, Frank. "Midway Sailor Recounts Events, Puzzles over His Seemingly Miraculous Survival Among 165 Dead." *Jax Air News*, November 4, 1999.

Greenbacker, Capt. John E. Oral history interview with Donald R. Lennon, November 8, 1995. East Carolina University Manuscript Collection.

Joe Hartlove, recollections, *Yorktown* (VA) *Crier*, Spring 2002, 15.

Heller, Warren. "Stories for My Family," unpublished memoir, circa 1980s. Personal story, courtesy of his son, Warren G. Heller.

"Illinois Marines Describe Leaving Mighty Yorktown." *Dixon* (IL) *Evening Telegraph*, October 12, 1942. Kiefer, Dixie. "Noteworthy Incident Occurring During Engagement on May 8, 1942, and in the Operations Leading Up Thereto Involving Individual Instances of Personnel Deserving of Praise— Report of." May 19, 1942.

Lorenz, John d'Arc. "I Was on the *Yorktown.*" *Sea Power*, May 1943.

McCuskey, Elbert Scott. Interview with Eric M. Hammell, June 22, 1990, American Fighter Aces Association, Museum of Flight, Seattle, WA.

McKelvey, Wallace. "Ocean City Survivor of Midway Abandoned *Yorktown* Under Torpedo Fire." *The Press of Atlantic City*, June 6, 2012.

Meranski, Sophie Ruth. "Red Headed Stepchild: The Barrett Family Memoir of Navy Life."

Merrill, Milford Austin. National WWII Museum interview, New Orleans.

Montalvo, Peter. "Memories of the Battle of Midway." *Yorktown* (VA) *Crier*, Spring 2015.

Mullen, Admiral Mike. "Why Midway Matters." *Naval History*, June 2002.

Patterson, James Edward. Veteran History Project oral history interview, Washington, DC.

Pollard, Lt. Joseph P., MC, USN. "Recollections of the Battle of Midway." Oral history from the Historian, Bureau of Medicine and Surgery, Naval History Heritage Command.

"Purple Heart Award to Air Station Chief." *Ottumwa* (IA) *Daily Courier*, July 10, 1943.

"Rabbit Is Tucked in Gas Mask Bag, Saved by Sailor." *Ames* (IA) *Daily Tribune*, July 24, 1942.

Ramsey, Lt. Cdr. D. J. "Operations in Connection with USS *Yorktown* from Time of Abandonment About 0301, GCT, June 5, 1942, Until Sinking at 1659, GCT, June 7, 1942." From USS *Hughes* war diary, June 1942.

Ray, Rear Adm. Clarence C. USN (Ret.). "Saga of the *Yorktown* (CV-5) Part I, April 1941–May 1942." *Shipmate*, May 1982.

———. "Saga of the *Yorktown* (CV-5) Part II, Midway." *Shipmate*, June 1982.

Rowe, Peter. "The Battle of Midway's Unsinkable San Diegan." *Growth Spotter*, June 2, 2012.

Roy, William G. National Museum of the Pacific War oral history, September 18, 2004. Fredericksburg, TX.

Roy, William G. National WWII Museum interview, September 18, 2004. New Orleans.

Roy, William G. Veterans History Project oral history interview, Washington, DC.

Sloan, Senior Airman Dennis. "War Hero Relives Battle 70 Years Later." Joint Base Charleston Public Affairs, June 6, 2012.

Stancil, Clyde L. "Graduating Grandpa. Moulton Man, 81, Receives Diploma After Leaving High School to Serve in WWWII." *The Decatur* (AL) *Daily News*, May 26, 2006.

Steinway, Roger. "Pearl Harbor to Midway." *Military History*, June 2001.

Tanabe, Yahachi. "I Sank the *Yorktown* at Midway." *Proceedings*, May 1963.

Toll, Ian W. "Rear-Seat Gunners at Midway." *Naval History* 27, no. 3 (May 2013).

"Veteran Mascot of Navy Battle Gets Discharge." *Berkeley Daily Gazette*, April 10, 1943.

Wadleigh, Rear Adm. John R., USN (Ret.). "Memories of Midway Thirty Years Ago." *Shipmate*, June 1972.

Weise, George K. "I Was Left On Board." *Yorktown* (VA) *Crier*, May 1988.

Wilken, John. "Andy Mills, Battle of Midway Survivor, Dies at 103." *San Diego Union-Tribune*, May 24, 2018.

Yorktown (VA) *Crier* reunion newsletter, various issues as listed in notes.

Yost, Victor J. National WWII Museum interview. New Orleans.

WALTER LORD "INCREDIBLE VICTORY" PAPERS: NAVAL HISTORY HERITAGE COMMAND

Aldrich, Rear Adm. Clarence E., USN (Ret.)

Arnold, Rear Adm. Ralph J., USN (Ret.)

Bateman, CWO George Edward, USN

Bennett, Capt. Vane M., USN (Ret.)

Bennett, Lt. (jg) Floyd H., USN (Ret.)

Briggs, Capt. Chester E., Jr., USN (Ret.)

Buckmaster, Admiral Elliott, USN (Ret.)

Crenshaw, Capt. William R., USN (Ret.)

Crosby, Lt. Cdr. Edmund B., USN (Ret.)

Cundiff, Rear Adm. Charles R., USN (Ret.)

Davis, CWO Raymond C., USN (Ret.)

Davis, Rear Adm. William Dalton (MC), USN (Ret.)

Delaney, Rear Adm. John F., USN (Ret.)

Greenbacker, Capt. John E., USN (Ret.)

Hare, ENCS Worth E., USN

Holmes, Lt. (jg) Pressley E., USN (Ret.)

Hurlbert, Capt. Elgin B., USN (Ret.)

Kisela, Cdr. Joseph, USN (Ret.)

Lancaster, Cdr. William W., USN (Ret.)
Lorenz, John d'Arc, USN
Martin, Master CQM William C., USNR
McDonald, Cdr. Philip N., USN (Ret.)
McKenzie, Lt. Cdr. Boyd M., USN (Ret.)
Patterson, Cdr. Ralph E., USN (Ret.)
Ray, Rear Adm. Clarence C., USN (Ret.)
Thore, Lt. Oliver C., USN (Ret.)
Weise, George K., USN (Ret.)
Wilson, Lt. James E., USN (Ret.)
Wingo, Leonard A., USN
Witting, Maurice E.

BOOKS / UNIT HISTORIES

Ballard, Robert D., and Rick Archbold. *Return to Midway: The Quest to Find the Yorktown and the Other Ships from the Pivotal Battle of the Pacific War.* Washington, DC: National Geographic/Madison Press, 1999.

Cressman, Robert. *That Gallant Ship: USS Yorktown (CV-5).* Missoula, MT: Pictorial Histories Publishing Company, 1985.

Crisman, Bryan, Ensign (SC) USNR. *"Intervention" Won the Battle of Midway.* Privately published, 2002.

Domienik, E. H. *I Remember the Yorktown.* Privately published, 2006.

Edwards, Ted. *Seven at Santa Cruz: The Life of Fighter Ace Stanley "Swede" Vejtasa.* Annapolis, MD: Naval Institute Press, 2018.

Frank, Pat, and Joseph D. Harrington. *Rendezvous at Midway: The U.S.S. Yorktown and the Japanese Carrier Fleet.* New York: The John Day Company, 1967.

Johnston, Stanley. *The Grim Reapers.* New York: E. P. Dutton & Co., Inc., 1943.

Keith, Don, with David Rocco. *The Indestructible Man: The True Story of World War II Hero "Captain Dixie."* Indian Springs Village, AL: Erin Press, 2017.

Linzey, Stanford E., Captain, USN (Ret.). *God Was at Midway: The Sinking of the USS Yorktown (CV-5) and the Battles of the Coral Sea and Midway,* second edition. San Diego: Black Forest Press, 1999.

Lord, Walter. *Incredible Victory.* New York: Harper & Row, 1967.

Ludlum, Stuart D. *They Turned the War Around at Coral Sea and Midway: Going to War with Yorktown's Air Group Five.* Bennington, VT: Merriam Press, 1991.

Lundstrom, John B. *Black Shoe Carrier Admiral: Frank Jack Fletcher at Coral Sea, Midway, and Guadalcanal.* Annapolis, MD: Naval Institute Press, 2006.

———. *The First Team: Pacific Naval Air Combat from Pearl Harbor to Midway.* Annapolis, MD: Naval Institute Press, 1984.

Moore, Stephen L. *Pacific Payback: The Carrier Aviators Who Avenged Pearl Harbor at the Battle of Midway.* New York: NAL Caliber, 2014.

BIBLIOGRAPHY

Nesmith, Jeff. *No Higher Honor: The U.S.S.* Yorktown *at the Battle of Midway.* Atlanta: Longstreet, Inc., 1999.

Shaw, Norman W., Ens., USN (Ret.). *Screened Her Going Down.* Albany, NY: Fort Orange Press, Inc., 1984.

Tillman, Barrett. *The Dauntless Dive Bomber of World War II.* Annapolis, MD: Naval Institute Press, 1976.

War diaries of USS *Russell, Benham, Morris, Astoria,* and *Balch,* June 5, 1942.